BASIC
CAR CARE

TIME
LIFE
BOOKS ®

Other Publications:

MYSTERIES OF THE UNKNOWN

TIME FRAME

FIX IT YOURSELF

FITNESS, HEALTH & NUTRITION

SUCCESSFUL PARENTING

HEALTHY HOME COOKING

UNDERSTANDING COMPUTERS

LIBRARY OF NATIONS

THE ENCHANTED WORLD

THE KODAK LIBRARY OF CREATIVE PHOTOGRAPHY

GREAT MEALS IN MINUTES

THE CIVIL WAR

PLANET EARTH

COLLECTOR'S LIBRARY OF THE CIVIL WAR

THE EPIC OF FLIGHT

THE GOOD COOK

WORLD WAR II

HOME REPAIR AND IMPROVEMENT

THE OLD WEST

BASIC CAR CARE

TIME-LIFE BOOKS
ALEXANDRIA, VIRGINIA

Fix It Yourself was produced by
ST. REMY PRESS

MANAGING EDITOR	Kenneth Winchester
MANAGING ART DIRECTOR	Pierre Léveillé

Staff for *Basic Car Care*

Series Editor	Kathleen M. Kiely
Editor	Caroline Miller
Art Director	Diane Denoncourt
Research Editor	Nancy D. Kingsbury
Designer	Marie-Claire Amiot
Editorial Assistant	Cathleen Farrell
Contributing Writers	Beverley Bennett, Margaret Caldbick, Harriett Fels, Carol Halls, Joan Irving, Emer Killean, Michael Kleiza, S. Kim Leslie, Grant Loewen, Daniel McBain
Contributing Illustrators	Gérard Mariscalchi, Jacques Proulx
Technical Illustrator	Robert Paquet
Cover	Robert Monté
Index	Christine M. Jacobs
Administrator	Denise Rainville
Coordinator	Michelle Turbide
Systems Manager	Shirley Grynspan
Systems Analyst	Simon Lapierre
Studio Director	Daniel Bazinet
Photographer	Maryo Proulx

Time-Life Books Inc. is a wholly owned subsidiary of
TIME INCORPORATED

FOUNDER	Henry R. Luce 1898-1967
Editor-in-Chief	Henry Anatole Grunwald
Chairman and Chief Executive Officer	J. Richard Munro
President and Chief Operating Officer	N. J. Nicholas Jr.
Chairman of the Executive Committee	Ralph P. Davidson
Corporate Editor	Ray Cave
Group Vice President, Books	Kelso F. Sutton
Vice President, Books	George Artandi

TIME-LIFE BOOKS INC.

EDITOR	George Constable
Executive Editor	Ellen Phillips
Director of Design	Louis Klein
Director of Editorial Resources	Phyllis K. Wise
Editorial Board	Russell B. Adams Jr., Dale M. Brown, Roberta Conlan, Thomas H. Flaherty, Lee Hassig, Donia Ann Steele, Rosalind Stubenberg, Kit van Tulleken, Henry Woodhead
Director of Photography and Research	John Conrad Weiser
PRESIDENT	Christopher T. Linen
Chief Operating Officer	John M. Fahey Jr.
Senior Vice President	James L. Mercer
Vice Presidents	Stephen L. Bair, Ralph J. Cuomo, Neal Goff, Stephen L. Goldstein, Juanita T. James, Hallett Johnson III, Carol Kaplan, Susan J. Maruyama, Robert H. Smith, Paul R. Stewart, Joseph J. Ward
Director of Production Services	Robert J. Passantino

Editorial Operations

Copy Chief	Diane Ullius
Production	Celia Beattie
Quality Control	James J. Cox (director)
Library	Louise D. Forstall
Correspondents	Elizabeth Kraemer-Singh (Bonn); Maria Vincenza Aloisi (Paris); Ann Natanson (Rome).

THE CONSULTANTS

Consulting Editor **David L. Harrison** served as an editor of several Time-Life Books do-it-yourself series, including *Home Repair and Improvement*, *The Encyclopedia of Gardening* and *The Art of Sewing*.

Richard Day, a do-it-yourself writer for a quarter century, is a founding director of the National Association of Home and Workshop Writers, and the author of two books on auto mechanics. He wrote a series of automotive service and repair articles for Popular Science, where he was Consulting Editor, Home and Shop.

Evan Powell is the Director of Chestnut Mountain Research Inc. in Taylors, South Carolina, a firm specializing in the evaluation of equipment including automotive and recreational vehicles. He was a consulting editor for Popular Science's Car Care Handbook and is the producer of "Road Test," a syndicated television series.

Mort Schultz has been a contributing editor to Popular Mechanics for 25 years and has a weekly radio show, American Know-How, broadcast nationwide. He has written three books on car repair and maintenance and has served as a contributing writer and consultant to several others.

Larry Savoy and **Robert Dethier** have taught auto mechanics to vocational students in Montreal since 1977. Both have worked in the automotive industry as licensed mechanics.

Laurier MacDonald Comprehensive High School, a vocational-technical high school in St. Leonard, Quebec, provided the garage, tools and resources used in the production of this book.

Library of Congress Cataloging-in-Publication Data
Basic car care
      p. cm. – (Fix it yourself)
  Includes index.
  ISBN 0-8094-6224-9
  ISBN 0-8094-6225-7 (lib. bdg.)
1. Automobiles – Maintenance and repair – Handbooks, manuals etc. I. Time-Life Books. II. Series.
TL152.B26597   1988
629.28'722–dc 19   87-28732
                              CIP

For information about any Time-Life book, please write:
Reader Information
541 North Fairbanks Court
Chicago, Illinois 60611

CONTENTS

HOW TO USE THIS BOOK

Basic Car Care is divided into three sections. The Emergency Guide on pages 8-17 provides information that can be indispensable in the event of a roadside breakdown or an emergency that may arise while you are repairing your car. Take the time to study this section carefully *before* you need the important advice it contains.

The Repairs section—the heart of the book—is a system for troubleshooting and repairing all the systems in your car. Pictured below are four sample pages from the chapter on the cooling system, with captions describing the various features of the book and how they work. If your radiator is overheating, for example, the Troubleshooting Guide will offer a number of possible causes. If the problem is a defective thermostat, you will be directed to page 88 for detailed, step-by-step directions for testing and, if necessary, replacing the thermostat.

Each job has been rated by degree of difficulty and the average time it will take for a do-it-yourselfer to complete. Keep in mind that this rating is only a suggestion. Before deciding whether you should attempt a repair, first read all the instructions carefully. Then be guided by your own confidence, and the tools and time available to you. For more complex or time-consuming repairs, such as removing and

Introductory text
Describes the cooling system, its most common problems and basic repair procedures.

Cutaway anatomy diagrams
Locate the components of the cooling system.

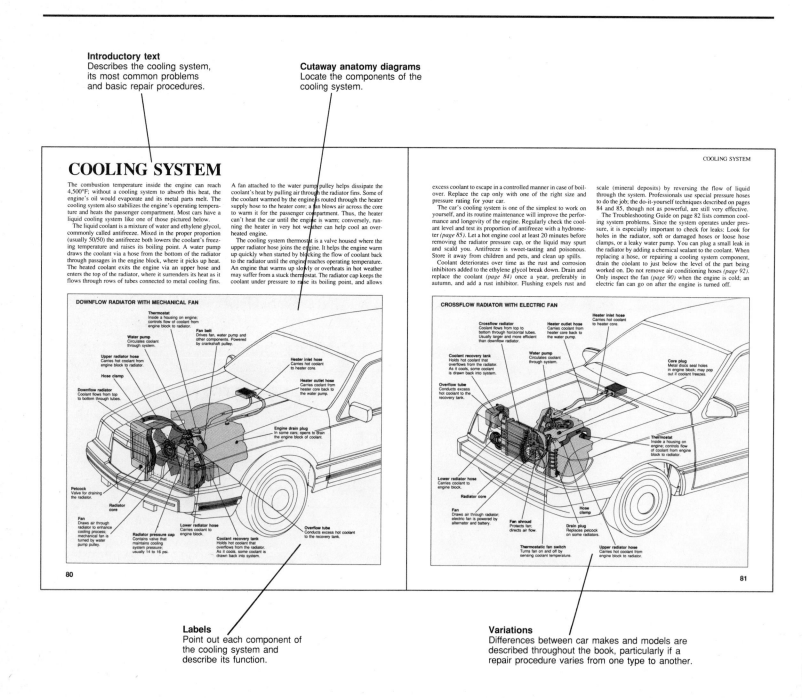

Labels
Point out each component of the cooling system and describe its function.

Variations
Differences between car makes and models are described throughout the book, particularly if a repair procedure varies from one type to another.

replacing a damaged muffler or changing the automatic transmission fluid and filter, you may wish to call for professional service. You will still have saved time and money by diagnosing the problem yourself.

Most of the repairs in *Basic Car Care* can be made with simple tools such as screwdrivers and wrenches. For some checks and repairs, you will need to raise the car on jack stands or ramps. You will also need specialized, but inexpensive, equipment such as a hydrometer and a vacuum gauge for some tests. Basic automotive tools—and the proper way to use them—are presented in the Tools & Techniques section

starting on page 132. If you are a novice when it comes to car repair, read this section in preparation for a major job.

Car repair can lead to serious injury unless you take certain basic precautions. Wear safety goggles when working underneath your car, and put on a pair of heavy-duty work gloves when working on the battery to prevent burns. If a test or repair must be done with the engine running, keep fingers away from moving parts. Do not wear loose clothing or dangling jewelry, and tie back long hair. Work in a well-ventilated area. Most important, follow all safety tips in the Emergency Guide and throughout the book.

Troubleshooting Guide
To use this chart, locate the symptom that most closely resembles your problem, review the possible causes in column 2, then follow the recommended procedures in column 3. Simple fixes may be explained on the chart; in most cases you will be directed to an illustrated, step-by-step repair sequence.

Name of repair
You will be referred by the Troubleshooting Guide to the first page of a specific repair job.

Insets
Illustrate variations and provide close-up views of specific steps.

Cross-references
Direct you to important information elsewhere in the book, such as instructions for replacing hoses.

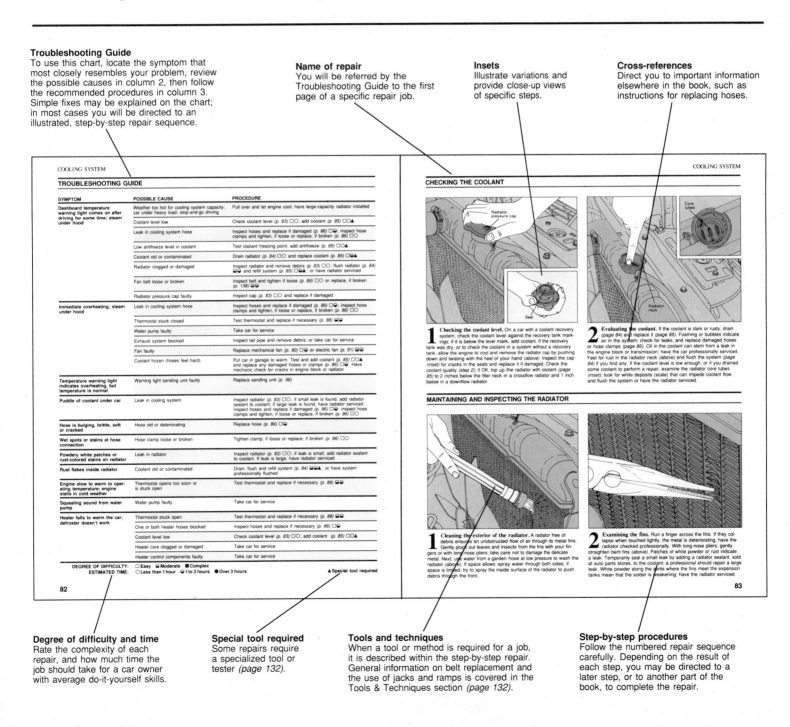

Degree of difficulty and time
Rate the complexity of each repair, and how much time the job should take for a car owner with average do-it-yourself skills.

Special tool required
Some repairs require a specialized tool or tester (*page 132*).

Tools and techniques
When a tool or method is required for a job, it is described within the step-by-step repair. General information on belt replacement and the use of jacks and ramps is covered in the Tools & Techniques section (*page 132*).

Step-by-step procedures
Follow the numbered repair sequence carefully. Depending on the result of each step, you may be directed to a later step, or to another part of the book, to complete the repair.

EMERGENCY GUIDE

Preventing on-the-road emergencies. The importance of regular car inspection and routine preventive maintenance cannot be overstressed. Refer to the owner's manual that came with the car for the manufacturer's maintenance schedules, a series of simple routine checks to be conducted at specific intervals throughout the lifetime of the vehicle. Proper maintenance will extend the life of your car, reduce gas consumption, prevent frequent and costly repairs and, most important, lessen the risk of a serious accident.

But even a well-maintained car is not immune to sudden mechanical failure. Be prepared to deal with emergencies. Carry the emergency kits detailed on page 11, and learn how to use their contents before they are needed—the steps in this chapter cover setting out road flares, using a fire extinguisher and changing a flat tire, among other techniques. Learn to read the warnings of potential trouble: excessive gas consumption, repeated loss of coolant or other fluids, new or unusual noises, or any change in normal performance all signal that your car needs repair.

Safety is the first consideration when undertaking car repair, whether on the road or in the garage. Read the list of safety tips at right before attempting any inspection or repair described in this book. Also, familiarize yourself with the equipment in the Tools & Techniques section *(page 132)*. The Troubleshooting Guide on pages 9 and 10 puts emergency procedures at your fingertips. It lists quick-action steps to take and refers you to the pages that follow for more detailed instructions. Read the emergency procedures in this chapter thoroughly before you need to put them into practice.

Before leaving on a long trip, check the condition of all your car's replaceable components: belts and hoses, fluid levels and coolant mixture, light bulbs and wiper blades, tire tread and pressure (don't forget the spare). Replace partially worn parts so they won't fail on the road.

For safety reasons, electronic or computer-controlled equipment such as electronic fuel injection or the automatic braking system (an anti-skid control) should be serviced only by professional technicians. When you decide to repair a mechanical or electrical component, remember that it would be impossible to illustrate all the variations among cars in this book. Your car's service manual, available from the dealer or at an auto parts store, is an important tool; many of the repair steps recommend that you refer to the service manual for more precise specifications. If a step does not refer to parts similar to those on your vehicle, do not improvise the repair. If you are not sure what is causing the problem or you lack the skills, confidence or tools to do the job, do not hesitate to call for professional service.

SAFETY TIPS

1. Read your car owner's manual from cover to cover for important operational, maintenance and safety information. Keep the manual in the glove compartment. If you have misplaced it, obtain another copy from the dealer or from the car's manufacturer.

2. Before attempting any repair in this book, read the entire repair procedure and familiarize yourself with the safety precautions in the chapter. Use the right tool for the job; using makeshift equipment can produce a hazard both during the repair and on the road.

3. Do not smoke or cause sparks when servicing or inspecting a car. Keep an ABC fire extinguisher and a first-aid kit nearby.

4. If it is essential to heat the work space, do not use a heater with an open flame; use an electric heater and position it away from the car.

5. Do not work under a car supported by an emergency jack, and do not allow passengers to remain in the car while it is being jacked. Do not work under a car raised on cement blocks or a makeshift stand. Chock the wheels securely *(p. 137)*.

6. Allow the engine to cool completely before working on a car. Do not remove a radiator cap until the system has cooled for at least 90 minutes.

7. Disconnect the negative battery cable before working on the fuel and electrical systems, or if you smell burning wiring.

8. Wear rubber or heavy-duty work gloves and safety goggles when working on the battery or near corrosive or flammable liquids. If brake fluid, battery acid or any other corrosive material gets on your skin or eyes, flush the affected area with water immediately.

9. Do not wear loose clothing, a watch or jewelry when making car repairs. Secure long hair and roll up shirtsleeves.

10. To prevent carbon monoxide poisoning, work in a well-ventilated area—outdoors is best. Do not run an engine inside an unventilated garage or in any enclosed space.

11. Catch draining fluids in a sturdy basin and wipe up spills immediately. Store all car fluids away from children and pets. Discard used oil and other fluids according to local environmental regulations.

12. When jump-starting a car, remember that the battery contains sulfuric acid, which is corrosive and can give off highly explosive hydrogen gas. Wear protective gloves and goggles and do not smoke.

13. Before using jumper cables, refer to the correct procedure *(page 17)*. Double check that the positive (+) terminals are connected by the positive cable, and that the negative (-) terminal of the operative car is connected to the engine block of the disabled car before turning either car's ignition.

14. When making a roadside repair on a car with an electric fan, disconnect the negative battery cable. The fan can turn on even after the engine is turned off.

15. When using this book as a reference, never attempt a repair that is not described specifically. If there is a discrepancy between the illustration and your car's components, seek professional service. If a part is under warranty, do not repair it yourself—you will void the warranty.

TROUBLESHOOTING GUIDE

SYMPTOM	PROCEDURE
Brakes fail	Pump brakes several times hard and fast
	Downshift
	Gently engage and disengage parking brake; summon help
Brakes fade (gradually lose power)	Pull car off road to place of safety and let brakes cool
Steering fails	Apply gentle, even pressure to brakes
	Turn on four-way flashers and honk horn
	Downshift
	Pull car off road to place of safety; summon help
Tire blows out	Lift foot off accelerator
	Grip steering wheel firmly and apply gentle, even pressure to brakes
	Pull car off road to place of safety
	Set up and light flares *(p. 12)*, or set up reflective triangles
	Replace flat tire *(p. 13)*
Accelerator sticks	Do not turn off ignition
	Shift into NEUTRAL (manual) or stay in DRIVE (automatic)
	Apply gentle, even pressure to brakes
	Try to pull up pedal with foot
	Coast off road to place of safety; summon help
Hood pops open	Look through side window or narrow opening between top of dashboard and edge of hood
	Slow car and pull off road to place of safety
	Repair hood latch *(p. 124)* or tie hood closed with rope
Headlights go out	Pump brakes several times hard and fast
	Try to drive in a straight line unless positive of upcoming curve
	When car slows down, pull off road to place of safety
	Set up and light flares *(p. 12)* or set up reflective triangles
	Check fuses *(p. 106)* and summon help if necessary
Fire in passenger compartment or under hood	Immediately pull car off road to place of safety
	Turn off ignition
	Get passengers out; extinguish fire *(p. 12)*
Fire near gas tank	Immediately pull car off road to place of safety
	Seek shelter at least 500 feet away from car
	Call fire department
Engine doesn't start (cold car)	Turn off ignition
	Depress gas pedal to floor, then release and try ignition again
	Inspect spark plugs and distributor cap *(p. 115)* and dry them if wet
Engine cranks, but doesn't start (hot car)	Check for engine flooding and pry up choke plate if necessary *(p. 15)*
Engine loses power or stalls in hot weather	Pull car off road to place of safety
	Turn off ignition; allow engine to cool
	Pour cool water on fuel pump and fuel lines to break vapor lock *(p. 14)*
Starter clicks, but engine doesn't crank and headlights do not operate or grow dim	Shift into NEUTRAL (manual) or PARK (automatic)
	Switch off all accessories and ignition
	Jump-start battery *(p. 17)*; be sure to follow safety instructions

TROUBLESHOOTING GUIDE (continued)

SYMPTOM	PROCEDURE
Gas gauge reads EMPTY	Turn on emergency flashers
	Coast in slow lane at 10 mph, then speed up to 30 mph, coast to 10 mph, and repeat until gas can be added
	Do not turn off ignition; car will be hard to restart
Oil pressure light comes on	Stop engine immediately and coast off road to place of safety
	Check dipstick and add oil if necessary (p. 58); look for leaks
	If oil warning light comes on again, stop immediately and summon help
Water temperature light comes on	Immediately pull car off road to place of safety
	Turn off engine; allow it to cool 90 minutes
	Remove radiator cap (p. 15) and add coolant (p. 85)
	If light stays on, check for leaks in the cooling system radiator or hoses (p. 83)
Alternator (generator) light comes on	Pull car off road to place of safety and turn off engine
	Check for broken or missing drive belts
	Make emergency fan belt if necessary (p. 14)
Brake light comes on	Make sure parking brake is off
	Pressure in brake lines may be low; reduce speed immediately and drive directly to a service station to have brakes checked
Scraping sound from under car	Pull car off road to place of safety
	Turn off engine; allow car to cool
	Inspect exhaust system for dragging tail pipe; wire up tail pipe (p. 13)
	Leave a window rolled down
	Drive car to service station and have exhaust system professionally serviced
Windshield washers don't work	Check windshield washer reservoir; if empty, refill
	Check windshield washer nozzles for blockage; if frozen or clogged, unplug them (p. 16)
Car stuck in snow	Try rocking the car (p. 16)
	Use traction grates to free badly stuck wheels (p. 16)
Door lock frozen	Unfreeze lock (p. 16)
Exhaust sounds loud	Pull car off road to place of safety
	Turn off engine; allow car to cool
	Inspect muffler or exhaust pipe for hole
	Drive home with window down; replace muffler, if not welded on (p. 79), or have exhaust system serviced professionally
Banging sound from under hood	Pull car off road to place of safety
	Check to see if mechanical parts, such as fan blades, are hitting other components
Engine stops after driving through water	Coast off road to place of safety
	Allow engine to cool
	Dry spark plug cables, coils, and inside and outside of distributor cap

FIRST-AID KIT

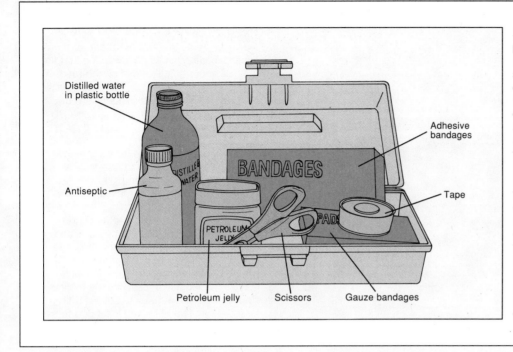

Distilled water in plastic bottle

Antiseptic

BANDAGES

Adhesive bandages

Tape

Petroleum jelly   Scissors   Gauze bandages

Stow a first-aid kit in the passenger compartment where it can be reached quickly. Pre-assembled first-aid kits are sold in stores, but you might want to put together one of your own, based on your family's health needs and the type of traveling you do. Most convenient are sterilized, disposable supplies that are individually packaged, such as adhesive bandages, moist towelettes, eye wash solutions and the like. For hot weather travel, include sunburn lotion and insect bite medication; for cold weather, lip balm and cold medicines that do not cause drowsiness. Aspirin or acetaminophen round out the kit. Store the articles in a sturdy, waterproof box *(left)*, with the contents clearly labeled. Keep the box unlocked to prevent hunting for the key. Before long trips, remember to include any prescribed medication that family members use—and a spare pair of eyeglasses if the driver wears them.

EMERGENCY SUPPLY KIT

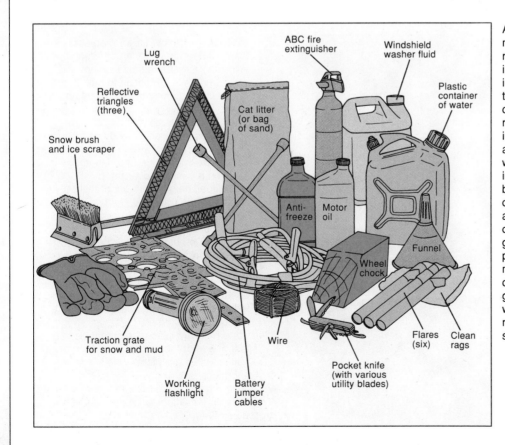

Lug wrench

Reflective triangles (three)

ABC fire extinguisher

Windshield washer fluid

Plastic container of water

Snow brush and ice scraper

Cat litter (or bag of sand)

Anti-freeze   Motor oil

Funnel

Wheel chock

Traction grate for snow and mud

Working flashlight

Wire

Battery jumper cables

Pocket knife (with various utility blades)

Flares (six)   Clean rags

A well-stocked emergency supply kit is a must in the event of an accident or on-the-road breakdown. The choice of items to include can vary based on the type of driving you do, but certain equipment is essential. In addition to the items shown at left, consider including penetrating oil (to loosen rusted lug nuts), a tire pressure gauge, insulated screwdrivers and pliers and an adjustable wrench. In regions with severe winters, pack blizzard survival gear, including a shovel and a large plastic garbage bag, which can double as a heat-retaining outer garment in cold or wet weather. In any climate, a container of drinking water can be a lifesaver. Carry change for emergency phone calls, as well as a pad of paper and a pen. Most tools and materials may be stored in the trunk, but keep flares or reflective triangles and the fire extinguisher in the passenger compartment, where they are accessible in case of a rear-end collision. Replace emergency supplies as they are used up.

COMBATING A CAR FIRE

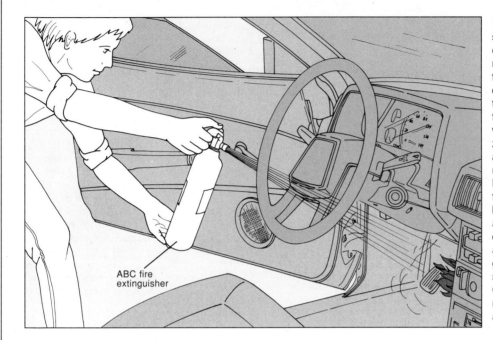

ABC fire
extinguisher

Using a fire extinguisher. An acrid smell, or the sudden failure of one or more electrical components, is a warning that fire may be about to strike. Pull off the road, turn off the ignition and get all passengers out of the car. To smother flames inside the passenger compartment, aim an ABC fire extinguisher through an open door or window *(left)*. Hold it upright, direct the nozzle at the base of the fire, press the lever and spray with a sweeping side-to-side motion. Wait a few minutes after the fire has been put out and, if it rekindles, use the extinguisher again. If flames have broken out in the engine compartment, get away; if it is smoking, raise the hood and disconnect the negative battery cable to allow hot wiring to cool. Use the extinguisher to snuff smoldering components, standing at least five feet from the engine. **Caution:** Do not attempt to put out a fire near the fuel tank. Move at least 500 feet away from the car and summon help.

HANDLING ROADSIDE EMERGENCIES

Reflective
warning
triangle

Flare

Setting up flares. To warn other drivers that you need to make an emergency stop, switch on the emergency flashers and hand signal your intention to pull off the road. On a paved shoulder, maintain traffic speed until leaving the road, then stop well away from the stream of traffic. If the shoulder is unpaved, slow down first, then drive off the road. Turn off the ignition and set the parking brake. In a dangerous location––on a curve or over the crest of a hill—get all passengers out of the car and far away from traffic. At night, leave the headlights on and turn on the interior lights. Set up at least three flares.
Caution: Do not ignite flares near gasoline. Set the flares on the shoulder close to the road's edge; where there is no shoulder, set them on the pavement. Keeping an eye on traffic behind you, set the first flare 10 feet behind the car, and the second 300 feet back from the first *(left)*. On an undivided highway, place the third flare 100 feet ahead of the car, to warn oncoming traffic. Flares are highly visible both day and night, but burn for only 15 to 20 minutes. If using less visible reflective warning triangles *(inset)*, position them as you would flares.

CHANGING A FLAT TIRE

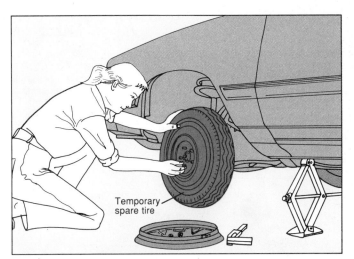

Temporary spare tire

Scissor-type jack

1 **Using the emergency jack.** Set the parking brake and put the car in PARK (automatic transmission) or NEUTRAL (manual transmission). Chock the wheel diagonal to the one being changed *(page 137)*. Then, with a screwdriver or the jack handle, pry off the wheel cover. Use a lug wrench (often the end of the jack handle) to loosen the lug nuts a full turn; if the nuts are stubborn, apply penetrating oil, wait a few minutes, and try again. Do not remove the nuts entirely. Position the jack under the jacking point nearest the wheel (the owner's manual locates these points) and crank the handle clockwise until the jack fits into the jacking point *(above)*. Keep turning until the wheel barely lifts off the ground. Remove the lug nuts, and pull the wheel off the studs.

2 **Putting on the spare tire.** Lift the spare tire onto the wheel studs. With one hand, hold it in place; with the other, *(above)* finger-tighten the nuts (their tapered ends toward the wheel). Let the jack down slowly until the full weight of the car rests on the ground. Then, with the lug wrench, finish tightening the lug nuts in a crisscross pattern *(page 28)*, but do not overtighten. Slip the tire valve through the hole in the wheel cover and hammer the cover onto the wheel with the heel of your hand. Many cars are now equipped with a space-saving, temporary spare tire. These small emergency substitutes should be driven no faster than 50 mph and only as far as the nearest service station.

SECURING A DRAGGING TAIL PIPE

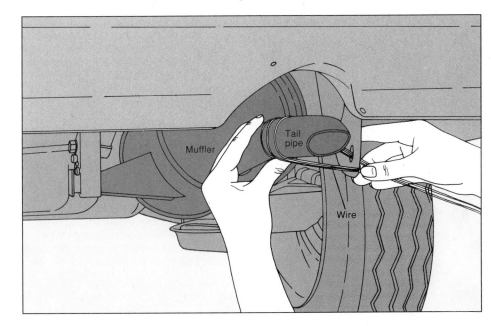

Muffler

Tail pipe

Wire

Wiring up a dragging tail pipe. Corrosion can weaken a hanger or bracket and allow the tail pipe to drag along the road. If you hear a grating sound from the rear of the car, park on level ground, turn off the ignition, set the parking brake and allow the engine to cool. To support the tail pipe, loop flexible wire around it and a nearby part of the car frame, or lash the wire to the trailer hitch or towing hook *(left)*. Raise the car with the emergency jack if necessary, but do not crawl under it. Or, drive a front and back wheel onto the curb to give you access. Make sure no part of the exhaust system touches the fuel lines, fuel tank or brake lines. This is a temporary remedy only; drive with a window open and have the system professionally repaired.

REPLACING A BROKEN FAN BELT

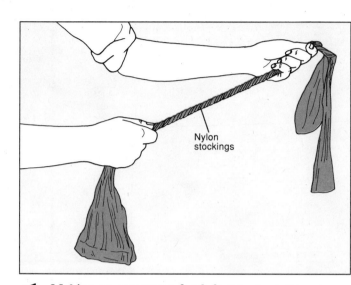

Nylon stockings

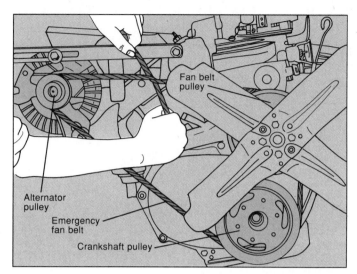

Fan belt pulley

Alternator pulley

Emergency fan belt

Crankshaft pulley

1 **Making an emergency fan belt.** If the fan belt breaks or loosens, several dashboard warning signals—the alternator light, the coolant temperature light, or a light marked ENGINE—will come on within seconds of each other. Pull off the road at once, turn off the ignition, allow the engine to cool and check whether the belt is damaged or missing (a broken belt will have fallen off). Fashion a substitute belt from nylon stockings or pair of tights, twisting the fabric into a tight rope *(above)*. A fiber (not plastic) clothes line or a nylon rope may also be used.

2 **Installing an emergency fan belt.** The fan belt, located behind the radiator, drives the fan, the water pump and the alternator *(page 80)*. Cars with power steering, air conditioning, and other accessories have additional pulleys; do not attempt to wrap a temporary fan belt around these. Slip the makeshift fan belt around the crankshaft pulley, then up around the alternator and fan belt pulleys *(above)*. Stretch it as tightly as possible and tie a firm knot. Trim off loose ends, replace any lost coolant *(page 83)* and slowly drive to the nearest service station.

BREAKING A VAPOR LOCK (Engine with carburetor)

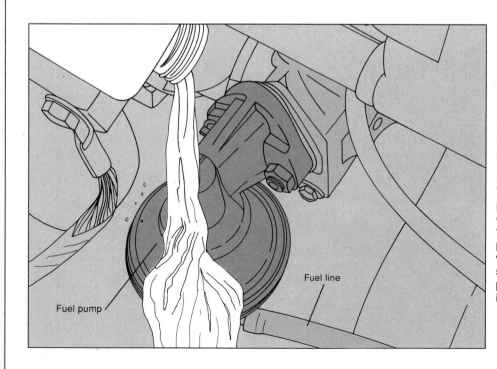

Fuel pump

Fuel line

Condensing the vaporized fuel. Vapor lock occurs when excessive heat in the engine compartment causes gasoline in the fuel lines to vaporize, blocking the passage of liquid fuel to the carburetor. If vapor lock occurs frequently or soon after refueling, try a different brand of gasoline. To break a vapor lock, you must condense the pocket of vaporized fuel in the fuel line or at the fuel pump. Park in a safe place (in the shade is ideal), turn off the ignition and wait at least 30 minutes before trying the starter again. Then, open the hood and locate the fuel pump; generally it is bolted to the side of the engine block *(page 62)*. Pour cool water on the fuel pump and the fuel lines into the pump *(left)*, or wrap the pump and lines with wet rags. If the engine continues to starve for fuel, test the fuel pump and replace it if necessary *(page 67)*. If the pump is sound, take the car for service.

CORRECTING A FLOODED ENGINE (Engine with carburetor)

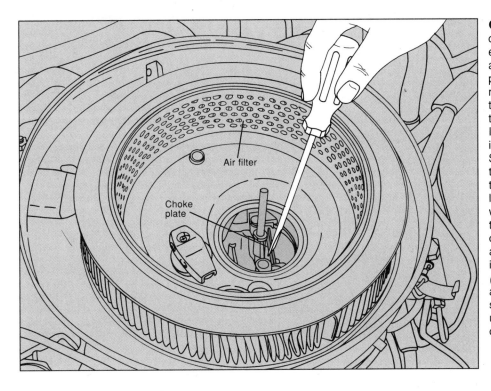

Air filter

Choke plate

Quick fix for a flooded engine. If the car's engine cranks but fails to start, the engine may be flooded. Press the accelerator pedal to the floor; hold it there, without pumping it, while cranking the engine. Do not run the starter continuously for more than 10 seconds; this could drain the battery, or worse, damage the ignition system. If the engine will not turn over, turn off the ignition, wait 10 minutes and try again. Should the engine still not start, remove the air cleaner cover *(page 74)* and inspect the carburetor. **Caution:** Do not smoke or light a flame. The carburetor may be wet with fuel and you will smell raw gasoline if the engine is flooded. If the choke plate is closed, the air/fuel mix may be too rich, another cause of engine flooding. Wedge it fully open with the tip of a screwdriver *(left)*, hold the accelerator pedal to the floor and try the starter again; the car should start immediately. Repeated flooding is usually the result of a jammed float valve or damaged float; take the car for service.

COOLING DOWN AN OVERHEATED CAR

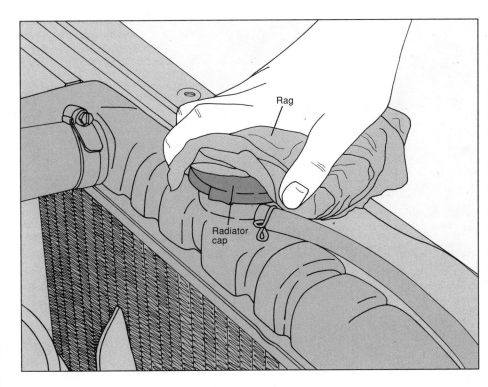

Rag

Radiator cap

Removing the radiator cap. At the first sign of overheating, when the dashboard oil light or coolant temperature light comes on, pull the car off the road to a safe spot. If the cooling system has boiled over, steam will be coming from the radiator; wait at least 15 minutes before lifting the hood. Check for leaking hoses, broken or missing drive belts or apparent leaks in the radiator itself. If all such components are sound, the coolant level may be low. **Caution:** Do not remove the radiator cap to check the level if the engine is hot; pressurized coolant can instantly boil up, expelling a sudden burst of steam. Wait at least 90 minutes before releasing the cap. Wrap a thick rag around the cap *(left)* and turn it counterclockwise to the first stop; some steam will now escape. When the hissing stops, push down on the cap and turn it fully to remove it. Check the coolant level *(page 83)* and top it up if necessary *(page 85)*.

MANEUVERING OUT OF SNOW

Cat litter

Traction grate

Providing a grip for the wheels. To free a car mired in snow, first try gently rocking it backward and forward: Keep the front wheels straight and shift the transmission back and forth between low and reverse (automatic transmission), or between first and reverse (manual transmission). Press on the accelerator pedal only enough to move the car without spinning the wheels. Keep the revolutions per minute as low as possible and the wheels as straight as possible. If the wheels spin, stop; repeated rocking raises the transmission fluid temperature and can cause serious damage to an automatic transmission. Instead, place collapsible traction grates under the drive wheels *(left)*.
Caution: Don't allow anyone to stand near the car when driving over the grates; a rotating tire can hurl them at high speed. Drive slowly over the grates. When the car is free, retrieve the grates. Rock salt, sand or cat litter can also be used to provide traction *(inset)*; keep a 25-pound bag of it in the trunk.

UNSTICKING FROZEN MECHANISMS

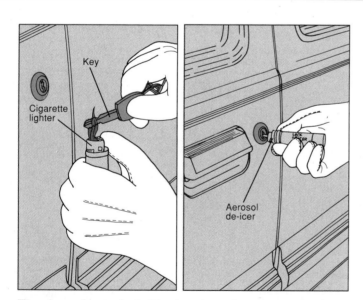

Key

Cigarette lighter

Aerosol de-icer

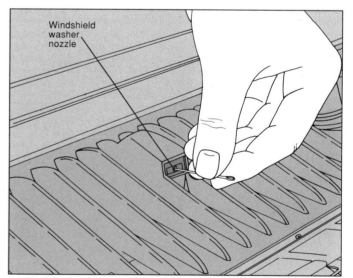

Windshield washer nozzle

Thawing a frozen lock. Wearing gloves, heat the car door key with a match or a cigarette lighter, then insert it quickly into the lock *(above, left)*. Alternatively, squirt a commercial lock de-icer into the keyhole *(above, right)*, and insert the key.

Unblocking a windshield washer nozzle. Heat a pin with a match or cigarette lighter. Insert the tip into an ice-blocked nozzle *(above)*. If the nozzle still does not squirt properly, the fluid may be frozen in the reservoir or the lines. Move the car to a warm location and allow the fluid to thaw. Use commercial windshield washer fluid in the winter; it contains an antifreeze. Unplug a nozzle that is clogged with dirt by wiggling a pin or thin wire into the opening; a pin can also be used to adjust the nozzle aim.

JUMP-STARTING A CAR

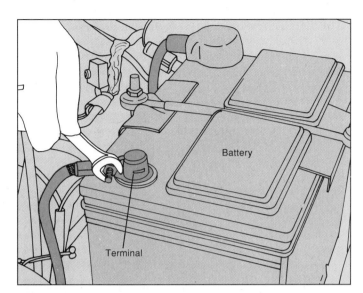

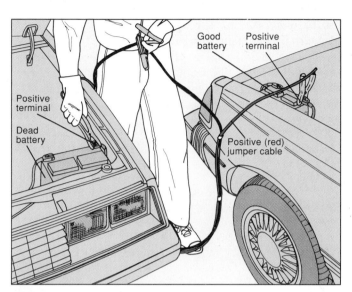

1 **Tightening the battery cable terminals.** If the starter does not work or the engine barely turns over, first make sure the car is not out of gas. Put the car in PARK (automatic transmision) or NEUTRAL (manual transmission), open the hood and inspect the battery cables and terminals. **Caution:** Wear safety goggles and rubber or heavy-duty work gloves, and do not smoke. Clean the battery posts and terminals *(page 100)*, then tighten the cable clamps with a wrench *(above)*. Do not overtighten. Try to start the car. If the engine still cranks weakly, and the headlights fade, jump-start the battery *(step 2)*.

2 **Connecting the positive jumper cable. Caution:** First consult the owner's manual to make sure your car can be jump-started. If so, verify that both your car and the car providing the jump start have compatible batteries of the same voltage. Position the cars close together, but not touching: hood to hood or side by side. Set the transmissions of both cars in PARK (automatic) or NEUTRAL (manual), switch off their ignitions, turn off all accessories and engage the parking brakes. Identify the positive battery post in each car; it is generally the larger and labelled (+) or POS. Attach one jaw of the positive (red) jumper cable to the positive terminal of the good battery and its other (red) jaw to the positive terminal of the dead battery *(above)*.

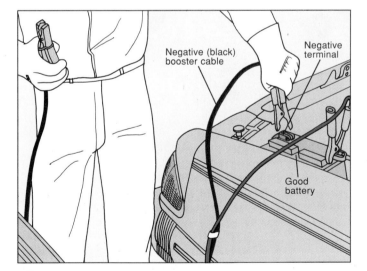

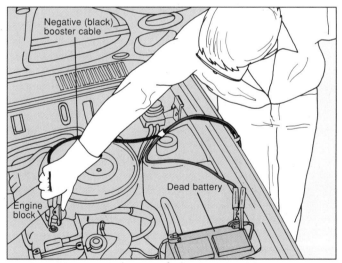

3 **Attaching the negative jumper cable.** The negative jumper cable is usually black. First attach one of its jaws to the negative terminal (marked - or NEG) of the good battery *(above)*. Now check for cross-wiring, which could permanently damage the alternators of both cars or even cause personal injury: The positive (red) jumper cable must connect the positive (+) terminal on the good battery to the positive terminal on the dead battery, and the first jaw of the negative (black) jumper cable must be attached to the negative (-) terminal of the good battery.

4 **Boosting the battery.** On the disabled car, attach the second jaw of the negative (black) jumper cable to a good ground—an unpainted bolt on the engine block or chassis *(above)*. **Caution:** Do not attach the negative jumper cable to the dead battery. Attach the jaw at least 12 inches from the dead battery. Do not attach the jaw to the alternator or any other electrical component. Start the engine of the good car and gently rev it. Then start the engine of the disabled car. Disconnect the jumper cables by reversing the steps you followed to install them.

YOUR CAR

A typical family car has more than 3,000 parts, and nearly 60 materials—from rubber and plastic to steel and chrome—are used in its construction. The heart of the car, its gasoline-fueled internal combustion engine, has evolved surprisingly little since the turn of the century. But with the recent development of computerized engine controls, the car now has a brain as well: Most cars manufactured since 1981 have an electronic control module, or ECM. This minicomputer adjusts the air/fuel mixture, spark timing, emission controls and many other

functions as you drive, providing optimum performance under a wide range of conditions. It even diagnoses malfunctions, recording them in codes that can be read by a repair technician using special equipment.

Despite such electronic wizardry, the car remains largely a system of mechanical parts that wear, break and go out of adjustment. Keeping your car in peak condition depends mainly on your own ability to diagnose problems and perform basic maintenance and repair procedures. These tasks, detailed

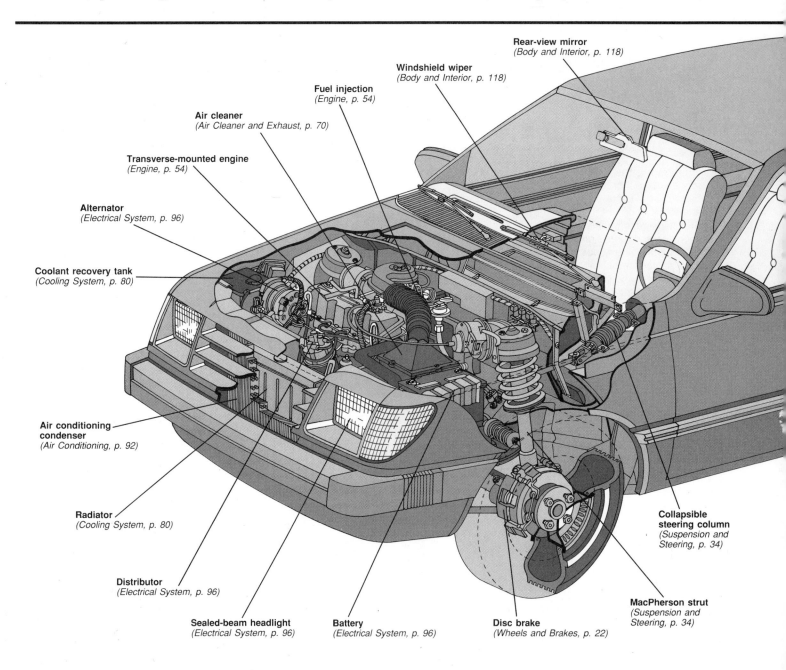

Rear-view mirror
(Body and Interior, p. 118)

Windshield wiper
(Body and Interior, p. 118)

Fuel injection
(Engine, p. 54)

Air cleaner
(Air Cleaner and Exhaust, p. 70)

Transverse-mounted engine
(Engine, p. 54)

Alternator
(Electrical System, p. 96)

Coolant recovery tank
(Cooling System, p. 80)

Air conditioning condenser
(Air Conditioning, p. 92)

Radiator
(Cooling System, p. 80)

Distributor
(Electrical System, p. 96)

Sealed-beam headlight
(Electrical System, p. 96)

Battery
(Electrical System, p. 96)

Disc brake
(Wheels and Brakes, p. 22)

Collapsible steering column
(Suspension and Steering, p. 34)

MacPherson strut
(Suspension and Steering, p. 34)

step-by-step in this book, are well within the abilities of the average car owner and fix-it enthusiast. Mastering them can add thousands of miles to the life of your car, and save you money in the process.

Economic influences have shaped the modern car, shown below, both inside and out. Its smaller body has been aerodynamically designed to reduce drag and lower fuel consumption. The transverse-mounted, four-cylinder engine saves both gas and space under the hood. Front-wheel drive, which elimi-

nates a drive shaft running to the rear axle, allows a roomier passenger compartment and provides better handling in snow and rough terrain. And fuel injection, once only seen in race cars and exotic European imports, meters gas to the engine precisely so that fuel waste is kept to a minimum. Fuel injection also decreases emissions and squeezes more mileage from each gallon of gasoline. These and other components are labeled below, with the page number of the chapter where they are pictured and described in greater detail.

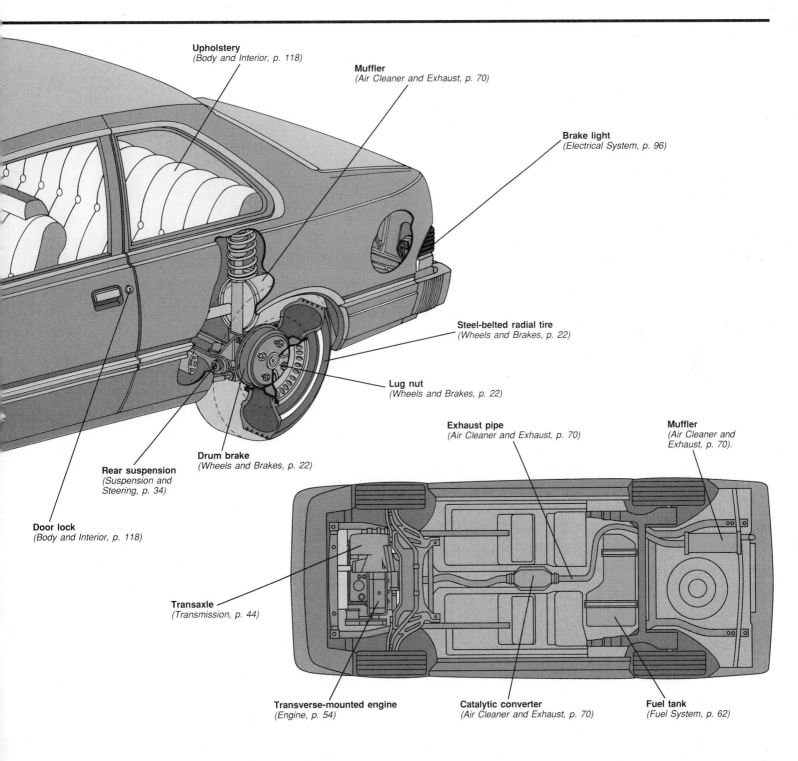

Upholstery
(Body and Interior, p. 118)

Muffler
(Air Cleaner and Exhaust, p. 70)

Brake light
(Electrical System, p. 96)

Steel-belted radial tire
(Wheels and Brakes, p. 22)

Lug nut
(Wheels and Brakes, p. 22)

Door lock
(Body and Interior, p. 118)

Rear suspension
(Suspension and Steering, p. 34)

Drum brake
(Wheels and Brakes, p. 22)

Exhaust pipe
(Air Cleaner and Exhaust, p. 70)

Muffler
(Air Cleaner and Exhaust, p. 70).

Transaxle
(Transmission, p. 44)

Transverse-mounted engine
(Engine, p. 54)

Catalytic converter
(Air Cleaner and Exhaust, p. 70)

Fuel tank
(Fuel System, p. 62)

Of course, there are many variations in automobile systems. Some cars have automatic transmission, while others have manual transmission. And instead of front-wheel-drive, many cars have rear-wheel-drive, and some have four-wheel drive. The car pictured below has many features more typical of cars manufactured several years ago. It has a carburetor rather than fuel injection, along with a more powerful, eight-cylinder engine, mounted longitudinally. Such a large engine is essential for powering a traditional full-size car. It is also ideal for cars that tow a trailer or carry a heavy load of power accessories. Four-wheel disc brakes, a recent innovation on the standard family car, provide optimum stopping power since they dissipate heat better and are less affected by water than drum brakes. Rear-wheel drive, with its drive shaft running to a differential on the rear axle, makes for a simpler transmission, and dispenses with the expensive constant velocity (CV) joints on the front axle. However, the drive shaft robs some space from the passenger compartment. In addition, rear-

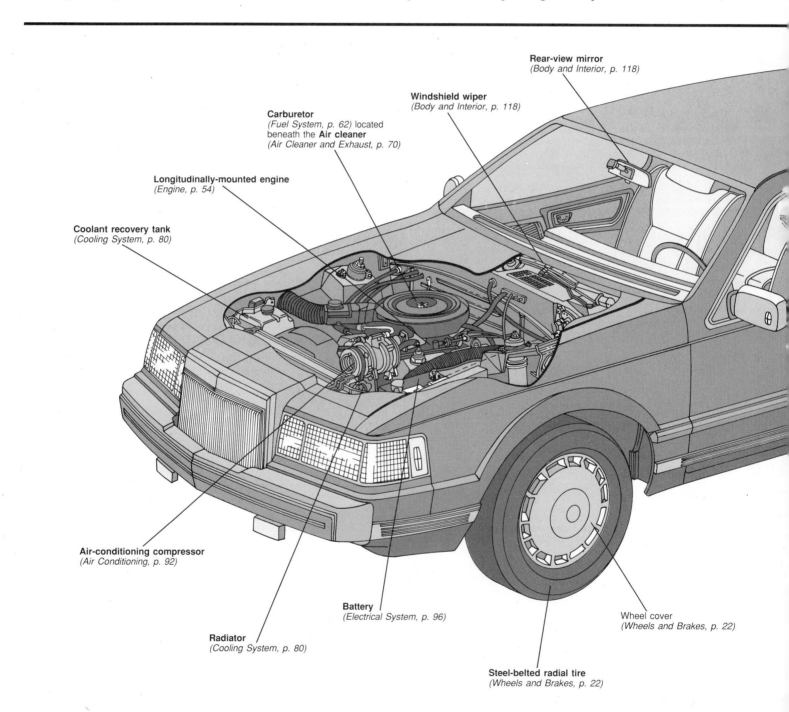

Rear-view mirror
(Body and Interior, p. 118)

Windshield wiper
(Body and Interior, p. 118)

Carburetor
(Fuel System, p. 62) located beneath the **Air cleaner**
(Air Cleaner and Exhaust, p. 70)

Longitudinally-mounted engine
(Engine, p. 54)

Coolant recovery tank
(Cooling System, p. 80)

Air-conditioning compressor
(Air Conditioning, p. 92)

Battery
(Electrical System, p. 96)

Radiator
(Cooling System, p. 80)

Wheel cover
(Wheels and Brakes, p. 22)

Steel-belted radial tire
(Wheels and Brakes, p. 22)

wheel drive provides a smoother ride, with less vibration transferred to the steering. For these reasons, rear-wheel drive is still used in larger, luxury cars.

Like nearly all cars on American roads today, both cars pictured use unleaded gasoline, and have sealed-beam headlights, modern emission-control equipment and impact-absorbing bumpers. Not seen here are the automatic passive restraints—seat belts or air bags. The computer-controlled anti-lock braking system, or ABS, will soon be a standard safety feature as well. The ABS improves emergency stopping ability by allowing the driver to use maximum braking force without the wheels locking. Four-wheel steering is another innovation being introduced in foreign cars.

Examine the illustrations in this chapter and the other chapters in this book, and try to pinpoint similar components under the hood of your car. Understanding the maze of systems, their relative positions and how they interact is your first step toward maintaining a healthy car.

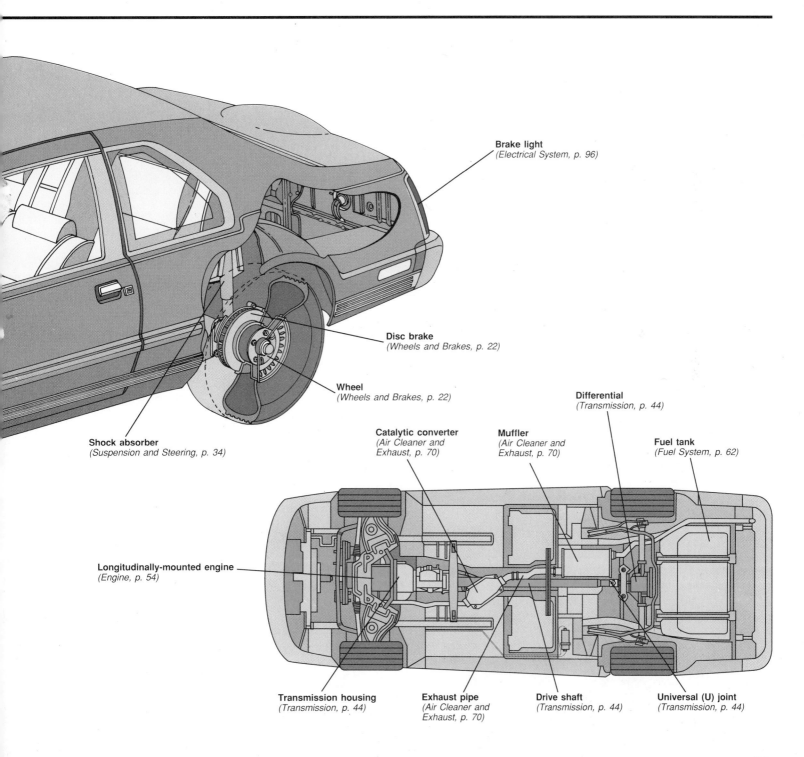

Brake light
(Electrical System, p. 96)

Disc brake
(Wheels and Brakes, p. 22)

Wheel
(Wheels and Brakes, p. 22)

Differential
(Transmission, p. 44)

Shock absorber
(Suspension and Steering, p. 34)

Catalytic converter
(Air Cleaner and Exhaust, p. 70)

Muffler
(Air Cleaner and Exhaust, p. 70)

Fuel tank
(Fuel System, p. 62)

Longitudinally-mounted engine
(Engine, p. 54)

Transmission housing
(Transmission, p. 44)

Exhaust pipe
(Air Cleaner and Exhaust, p. 70)

Drive shaft
(Transmission, p. 44)

Universal (U) joint
(Transmission, p. 44)

WHEELS AND BRAKES

The hydraulic brake system goes to work when the brake pedal is depressed, forcing pistons in the master cylinder to exert tremendous force on the brake fluid in the brake lines. On drum brakes, the pressure on this fluid is forced into the wheel cylinder pistons and transferred to the brake shoes, which press against the inside of the brake drum. On disc brakes, the hydraulic pressure pushes on a caliper piston, which transfers the pressure to brake pads that grip a rotating disc, or rotor. The friction of the lining against the brake drum or rotor makes the wheel stop turning.

Disc brakes are exposed to the open air instead of being enclosed by drums, making them less likely to overheat and fade, or lose efficiency. They also work better in bad weather because the centrifugal motion of the disc throws off rain and mud. Since the car's front brakes do most of the work of stopping the car, many cars are equipped with disc brakes on the front wheels and drum brakes on the rear wheels, as pictured below. The owner's manual will tell you what kind of brakes your car has.

The Troubleshooting Guide on pages 24 and 25 lists some common problems with brakes, wheels and tires. Do not remove a drum-brake drum or work on its inner mechanism; for safety reasons, this is a job better left to the advanced do-it-yourselfer or a professional.

Hydraulic brakes are a sealed system. If you must repeatedly top up the brake fluid, check for a leak in the brake lines and hoses *(page 30)*. Use only the brake fluid recommended by your car's manufacturer, and never put any other fluid in the brake system. Brake fluid is alcohol based, and deteriorates on exposure to air and moisture; discard any leftover fluid.

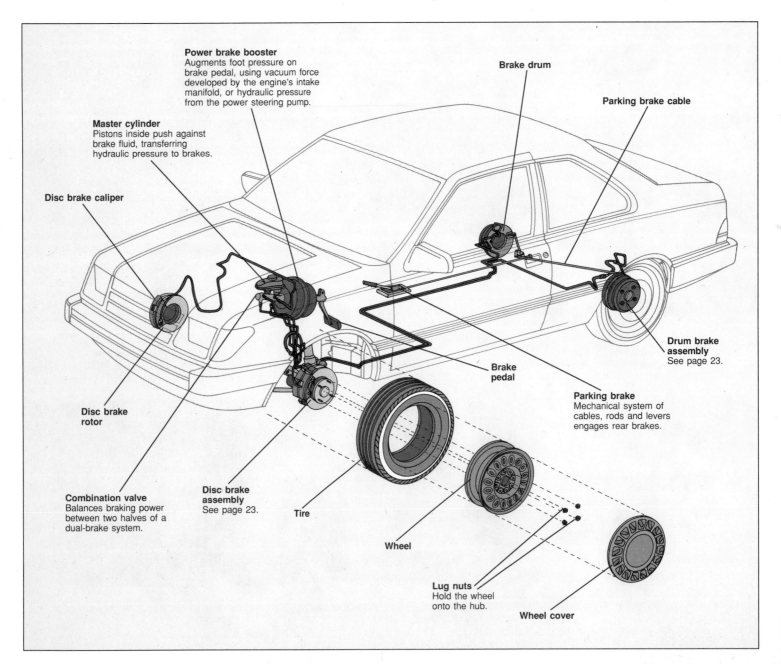

Power brake booster
Augments foot pressure on brake pedal, using vacuum force developed by the engine's intake manifold, or hydraulic pressure from the power steering pump.

Master cylinder
Pistons inside push against brake fluid, transferring hydraulic pressure to brakes.

Disc brake caliper

Disc brake rotor

Combination valve
Balances braking power between two halves of a dual-brake system.

Disc brake assembly
See page 23.

Tire

Wheel

Lug nuts
Hold the wheel onto the hub.

Wheel cover

Brake drum

Parking brake cable

Drum brake assembly
See page 23.

Parking brake
Mechanical system of cables, rods and levers engages rear brakes.

Brake pedal

Have all the fluid in the brake system replaced professionally every two or three years.

On a car with drum brakes, the parking brake is connected to the rear wheels. Cars equipped with disc brakes on all four wheels have a different type of parking brake: either an extra drum brake built onto each back wheel, or a special lever connected to the disc brake caliper. If your car has four-wheel disc brakes, have the parking brake professionally serviced.

The front tires on cars equipped with front-wheel drive can wear out twice as fast as the rear tires. To maximize tire life and balance the tread wear, have the tires rotated every 6,000 miles. If your spare tire is full size, include it in the rotation. The wheels should be balanced every time a tire is changed, and when switching from summer to winter tires. Keep the tires correctly inflated *(page 26).*

Almost all tire problems occur during the last 10 percent of tread life, so it is important to replace your tires when the tread wears down. Periodically inspect the tires for signs of wear and learn to read their tread wear patterns *(page 27).* The replacement tires you choose will depend upon your driving habits. For high-speed highway driving, or rough, winding roads, steel-belted radial tires provide safer traction and longer wear. If you drive at slow speeds, or mostly in stop-and-go city traffic, less expensive bias-ply tires may suit your needs. Make sure both tires on the same axle are the same size and type. Because of their different handling performance, radials should never be mixed with other types of tire on the same car.

Have the wheels aligned once a year. Proper alignment helps prevent wear throughout the suspension and steering systems, lengthens tire life and improves fuel economy.

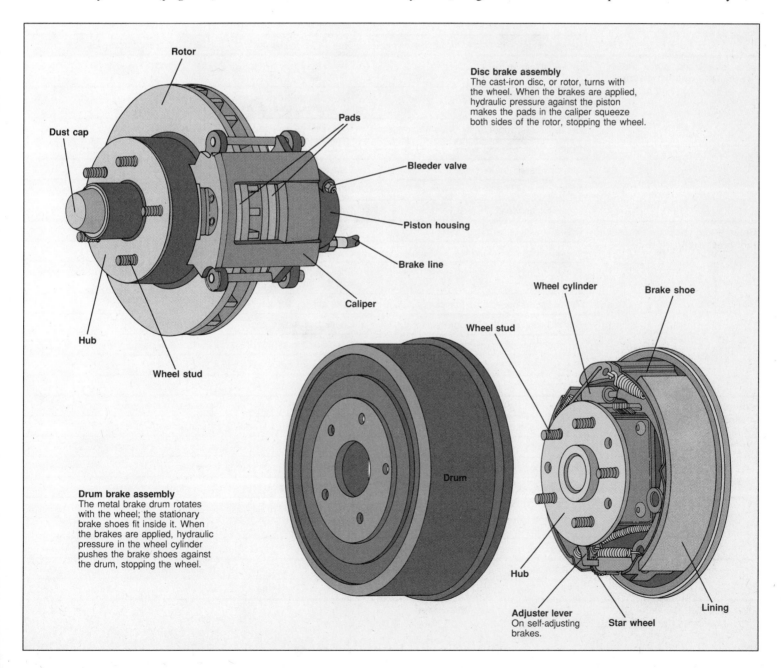

Rotor

Disc brake assembly
The cast-iron disc, or rotor, turns with the wheel. When the brakes are applied, hydraulic pressure against the piston makes the pads in the caliper squeeze both sides of the rotor, stopping the wheel.

Pads

Dust cap

Bleeder valve

Piston housing

Brake line

Hub

Caliper

Wheel stud

Wheel cylinder

Brake shoe

Wheel stud

Drum

Hub

Drum brake assembly
The metal brake drum rotates with the wheel; the stationary brake shoes fit inside it. When the brakes are applied, hydraulic pressure in the wheel cylinder pushes the brake shoes against the drum, stopping the wheel.

Adjuster lever
On self-adjusting brakes.

Star wheel

Lining

TROUBLESHOOTING GUIDE

SYMPTOM	POSSIBLE CAUSE	PROCEDURE
Uneven tire wear	Wheels out of alignment	Take car for service to align wheels
	Tires not inflated properly	Check and adjust tire air pressure (p. 26) □○
	Poor driving habits	Examine tread (p. 26) □○; change tire if necessary (p. 27) ◨○
	Suspension or steering defective	Check suspension and steering components (p. 34)
Wheel wobbles	Lug nuts loose or missing	Check wheel and tighten or replace nuts (p. 27) □○
	Wheels not balanced	Take car for service to balance wheels
	Wheels out of alignment	Take car for service to align wheels
	Suspension or steering defective	Check suspension and steering components (p. 34)
Complete loss of brakes	Broken brake line or major leak in cylinder	Check brake system for leaks (p. 30) ◨○
	Air or blockage in hydraulic brake system	Take car for service to bleed brakes
	Brakes wet	Drive with the brake pedal depressed slightly to dry the brakes
	Brakes fading due to overheating	Shift into lower gear and coast to a stop; let the brakes cool; do not ride the brake pedal
	Brake linings or pads oily or glazed	Check disc brake pads (p. 31) ◨○; take car for service
Excessive brake pedal travel; brakes fade under pressure	Brake fluid level low	Check brake fluid level (p. 29) □○; check brake system for leaks (p. 30) ◨○
	Drum brake self-adjuster faulty	Make several reverse stops to adjust drum brakes; if braking does not improve, take car for for service
	Brake fluid of poor quality or contaminated	Take car for service to bleed brakes
	Brake linings or pads worn	Check disc brake pads (p. 31) ◨○; take car for service
	Air in hydraulic brake system	Take car for service to bleed brakes
	Leak in brake system	Check brake system for leaks (p. 30) ◨○
	Brake hoses weak or mushy	Take car for service
Brake pedal requires excessive foot pressure to slow car	Brake fluid of poor quality or contaminated	Take car for service to bleed brakes
	Brake linings or pads worn	Check disc brake pads (p. 31) ◨○; take car for service
	Brakes fading due to overheating	Shift into lower gear and coast to a stop; let the brakes cool; do not ride the brake pedal
	Brake line or hose kinked or clogged	Take car for service
	Brake linings or pads oily or glazed	Check disc brake pads (p. 31) ◨○; take car for service
	Drum or rotor worn or damaged	Check disc brake rotor (p. 32) ◨○; take car for service
	Power brake vacuum booster faulty	Take car for service
	Brake pedal linkage binding	Take car for service
Car pulls to one side when brakes are applied	Brakes wet	Drive with the brake pedal depressed slightly to dry the brakes
	Tires not inflated properly	Check and adjust tire air pressure (p. 26) □○
	One front tire worn excessively	Examine tread (p. 26) □○; change tire if necessary (p. 27) ◨○
	Brakes not equally adjusted	Take car for service to adjust brakes
	Brake hose or line kinked or clogged	Take car for service
	Front wheels out of alignment	Take car for service to align wheels
	Suspension or steering defective	Check suspension and steering components (p. 34)
	Leak in half of dual brake system	Check brake system for leaks (p. 30) ◨○
Brakes grab	Brake pads or linings worn or damaged	Check disc brake pads (p. 31) ◨○; take car for service
	Parking brake frozen or stuck	Adjust parking brake (p. 33) ◨○

DEGREE OF DIFFICULTY: □ Easy ◨ Moderate ■ Complex
ESTIMATED TIME: ○ Less than 1 hour ◐ 1 to 3 hours ● Over 3 hours

SYMPTOM	POSSIBLE CAUSE	PROCEDURE
Brakes grab (cont.)	Drum or rotor worn or damaged	Check disc brake rotor (p. 32) ■○; take car for service
	Tires not inflated properly	Check and adjust tire air pressure (p. 26) □○
	One front tire worn excessively	Examine tread (p. 26) □○; change tire if necessary (p. 27) ■○
	Brake pedal linkage binding	Take car for service
	Wheels out of alignment	Take car for service to align wheels
Brake pedal vibrates; brakes thump or chatter	Brake pads or linings worn	Check disc brake pads (p. 31) ■○; take car for service
	Air in hydraulic brake system	Take car for service to bleed brakes
	Brake hoses weak or mushy	Take car for service
	Wheel bearings loose or worn	Take car for service
	Drum or rotor damaged	Check disc brake rotor (p. 32) ■○; take car for service
Parking brake does not hold	Parking brake cables loose	Adjust parking brake (p. 33) ■○
	Parking brake cable broken	Take car for service
Brakes squeal or scrape when applied	Brake pads or linings worn	Check disc brake pads (p. 31) ■○; take car for service
	Drum or rotor worn or damaged	Check disc brake rotor (p. 32) □○; take car for service
	Drum brake mechanism damaged	Take car for service

DEGREE OF DIFFICULTY: □ **Easy** ■ **Moderate** ■ **Complex**
ESTIMATED TIME: ○ **Less than 1 hour** ◐ **1 to 3 hours** ● **Over 3 hours**

TIRE CONSTRUCTION

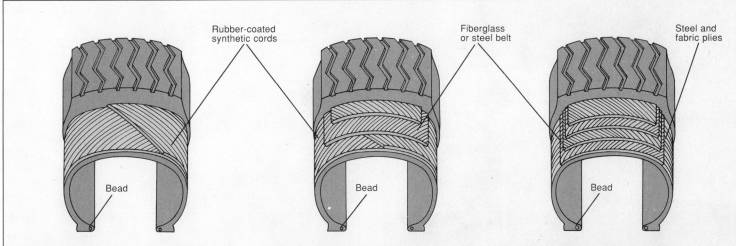

Bias-ply tires have two or more plies (layers) of rubber-coated rayon, nylon or polyester cords. The plies cross one another from bead to bead at an angle (bias) of 35 to 40 degrees to the tread's centerline. Nylon-ply tires can develop flat spots on the bottom if the car is parked for a long time; the spots smooth out after a few minutes of driving. Rayon-ply tires do not share this problem, are stronger and last longer than nylon-ply tires. Polyester-ply tires are the strongest and longest-lasting of the three.

Bias-belted tires offer a firmer ride, better traction, more puncture resistance and a longer life than bias-ply tires. They share the same crisscross ply construction but, in addition, possess two or more belts, usually made of fiberglass or steel. These are bonded around the circumference of the tire on top of the plies. Fiberglass belts provide better high-speed performance; steel belts offer greater strength and longer wear. You may mix bias-ply and bias-belted tires on the same car, but not on the same axle.

Radial-ply tires have cords that run straight across the tire from bead to bead at a right angle (radially) to the tread's centerline. The flexible sidewall that results reduces tread wear and provides the best handling and cornering, especially at high speed. Fiberglass or steel belts around the circumference of the tire stabilize the tread against the road, improving traction. Radial tires are the longest lasting. Because of their different handling characteristics, do not mix radials with other types of tires, even on different axles.

INSPECTING AND MAINTAINING TIRES

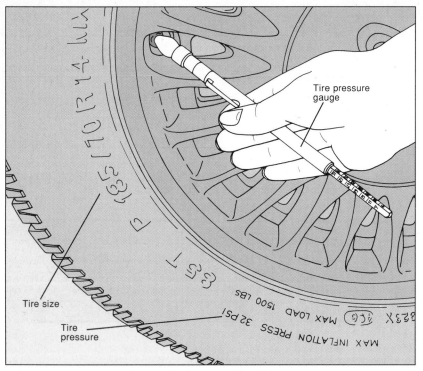

Tire pressure gauge

Tire size

Tire pressure

Checking the tire air pressure. Correct air pressure extends tire life, improves mileage and gives you better control when driving. You will find the recommended pressure for your car's tires on the tire itself, or in your owner's manual, on a sticker inside the glove compartment or on the driver's door. Tire air pressure is measured in pounds per square inch, or psi. Use a tire pressure gauge to check the pressure every two weeks. Also check it when driving between hot and cold climates; an increase in air temperature of 10°F raises tire pressure by one pound per square inch.

For an accurate reading, measure the pressure when the tires are cold. Locate the air valve on the tire and unscrew its cap. Fit the end of a tire pressure gauge firmly over the end of the valve and press. If the valve hisses, air is escaping and you will not get a good reading. The stem of a pencil-type gauge *(left)* will pop out; a dial-type pressure gauge will display the reading on its face. If the pressure is low, drive to a nearby garage to add air, then recheck the pressure. If it is too high, bleed some air by depressing the pin in the center of the air valve, and take another reading. Check the pressure in all the tires, including the spare.

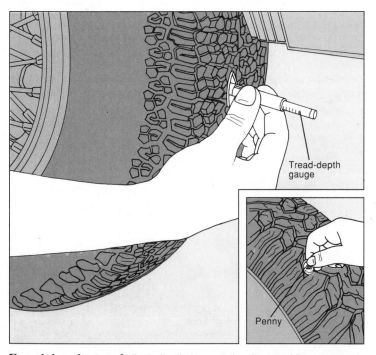

Tread-depth gauge

Penny

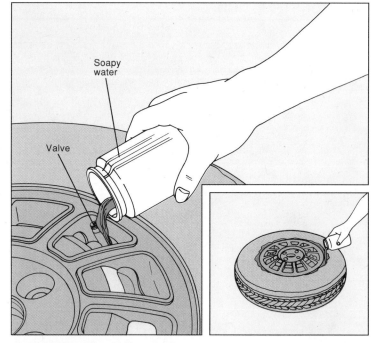

Soapy water

Valve

Examining the tread. Periodically inspect the tire tread for wear and foreign objects. Insert the end of a tread-depth gauge into the shallowest tread groove *(above)*. If the reading is less than 1/16 inch, replace the tire with one that matches the other on the same axle *(page 25)*. To check tread wear without a gauge, insert a penny, Lincoln's head down, into the groove *(inset)*. If the top of Lincoln's head shows, you need a new tire. Modern tires have built-in tread wear indicators; these usually appear as 1/2-inch bands across the tire when the tread has eroded to 1/16 inch.

Testing for leaks. To test the tire valve for escaping air, remove the wheel from the car *(page 27)* and lay it down. Unscrew the valve cap and pour a half-and-half solution of liquid detergent and water over the valve *(above)*. If bubbles appear around the valve, it leaks; have a professional replace the valve. If no bubbles appear at the valve, check for leaks where the tire bead seals the rim: Drip the soapy solution around the rim on both sides of the wheel *(inset)* and look for bubbles. If you spot a leak, have the wheel serviced professionally.

TIRE TREAD WEAR PATTERNS

Identifying the causes of tire wear. Improperly balanced wheels and incorrect front or rear alignment both produce uneven tire wear. Have a professional make the necessary adjustments. Poor driving habits also damage tires. Skidding on dry pavement with the wheels locked, for example, results in flat spots on the tire tread; spinning the wheels on dry pavement can tear off chunks of tread; and driving on an underinflated tire, or hitting potholes or curbs, weakens the sidewalls.

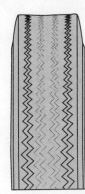

Excessive wear at the center of the tread indicates that a tire is overinflated. Most of the weight of the car is being carried on the centerline of the tire, wearing it out prematurely. Check the tire air pressure *(page 25)* and bleed off air as needed.

Premature wear on both edges of the tread points to an underinflated tire. This defect can cause the car to skid. Check the tire pressure *(page 25)* and add more air.

Feathering is a condition in which the edge of the inside or outside tread develops a ridge or ruffle. It results from excessive toe-in or toe-out caused by poor wheel alignment. Have the wheels professionally aligned.

Wear along one edge of the tread and not the other indicates incorrect wheel camber (the inward or outward tilt of the wheel). Have the wheels professionally aligned.

Cupping is a regular scalloping of the tread caused by worn suspension parts, a damaged steering linkage, faulty wheel bearings or unbalanced wheels. Have these components serviced and the tires rotated and balanced professionally.

CHANGING A TIRE

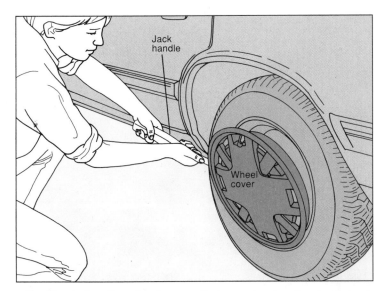

Jack handle

Wheel cover

1 Removing the wheel cover. Park on a level surface and chock the tire diagonally opposite the one being changed. Put a car with automatic transmission into PARK and a car with manual transmission into REVERSE, and engage the parking brake. If you are installing the spare tire, check its pressure *(page 26)*. Insert the flat end of the jack handle, or a utility bar, between the wheel and wheel cover and gently pry off the cover *(above)*.

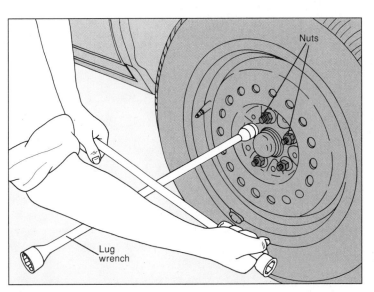

Nuts

Lug wrench

2 Loosening the lug nuts. With a lug wrench, partially loosen the nuts securing the wheel. If a letter "L" marks the nuts, they have left-hand threads and must be loosened in a clockwise direction. Unmarked nuts, which have right-hand threads, are loosened by turning them counterclockwise *(above)*. If the nuts are stubborn, apply penetrating oil, wait a few minutes, and try loosening them again. Do not remove the nuts entirely.

CHANGING A TIRE (continued)

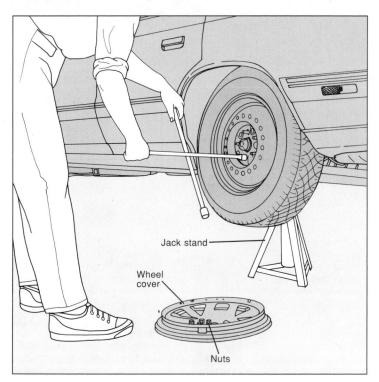

Jack stand

Wheel cover

Nuts

3 **Removing the lug nuts.** Install the car's jack *(page 137)* at its jacking point closest to the tire being changed. Jack the car until the tire clears the ground, position a jack stand *(page 137)* and lower the car. Remove the nuts with the lug wrench *(above)*. Store the nuts in the wheel cover for safekeeping. Pull off the wheel and tire. If the assembly is hard to remove, dislodge it by pushing the tire sidewall firmly with your foot.

4 **Installing the wheel.** Roll the replacement wheel into position. Lift the wheel, supporting it on your knees if necessary, and align its holes with the mounting studs on the car *(above)*. Push the wheel onto the studs. Holding the wheel firmly in place with one hand, screw the nuts onto the studs by hand, positioning the tapered ends of the nuts toward the wheel.

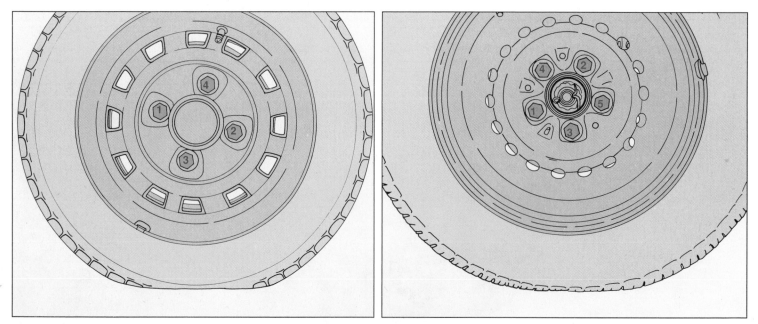

5 **Tightening the lug nuts in sequence.** To ensure that stress is distributed evenly around the wheel, use the lug wrench to tighten the nuts in one of the patterns shown above. Then raise the car with the jack, remove the jack stand and lower the car. Tighten all the nuts in sequence once again. Replace the wheel cover, inserting the tire valve through its hole in the cover. If the tire you removed was damaged, have it fixed or replaced as soon as possible; the spare tire is for temporary use only. If you installed a special temporary spare *(page 13)*, drive no farther than the nearest service station.

CHECKING THE BRAKE FLUID LEVEL (Screw-cap master cylinder)

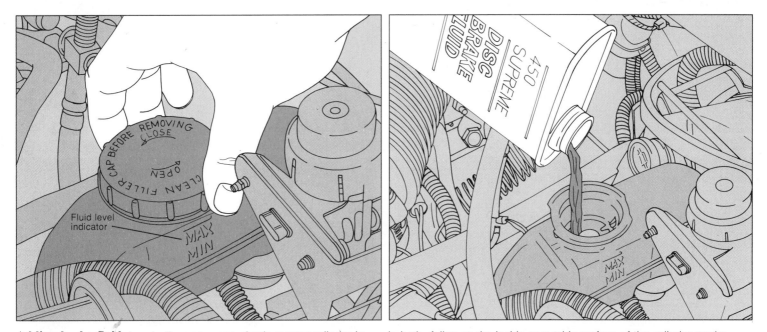

Adding brake fluid. Locate the screw-cap plastic master cylinder in the engine compartment, usually on the driver's side against the fire wall. You can check the brake fluid level without removing the cap if the cylinder is transparent. If not, wipe the cap before removing it to prevent debris from falling into the fluid. Unscrew the cap counterclockwise *(above, left)*. Where there are two reservoirs, check the fluid level in both. A line on the inside or outside surface of the cylinder marks the required fluid level; if the level falls below that line, add a fresh supply from a sealed container *(above, right)*. The owner's manual specifies which type of brake fluid to use—DoT 3, DoT 4 or DoT 5. Brake fluid corrodes paint; protect the car's finish and wash off spills immediately with water. Replace the cap on the master cylinder.

CHECKING THE BRAKE FLUID LEVEL (Bail-top master cylinder)

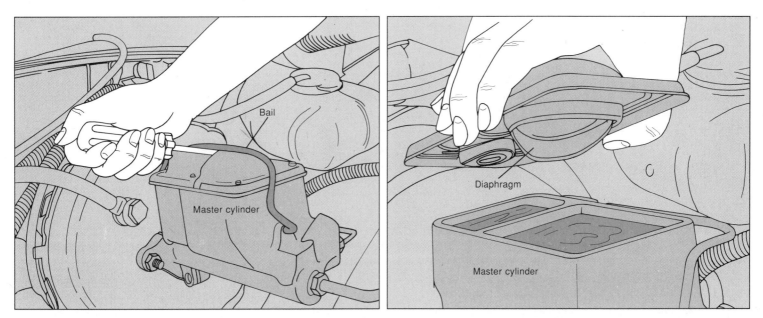

Adding brake fluid. Locate the bail-top metal master cylinder in the engine compartment, usually on the driver's side against the fire wall. Using a screwdriver as a lever, pry off the bail, or retainer, that holds the top down *(above, left)* and lift off the top. (On some cylinders, the top is fastened with screws; unscrew them.) The cylinder is divided into two reservoirs. Check the fluid level *(above, right)*; it should come within 1/2 inch of the top of each reservoir. Top off the brake fluid with a fresh supply from a sealed container. The owner's manual specifies which type of brake fluid to use—DoT 3, DoT 4 or DoT 5. Brake fluid corrodes paint; protect the car's finish and wash off spills immediately with water. A rubber diaphragm lines the top of the cylinder. Push the protruding cups of the diaphragm up into the top before replacing it.

FINDING LEAKS IN LINES AND HOSES

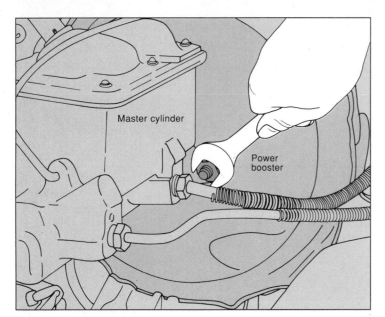

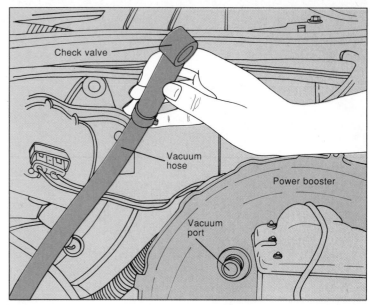

1 **Tightening the connections between master cylinder and power booster.** With the engine off and the transmission in neutral, pump the brakes several times, then hold the brake pedal down. It should not move more than halfway to the floor, and should maintain pressure for at least 30 seconds. If the pedal sinks slowly to the floor, the brake system may have a leak. First check for a leak where the master cylinder joins the power booster. If you see wet spots at the fittings, tighten the nuts with a wrench *(above)*. Next, wipe away the wet spots and pump the brake pedal as you did before. If the wet spots reappear, have the brakes serviced.

2 **Checking for brake fluid in the vacuum hose.** If fluid leaks from the master cylinder into the power booster, you will find brake fluid in the vacuum hose that leads from the booster. Pull the end of the vacuum hose off its vacuum port *(above)*, take off the check valve and examine the hose's interior for fluid. If you are not able to see inside clearly, carefully twirl a narrow screwdriver into the hose. If the tool has fluid on it when it is withdrawn, there is a leak; have the brakes serviced professionally.

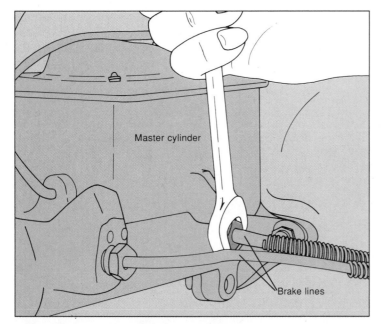

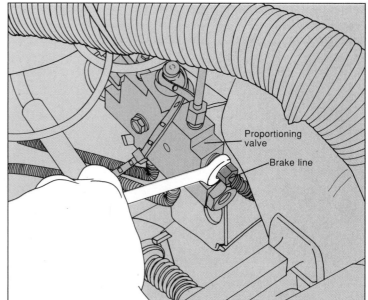

3 **Tightening the brake line fittings on the master cylinder.** Look for wet patches indicating brake fluid leaks at the fittings where the brake lines leave or enter the master cylinder. If there is any seepage, wipe it dry and then, with a tubing wrench or a combination wrench, tighten the fittings *(above)*. Now pump the brakes a few times. If the wet spots reappear, have the brakes serviced professionally. If there is no leak at this point in the system, go on to step 4.

4 **Tightening valve fittings.** Valves in the brake system monitor or control hydraulic pressure to improve braking efficiency. The proportioning valve, shown here, is typical in rear-wheel-drive cars. A front-wheel-drive car may have a pressure-differential valve, and many large cars have a combination valve. Locate the valve by following the brake lines from the master cylinder. If you spot leaks at the valve's fittings, wipe them dry, then tighten each fitting with a tubing wrench or a combination wrench *(above)*. Pump the brakes a few times. If the leaks reappear, have the brakes serviced professionally.

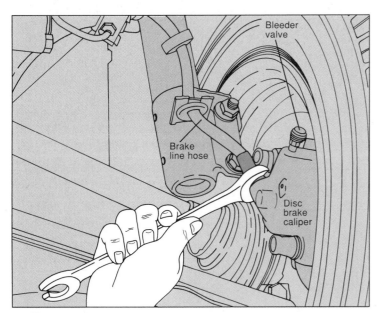

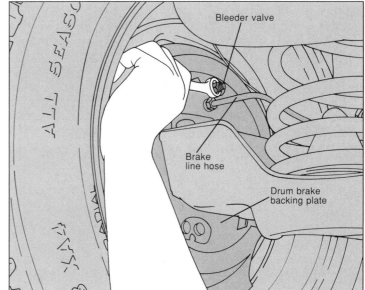

5 **Tightening the brake line fitting at the wheel.** Raise the car on jack stands *(page 137)*. Inspect all four wheels at the point where the flexible brake line, or hose, joins the brake. An oily, damp patch indicates a leak. Wipe the area clean. Gently tighten the fitting holding the brake line to the brake using a tubing wrench or a combination wrench *(above)*. (The adjustment is the same for drum brakes and disc brakes, shown here.) Now pump the brakes a few times; if the leak reappears, have the brakes serviced professionally.

6 **Tightening the bleeder valve connection.** On drum brakes, the bleeder valve is on the backing plate; on disc brakes, it is on the caliper assembly. Oily patches on the drum brake's backing plate indicate a leak from either the brake line, bleeder valve or brake cylinder inside the drum. Wipe the wet spots dry, then gently tighten the bleeder valve with a tubing wrench or a combination wrench *(above)*. On disc brakes, look for leaking brake fluid at the bleeder valve itself and on the caliper. Wipe away wet spots and tighten the bleeder valve. Pump the brakes a few times; if the leaks reappear, have the brakes serviced professionally.

INSPECTING DISC BRAKES

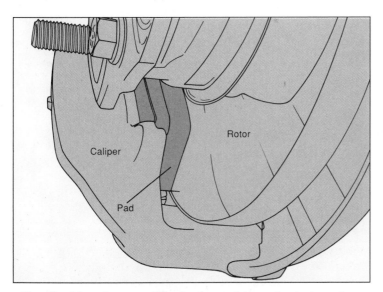

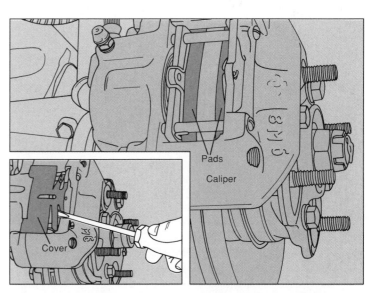

1 **Checking the outer disc brake pad.** Your disc brake calipers may be mounted in a different position from the example shown here, but the pads are inspected the same way. Raise the front of the car on ramps or jack stands *(page 137)* and remove the wheel *(page 27)*. Examine all visible edges of the outer brake pad *(above)*. If the pad has worn thinner than 1/16 inch at any point, or if it is soaked with grease or brake fluid, have the brakes serviced professionally. To check the inner brake pad, go to step 2.

2 **Checking the inner brake pad.** Examine the back edges of both the inner and outer brake pads by looking through the inspection hole in the caliper. The inspection hole may have a protective cover; snap it off with a screwdriver *(inset)*. Check all visible surfaces of each pad *(above)*. If a pad is worn thinner than 1/16 inch at any point, or if the pad is soaked with grease or brake fluid, have the brakes serviced professionally.

INSPECTING DISC BRAKES (continued)

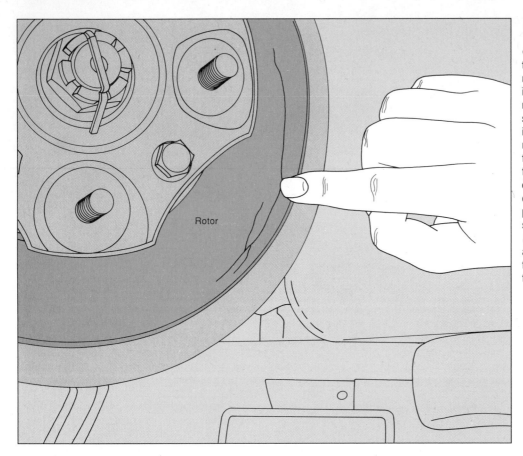

3 **Checking the rotor for damage.**
Worn out disc brake pads, or foreign material lodged between the pad and the disc, or rotor, may damage the brake rotor. You can inspect a rotor without removing the caliper. Examine both sides of the rotor for rust, uneven wear, ridges or deep scoring. Run a fingernail across each surface in several places to feel for defects you can not see *(left)*. Rub the rotor with your fingertips to detect grease spots or leaking brake fluid. Examine the surface of the rotor for dark patches or minute cracks caused by overheating. If you encounter any of these problems, have the brakes serviced professionally; if not, check the rotor for warpage *(step 2)*. Some rotors are manufactured with a groove machined into the center of the surface. Do not mistake this evenly incised circle for wear.

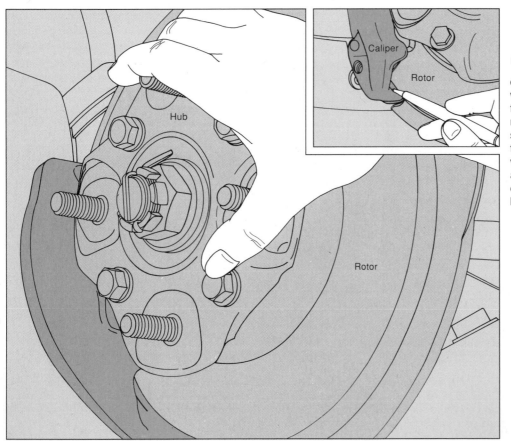

4 **Checking the rotor for warpage.**
Using the edge of the rotor as a guide, draw a line on the inside surface of the caliper with a felt-tip pen *(inset)*. Grasp the wheel hub firmly *(left)* and turn the rotor one full rotation. Watch the edge of the rotor as it moves past the line on the caliper; the rotor should not vary in distance from the line. If the rotor wobbles or wanders, it may be warped; have the brakes serviced professionally. Repeat steps 1 through 4 to check the other front disc brake; check the rear disc brakes as well, if your car has them.

ADJUSTING THE PARKING BRAKE (Pedal type)

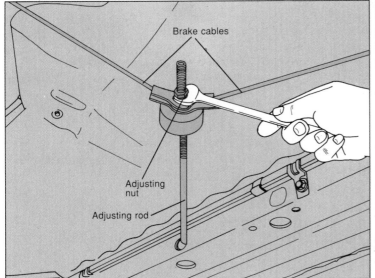

Brake cables

Adjusting nut

Adjusting rod

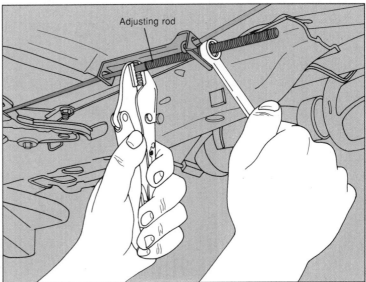

Adjusting rod

Adjusting the parking brake nut. On a car with rear disc brakes, have the parking brake adjusted by a professional. On a car with rear drum brakes, engage the parking brake halfway. Raise both rear wheels using jack stands *(page 137)*, and chock the front wheels. Locate the steel cable leading from each rear wheel to the parking brake pedal. On some cars, these cables meet near the middle at a tension adjuster *(above, left)*. To tighten the parking brake, loosen the locknut, if any, and turn the adjusting nut clockwise, using a combina-

tion wrench. Spin each rear wheel by hand until you feel resistance. Then release the parking brake and spin the rear wheels again; they should now rotate freely. Other cars have a separate cable adjuster for each rear wheel *(above, right)*. Hold the adjusting rod steady with a pair of locking pliers and tighten the parking brake by turning the adjusting nut clockwise with a combination wrench. If the nut is stubborn, apply penetrating oil to loosen it. Test-spin the wheel as above, then adjust and test the second brake cable the same way.

ADJUSTING THE PARKING BRAKE (Lever type)

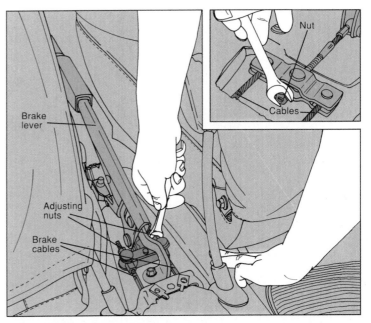

Plastic cover

Brake lever

Brake lever

Nut

Cables

Adjusting nuts

Brake cables

1 **Accessing the brake cable adjusting nuts.** On a car with rear disc brakes, have the parking brake adjusted by a professional. On a car with rear drum brakes, first unscrew the plastic cover around the base of the parking brake lever. Some of the screws may be hidden behind accessories—an ashtray, in the example shown here. Lift off the cover *(above)* to expose the brake cable adjusting nuts. If a light bulb or other electrical accessory is mounted on the cover, first disconnect it, if necessary, to free the cover.

2 **Tightening the adjusting nuts.** Engage the parking brake halfway. Raise both rear wheels using jack stands *(page 137)* and chock the front wheels. If the parking brake has two cables, one leading to each rear wheel *(above)*, tighten one adjusting nut at a time with a combination wrench, periodically spinning the corresponding rear wheel by hand until you feel resistance. Then release the parking brake and spin the rear wheels again; they should now rotate freely. On some cars, a single adjusting nut tightens both cables *(inset)*. Adjust the nut and test-spin both wheels as above.

SUSPENSION AND STEERING

A simple turn of the steering wheel sets a series of mechanisms in motion to move the car right or left. In rack-and-pinion steering, below, the pinion gear meshes with a rack, a steel bar with teeth cut into it, that is connected to the steering linkage. The steering wheel rotates the pinion along the rack, moving the rack side to side; the linkage, a series of rods and levers, transmits this motion to the front wheels.

In Pitman arm steering, also known as gearbox steering, the steering gearbox contains a worm gear resembling the spiral threads of a screw. In a worm-and-roller gearbox, these worm gears mesh with the threads of a roller mounted on the Pitman shaft. The steering wheel moves the roller along the worm gear to swivel the Pitman shaft, which transmits its movement to the steering linkage and the wheels. In a recirculating ball gearbox, the worm gear threads into a ball-nut rack containing ball bearings to reduce friction. The steering wheel rotates the worm gear, making the ball-nut rack move up or down the worm gear shaft. This movement swivels the Pitman shaft. Keep the steering apparatus in good working order by regularly checking the linkage points for signs of wear (page 37). Tighten loose parts, grease the fittings (page 40), and have worn components replaced.

Both systems can be adapted to receive power steering, which uses hydraulic pressure to help turn the steering gears. Consult the Troubleshooting Guide on page 36 to find a list of common malfunctions in the power and the manual steering

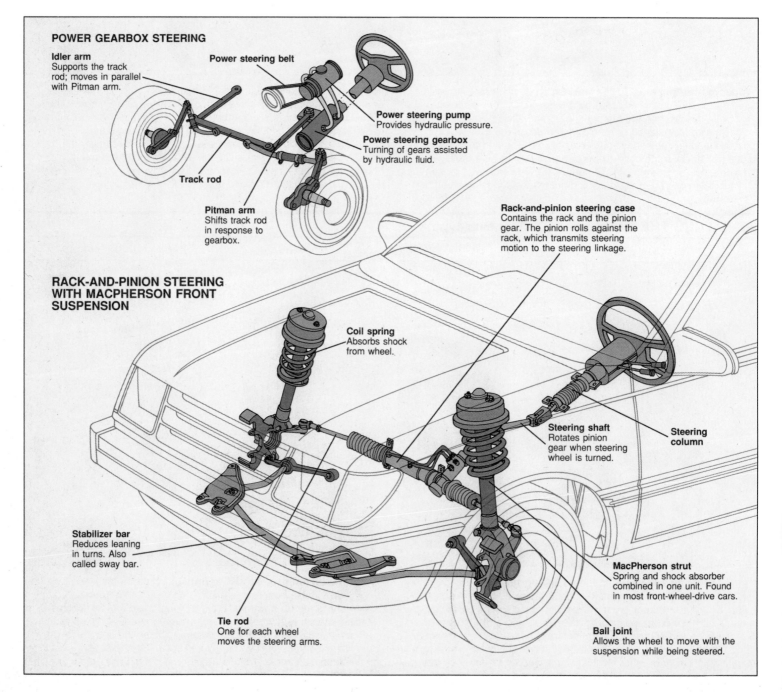

POWER GEARBOX STEERING

Idler arm
Supports the track rod; moves in parallel with Pitman arm.

Power steering belt

Power steering pump
Provides hydraulic pressure.

Power steering gearbox
Turning of gears assisted by hydraulic fluid.

Track rod

Pitman arm
Shifts track rod in response to gearbox.

Rack-and-pinion steering case
Contains the rack and the pinion gear. The pinion rolls against the rack, which transmits steering motion to the steering linkage.

RACK-AND-PINION STEERING WITH MACPHERSON FRONT SUSPENSION

Coil spring
Absorbs shock from wheel.

Steering shaft
Rotates pinion gear when steering wheel is turned.

Steering column

Stabilizer bar
Reduces leaning in turns. Also called sway bar.

MacPherson strut
Spring and shock absorber combined in one unit. Found in most front-wheel-drive cars.

Tie rod
One for each wheel moves the steering arms.

Ball joint
Allows the wheel to move with the suspension while being steered.

systems; it will direct you to the page in this chapter that describes their maintenance and repair.

The car's suspension system—the linkage, springs and shock absorbers—works to keep the wheels on the road and protect the car from jolts. The linkage controls the position of the wheels as they rise and fall, using ball joints to allow motion in more than one direction. The springs, most commonly coil springs, but also leaf springs or torsion bars, absorb the shocks taken by the wheels. The shock absorbers dampen the vibration of the springs.

Most cars have independent front suspension. Instead of a rigid connection between the two wheels, each is linked to the frame separately, so that if the road jolts one wheel, the other will not be affected. Two common designs, one incorporating a more recent innovation, the MacPherson strut, are illustrated below. Though the strut simplifies suspension construction by dispensing with the upper control arm, it cannot be replaced by the do-it-yourselfer. You can easily replace a conventional shock absorber, however (*page 43*).

The rear suspension system is usually much simpler than the front, since it does not incorporate steering components. Rear-wheel-drive cars may use live-axle rear suspension, in which an axle housing that incorporates the differential links wheel to wheel, or an independent rear suspension, in which the differential is mounted on the car's frame. Front-wheel-drive cars have a very simple independent rear suspension system.

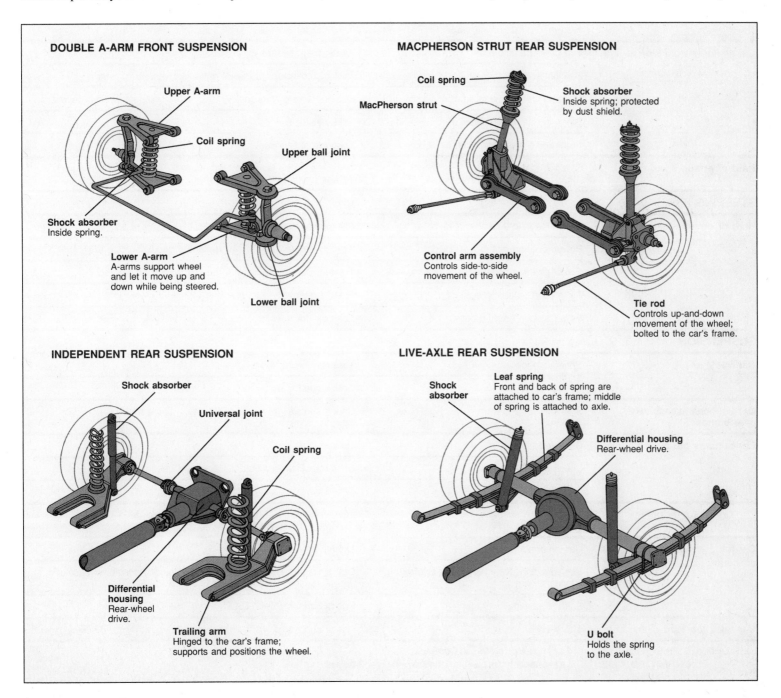

DOUBLE A-ARM FRONT SUSPENSION

Upper A-arm

Coil spring

Upper ball joint

Shock absorber
Inside spring.

Lower A-arm
A-arms support wheel and let it move up and down while being steered.

Lower ball joint

MACPHERSON STRUT REAR SUSPENSION

Coil spring

MacPherson strut

Shock absorber
Inside spring; protected by dust shield.

Control arm assembly
Controls side-to-side movement of the wheel.

Tie rod
Controls up-and-down movement of the wheel; bolted to the car's frame.

INDEPENDENT REAR SUSPENSION

Shock absorber

Universal joint

Coil spring

Differential housing
Rear-wheel drive.

Trailing arm
Hinged to the car's frame; supports and positions the wheel.

LIVE-AXLE REAR SUSPENSION

Shock absorber

Leaf spring
Front and back of spring are attached to car's frame; middle of spring is attached to axle.

Differential housing
Rear-wheel drive.

U bolt
Holds the spring to the axle.

TROUBLESHOOTING GUIDE

SYMPTOM	POSSIBLE CAUSE	PROCEDURE
STEERING (Manual and Power)		
Car pulls to one side	Tire pressure incorrect	Adjust tire pressure (p. 26) □○
	Tire tread uneven	Check tire tread (p. 26) □○
	Ball joints worn	Test ball joints (p. 41) ◨◖; have replaced if necessary
	Steering links loose or worn	Check steering links (p. 37) □○; have parts replaced if necessary
	Steering gear maladjusted	Take car for service
	Front end out of alignment	Take car for service
Steering wheel vibrates	Tire pressure incorrect	Adjust tire pressure (p. 26) □○
	Steering links loose or worn	Check steering links (p. 37) □○; have parts replaced if necessary
	Front end out of alignment	Take car for service
Car wanders from side to side	Tire pressure incorrect	Adjust tire pressure (p. 26) □○
	Ball joints worn	Test ball joints (p. 41) ◨◖; have replaced if necessary
	Steering links loose or worn	Check steering links (p. 37) □○; have parts replaced if necessary
	Steering gear maladjusted	Take car for service
	Front end out of alignment	Take car for service
Hard or erratic steering	Steering links dry	Grease steering linkage points (p. 40) □○; grease suspension linkage points at same time
STEERING (Power only)		
Hard or erratic steering	Power steering fluid low	Add power steering fluid (p. 38) □○
	Power steering belt loose or worn	Tighten belt (p. 38) □○ or replace if necessary (p. 138)
	Power steering hose loose or leaking	Tighten, if loose; replace, if leaking (p. 39) □○
	Air in power steering system	Bleed system (p. 40) □○
	Power steering pump faulty	Take car for service
SUSPENSION		
Car not level	Springs sagging	Test springs (p. 42) □○
	Control arms damaged	Check control arms (p. 42) □○
Car bounces excessively over bumps	Shock absorbers worn	Check shocks (p. 42) □○; replace if necessary (p. 43) ◨◖
Car bottoms out over bumps	Car overloaded	Lighten load
	Shock absorbers worn	Check shocks (p. 42) □○; replace if necessary (p. 43) ◨◖
	Springs worn	Test springs (p. 42) □○
Car squeaks over bumps	Steering and suspension boots or bushings worn	Inspect boots (p. 37) □○; inspect bushings (p. 41) □○
Car body leans when cornering	Car overloaded	Lighten load
	Stabilizer bar (sway bar) loose or broken; bushings worn	Check stabilizer bar (p. 41) □○; tighten, if loose; have replaced, if broken. Check stabilizer bar bushings (p. 41) □○
	Springs sagging	Check springs (p. 42) □○
Car rides too hard or too soft	Shock absorbers worn	Check shocks (p. 42) □○; replace if necessary (p. 43) ◨◖

DEGREE OF DIFFICULTY: □ Easy ◨ Moderate ■ Complex
ESTIMATED TIME: ○ Less than 1 hour ◖ 1 to 3 hours ● Over 3 hours

CHECKING LINKS ON RACK-AND-PINION STEERING

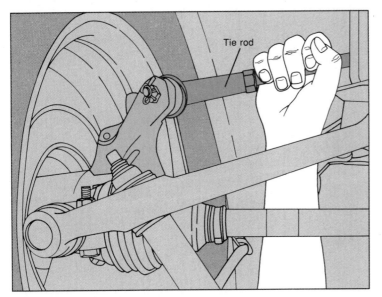

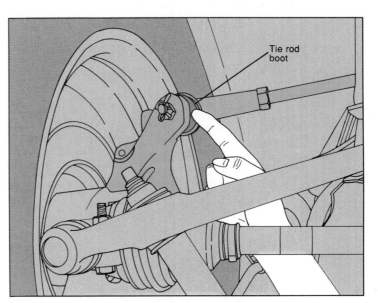

1 **Examining the tie rods.** There are two tie rods at the front of the car, one on each side. Each is connected to a wheel and to the rack. To locate them, set the parking brake, jack up the front end of the car and rest it on jack stands *(page 137)*. To test a tie rod for wear, twist it with your hand *(above)*; it should turn smoothly, but not move up and down. Repeat the procedure on the other rod. If you find incorrect movement, take the car for service.

2 **Inspecting the rubber boot.** Rack-and-pinion steering parts lie close to the road surface and are prone to corrosion. Look for signs of wear on the rubber boot that covers and protects each tie rod at its connection to the rack. With your fingers, examine the folds *(above)* for any cracks that may allow water or dirt to enter. Have damaged boots replaced and the joint inspected.

CHECKING LINKS ON PITMAN ARM (Gearbox) STEERING

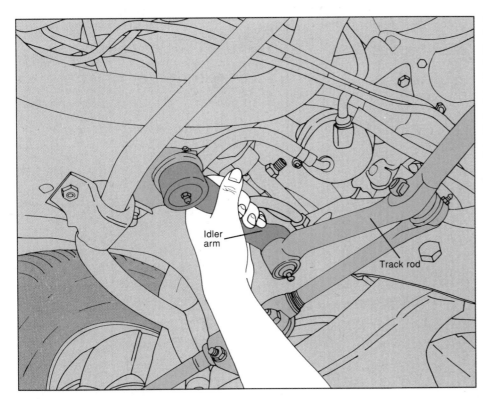

Testing the idler arm and Pitman arm.
The idler arm, located on the passenger side, is connected to the track rod at one end and to the frame at the other. To identify it, set the parking brake, jack up the front end of the car and rest it on jack stands *(page 137)*. To test the idler arm for looseness, grasp it firmly with one hand, then try to move it *(left)*. It should be rigid. Conduct the same test on the Pitman arm, which extends from the steering gearbox to the track rod on the driver's side. If you find movement in either component, take the car for service.

INSPECTING THE POWER STEERING FLUID AND BELT

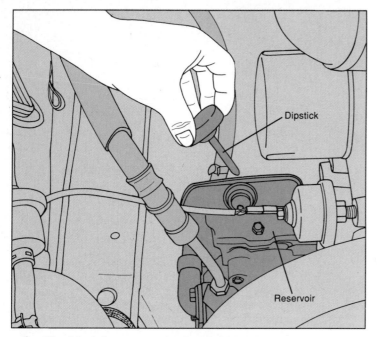

Dipstick

Reservoir

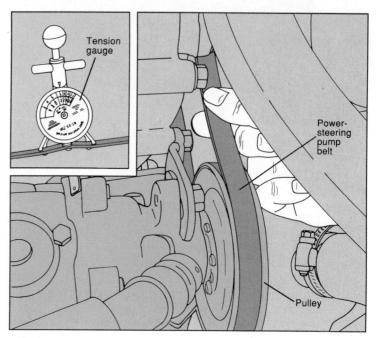

Tension gauge

Power-steering pump belt

Pulley

1 **Checking the power steering fluid level.** Allow the engine to cool, then locate the power steering fluid reservoir, next to the power steering pump. Wipe the cap, unscrew it and lift out the dipstick *(above)*. If the level is a little low, some fluid may have escaped through a loose cap. Top up the fluid and secure the cap tightly. Drive for an hour, then let the engine cool and recheck the fluid level; if it has fallen, there is a leak in the system. Take the car for service.

2 **Testing power-steering pump belt tension.** Allow the engine to cool. Grasp the belt at the midway point between its two pulleys with your thumb and forefinger *(above)* and press down with your thumb using moderate force. If space permits, use a tension gauge *(inset)* or ruler to obtain a more accurate reading *(page 132)*. If the belt can be depressed more than 1/2 inch, it is too loose; adjust it *(below)*.

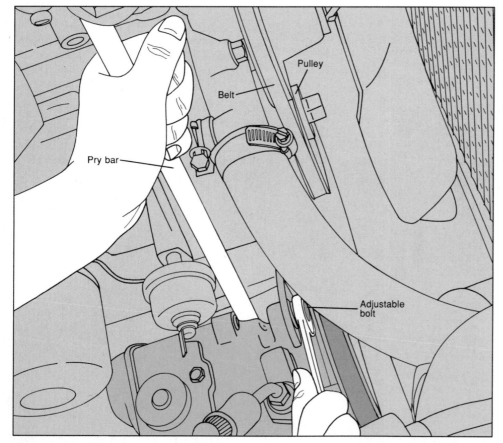

Pulley

Belt

Pry bar

Adjustable bolt

3 **Tightening the belt.** Locate the power steering pump adjustment and pivot bolts, either on the power steering pump pulley or on the belt's other pulley. With a socket wrench, loosen the bolts. Then, with one hand, push a pry bar against the bracket holding the power steering pump in place *(left)*, or press against another adjustable part of the belt system, such as the idler pulley; this will increase the belt's tension. With the other hand, tighten the bolts. Test the belt's tension *(step 2)* and readjust it if necessary. Test again after driving for one hour; if the belt is still too slack, it may need to be replaced *(page 138)*.

SERVICING POWER STEERING HOSES

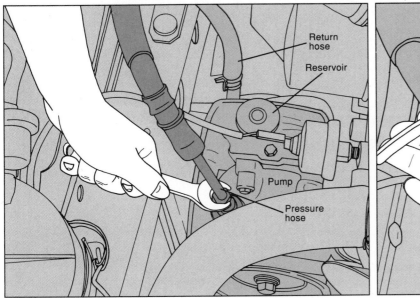

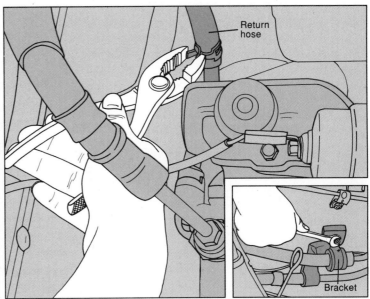

1 **Removing a damaged hose.** Locate the two hoses that lead from the power steering pump; generally, the hose held by a clamp is the return hose, and the one held by a metal fitting is the pressure hose. Examine both hoses for kinks, dryness, cracks and leaks. If either is damaged it must be replaced. Place a drain pan on the ground beneath the pump to catch steering fluid spills. To disconnect the pressure hose, unscrew its metal fitting with a tubing wrench *(above, left)*. To detach the return hose, loosen its clamp *(page 86)* with pliers *(above, right)* or a screwdriver. Also release the hose from any brackets that hold it to the car body *(inset)*.

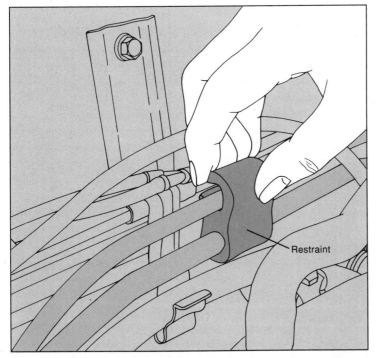

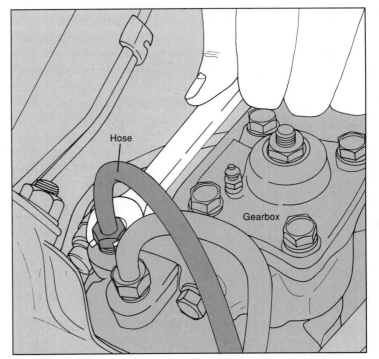

2 **Releasing the restraints.** Follow the path of the damaged hose or hoses until you locate the restraints; these hold the hoses away from hot engine parts and protect them from chafing or vibrating against the car body or frame. To release the hoses from the restraints, pry them off with your fingers *(above)*.

3 **Replacing a damaged hose.** Continue to follow the path of the damaged hose to the steering gearbox. Disconnect the hose from its metal fitting there with a tubing wrench *(above)* and allow any remaining fluid to drip into the drain pan. Do not reuse the fluid. Reverse the removal procedure to attach the new hose. Then fill up the fluid reservoir *(page 38)* and bleed air from the system *(page 40)*.

BLEEDING AIR FROM THE POWER STEERING SYSTEM

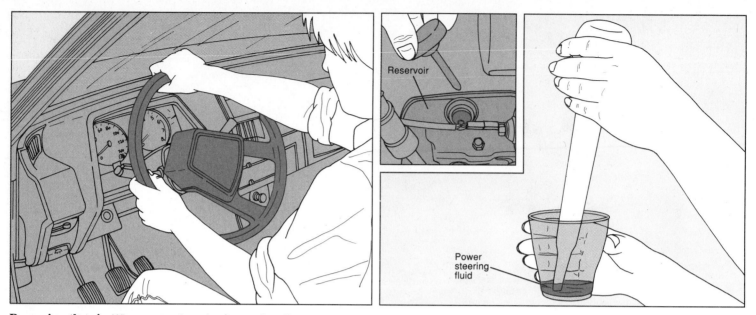

Reservoir

Power
steering
fluid

Removing the air. When a steering wheel starts handling erratically, especially after repairs, air in the power steering fluid may be the culprit. To bleed the air, first make sure the reservoir is full. Then set the parking brake, turn on the ignition, shift to park (automatic) or neutral (manual) and run the engine at fast idle. Grasp the steering wheel, turn it fully to each side a few times *(above, left)*, then return it to the center position. Idle the car a few more minutes and turn off the engine.

Remove the reservoir cap and examine the power steering fluid *(above, inset)*. If it is hard to see, drain out some fluid with a clean syringe and release it into a clear container *(above, right)*. If the fluid is milky, it still contains air and you will have to repeat the steering wheel bleeding procedure. Check for fluid leaks at the hose fittings before test-driving the car to see whether steering performance has improved. If not, take the car for service.

LUBRICATING THE SUSPENSION AND STEERING SYSTEM (Front suspension)

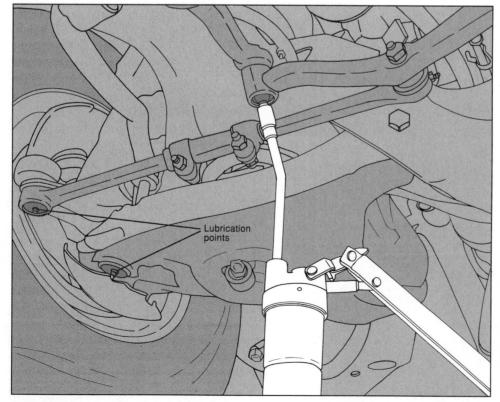

Lubrication
points

Greasing the joint fittings. Depending on the system, there may be as many as twelve or as few as two suspension and steering grease fittings. Pitman arm steering, for example, has more joints, hence more lubrication points. Set the parking brake, jack up the front end of the car and rest it on jack stands *(page 137)*. Locate the grease fittings on both sides of the car: at the ball joints, the control arm pivot points, the steering linkage and the tie rod ends. Your owner's manual will also locate them. If nipple-type fittings were installed, clean the fitting. Fill a grease gun with chassis grease and press its nozzle onto the fitting until it clicks into place; for hard-to-reach fittings, first attach a flexible hose to the gun. Inject the grease *(left)*, taking care not to rupture any rubber seal over the nipple or to cause a joint boot to swell. Then twist the nozzle off the fitting and wipe away any grease overflow.

If plug-type fittings were installed, take off the plug. To inject grease, attach a needle-nose nozzle to the gun's flexible extension and insert it into the opening. Alternatively, replace the plug fittings with nipple-type fittings, available at auto parts stores.

CHECKING BALL JOINTS (Front suspension)

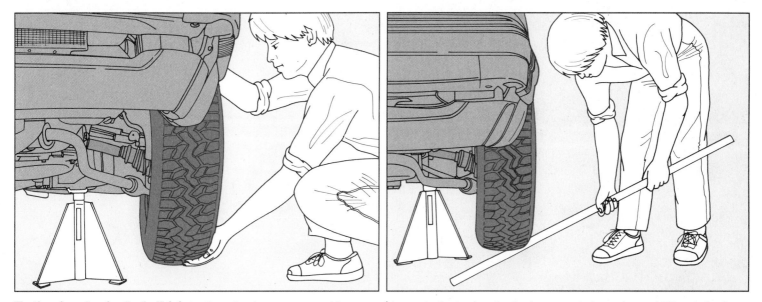

Testing for play in the ball joints. Cars that have upper and lower control arms have two ball joints on each side, one on the upper arm and one on the lower arm. If the spring is mounted on the lower control arm it is the lower ball joint that carries the weight of the car; if the spring is mounted on the upper control arm it is the upper ball joint that carries the weight of the car. (Cars with MacPherson struts have only one ball joint to carry the load; this is attached to the lower control arm on each side.) In either case, jack the wheel 2 inches off the ground,

place a jack stand under the lower control arm *(page 132)* and chock the rear wheels. To test for horizontal play in the load-bearing ball joint, grab the top and bottom of the tire *(above, left)* and rock it in and out. As you do so, have a helper look at the load-bearing ball joint; it should have no movement. To test for vertical movement in both upper and lower ball joints, place a steel bar or pipe under the tire and try to lift the wheel *(above, right)*. The joints should not move.

INSPECTING SUSPENSION POINTS

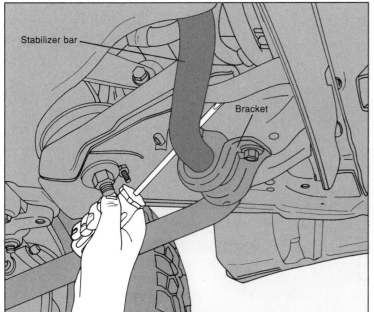

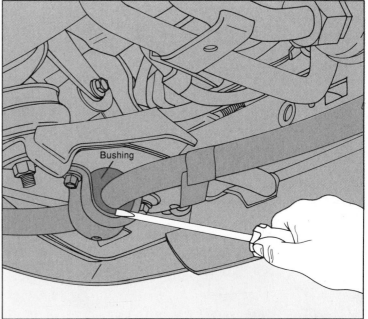

1 **Checking the stabilizer bar.** A stabilizer bar (also called a sway bar) may be found at the front or rear of the car, or at both ends. Bolted to the frame at each side with a bushing and bracket, it connects one side of the suspension system to the other and provides resistance to the leaning motion of the car on turns. To test the bar for excessive movement, first raise the car on jack stands *(page 137)*. Insert a screwdriver or pry bar between the stabilizer bar

and the car frame at one end *(above, left)*. Pull down several times on the tool. The stabilizer bar will give slightly. If the bar moves excessively, tighten the bolts on the bracket. Also check whether the rubber bushing that supports the end of the bar is worn; it should fit snugly. Gently poke the end of the screwdriver against the bushing *(above, right)*. If it is not firm, but spongy or cracked, have the bushing replaced. Examine the other end of the stabilizer bar the same way.

INSPECTING SUSPENSION POINTS (continued)

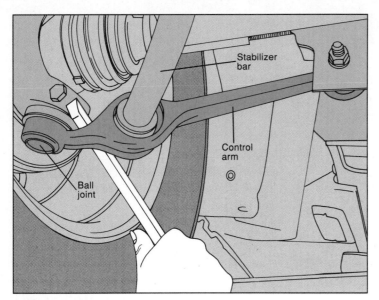

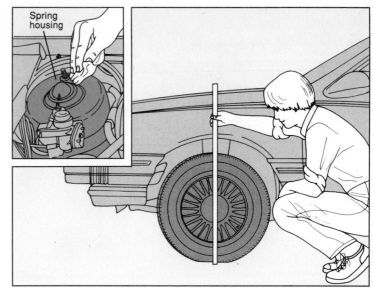

2 **Checking the control arms.** Older cars have upper and lower front control arms that form an A-shaped frame on each side; newer cars with MacPherson struts have eliminated the upper arm. With the car raised as in step 1, insert a pry bar between the control arm (or arms) and the car frame. Try to pry the arm outward *(above)* as well as in other directions. Any movement in the control arm indicates a loose or broken inner or outer tie rod end, or a damaged ball joint; take the car for service.

3 **Testing the car springs.** Lower the car. Remove extra weight from the trunk and check that the tire pressure is correct *(page 26)*. Measure from the ground to the top of each wheel housing, or fender *(above)*; the two front fenders should be the same height; so should the two rear fenders. Lift up the hood and examine each front coil spring or strut *(inset)* for damage. Check the rear springs or struts from underneath the car, raising the car on jack stands *(page 137)*. If you notice any damage, take the car for service.

CHECKING SHOCK ABSORBERS

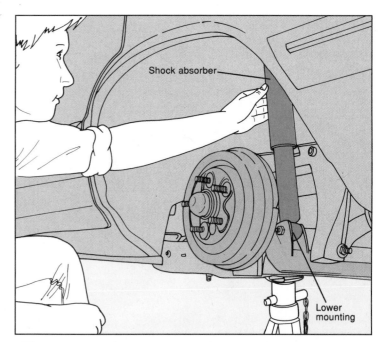

1 **Testing the shock absorbers.** Press down a few times on the bumper at one corner of the car until the car starts bouncing *(above)*. At the lowest point of the bounce, quickly release the bumper. The car should come up once, then return to the level position, indicating that the shock absorber in that corner is sound. Test the other three corners the same way. When replacing a worn shock absorber, you must also replace its partner on the same axle *(page 43)*.

2 **Inspecting a shock absorber for wear.** To access a shock absorber to confirm that it is worn, raise the car on jack stands *(page 137)* and remove the wheel *(page 27)*. Feel the shock body for dents *(above)* and check it for leaking hydraulic fluid. Inspect its mountings for loose nuts and bolts and for worn bushings; these can cause the car to squeak or rattle when driving over bumps. If the shock absorber is damaged, replace it *(page 43)*.

CHANGING SHOCK ABSORBERS

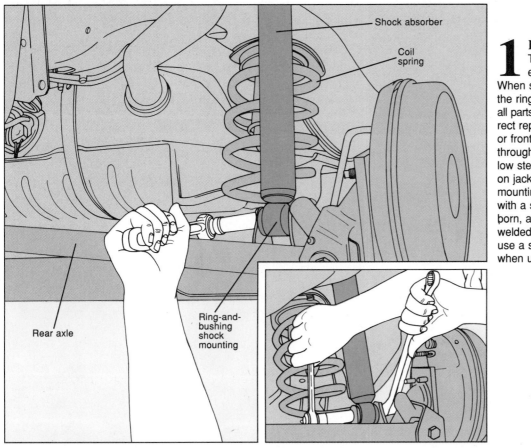

Shock absorber

Coil spring

Rear axle

Ring-and-bushing shock mounting

1 **Disconnecting the lower mounting.** Though simple to replace, shock absorbers vary widely in their mounting styles. When servicing any shock absorber, including the ring-and-bushing type shown here, line up all parts in order of their removal to ensure correct replacement. (On cars in which the rear or front upper mountings must be accessed through the trunk or engine compartment, follow step 2 first, then step 1.) Support the car on jack stands *(page 137)*. Remove the lower mounting bolt by turning it counterclockwise with a socket wrench *(left)*. If the bolt is stubborn, apply penetrating oil. If the nut is not welded to the axle, it may turn with the bolt; use a second wrench to restrict its movement when unscrewing the bolt *(inset)*.

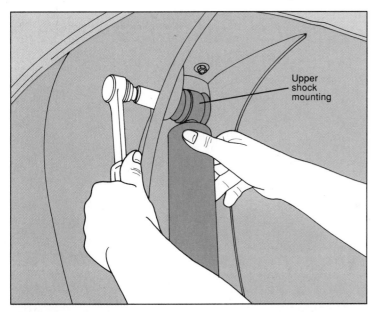

Upper shock mounting

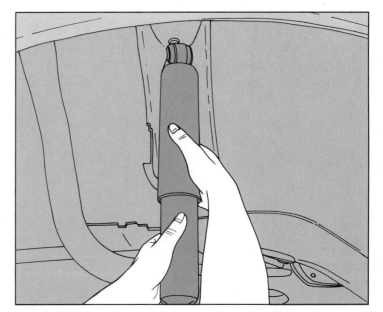

2 **Disconnecting the upper mounting.** Insert a socket wrench behind the mounting bracket and unscrew the bolt *(above)* just as you removed the lower bolt *(step 1)*. When installing a new shock absorber, replace its partner on the same axle as well; make sure the new shocks match the old ones exactly, and that all the correct fittings are included. For all mountings, including the ring-and-bushing type shown here, be sure to reinstall the parts in their correct sequence—refer to the order in which you set out the old parts.

3 **Installing a new shock absorber.** Position the top end of the shock absorber in the upper mounting slot or bracket *(above)*. If the nut is welded on, thread the bolt through the metal ring and rubber bushing into the nut; replace an unwelded nut. Finger-tighten the nut and bolt. Then attach the bottom mounting bolt to its nut and tighten it fully with a socket wrench; hold the nut in place if it is not welded. Next, return to the upper mounting and tighten that nut and bolt fully. Install the second shock the same way.

TRANSMISSION

The car's transmission system, which transfers power from the engine to the wheels, is one of the most complex in the car. Yet for the eager do-it-yourselfer, it provides many important and straightforward fix-it opportunities.

In a rear-wheel-drive car, the engine transmits power to the wheels through the transmission, near the front of the car, whose gears turn a drive shaft that runs back to the differential on the middle of the rear axle. Gears in the differential redirect the rotation of the drive shaft to turn the axle, and thus the rear wheels. Universal, or U, joints on the drive shaft allow it to flex as the wheels travel over bumps.

In a front-wheel-drive car, the engine is connected to the transaxle—a transmission and differential all in one. The front axle consists of two drive shafts, called half shafts, that transmit rotation from the differential to each front wheel.

Constant velocity, or CV, joints on the ends of the half shafts allow them to flex with the motion of the wheels while allowing the wheels to be steered.

Four-wheel-drive cars have an auxiliary transmission called a transfer case mounted on or near the transmission. When engaged, the transfer case directs power to the second set of wheels via a special driveshaft.

Both front-wheel-drive and rear-wheel-drive cars may have either manual or automatic transmission. Manual transmission permits the driver to alter the gear ratio by first depressing the clutch pedal to disengage the engine from the transmission, then moving the gearshift lever to reposition the transmission gears. Automatic transmission uses hydraulic pressure to shift the gears, the timing of which is governed by the position of the gas pedal relative to the speed of the car. Many automatic

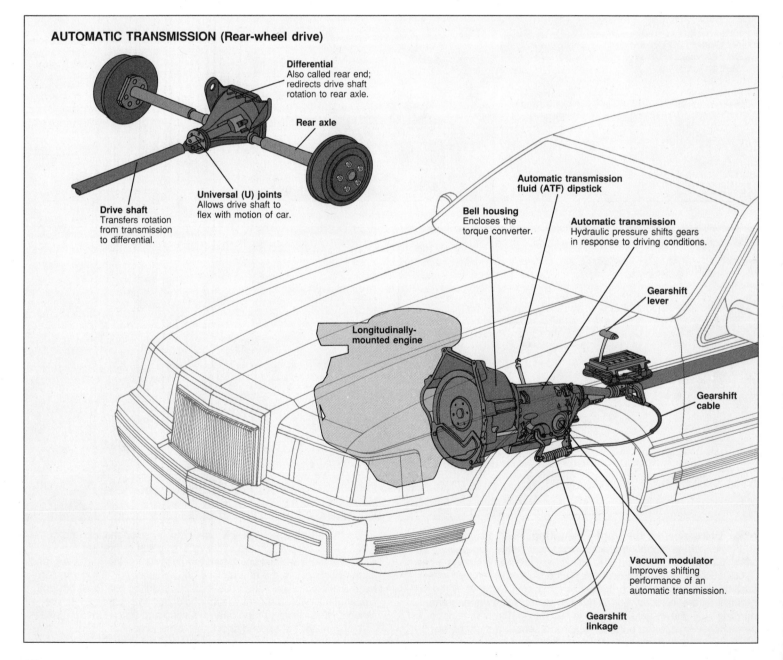

AUTOMATIC TRANSMISSION (Rear-wheel drive)

Differential
Also called rear end; redirects drive shaft rotation to rear axle.

Rear axle

Drive shaft
Transfers rotation from transmission to differential.

Universal (U) joints
Allows drive shaft to flex with motion of car.

Automatic transmission fluid (ATF) dipstick

Bell housing
Encloses the torque converter.

Automatic transmission
Hydraulic pressure shifts gears in response to driving conditions.

Gearshift lever

Longitudinally-mounted engine

Gearshift cable

Vacuum modulator
Improves shifting performance of an automatic transmission.

Gearshift linkage

transmissions have a vacuum modulator, which provides smoother and more efficient shifting. These major transmission variations are pictured below.

Repairs that require the dismantling of the transmission are best left to a specialist. But the do-it-yourselfer can correct less serious problems and perform routine maintenance. The Troubleshooting Guide on page 46 lists some common transmission malfunctions and directs you to the step-by-step procedures for correcting them.

On a manual transmission, you can easily adjust the free play of a cable-operated clutch pedal *(page 47)* or bleed and add fluid to a hydraulic clutch pedal *(page 47)*. Both types of transmission have fittings for inspecting and topping up the fluid in the system. If your car has manual transmission, consult the owner's manual for the specific lubricating oil to use

and the frequency of oil checks. Cars with automatic transmission use automatic transmission fluid (ATF), not only to lubricate, but to transmit hydraulic pressure to the gears. Inspect the fluid level each time you change the engine oil, or as often as once or twice a month if you regularly drive the car uphill, in city traffic or under heavy loads. Consult the owner's manual for the specific type of ATF required by your car. Proper transmission maintenance also includes checking the differential oil *(page 52)* and inspecting the U joints or CV joints for wear and damage.

In addition to some of the basic tools pictured in the Tools and Techniques chapter *(page 132)*, you will need a mechanic's syringe, a grease gun and a torque wrench, all sold at auto parts stores. When working under the car, wear safety goggles to protect your eyes from falling debris.

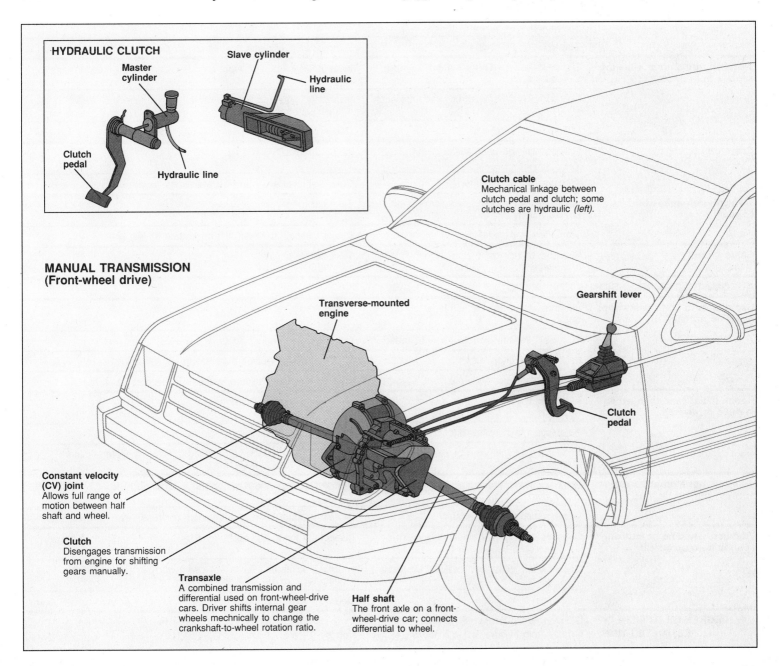

HYDRAULIC CLUTCH

Master cylinder

Slave cylinder

Hydraulic line

Clutch pedal

Hydraulic line

Clutch cable
Mechanical linkage between clutch pedal and clutch; some clutches are hydraulic *(left)*.

**MANUAL TRANSMISSION
(Front-wheel drive)**

Transverse-mounted engine

Gearshift lever

Clutch pedal

Constant velocity (CV) joint
Allows full range of motion between half shaft and wheel.

Clutch
Disengages transmission from engine for shifting gears manually.

Transaxle
A combined transmission and differential used on front-wheel-drive cars. Driver shifts internal gear wheels mechnically to change the crankshaft-to-wheel rotation ratio.

Half shaft
The front axle on a front-wheel-drive car; connects differential to wheel.

TROUBLESHOOTING GUIDE

SYMPTOM	POSSIBLE CAUSE	PROCEDURE
MANUAL TRANSMISSION		
Clutch slips, grabs or jolts	Cable clutch linkage out of adjustment	Test clutch pedal free play and adjust clutch cable (p. 47) ▭●
	Hydraulic clutch fluid level low	Check the fluid level and inspect hydraulic lines for leaks; bleed the system, if necessary (p. 47) ▭●
Gears grind or gearshift hard to operate	Cable clutch linkage out of adjustment	Test clutch pedal free play and adjust clutch cable (p. 47) ▭●
	Hydraulic clutch fluid level low	Check the fluid level and inspect hydraulic lines for leaks; bleed the system, if necessary (p. 47) ▭●
	Gearshift linkage bent, stuck or out of adjustment	Take car for service
	Transmission oil level low	Check oil level and add oil if necessary (p. 48) ▭●
	Transmission oil is wrong grade	Drain oil and refill with correct grade (p. 48) ▭●
	Transmission oil contaminated	Drain oil and refill with new oil (p. 48) ▭●
Transmission is noisy	Transmission oil level low	Check oil level and add oil if necessary (p. 48) ▭●
	Transmission oil is wrong grade	Drain oil and refill with correct grade (p. 48) ▭●
	Transmission oil contaminated	Drain oil and refill with new oil (p. 48) ▭●
Vibration, grinding or clunking sounds from under car	Constant velocity (CV) joints dirty or worn; CV boots worn	Inspect CV joints and boots (p. 53) ▢○; have replaced if necessary
	Universal (U) joints worn or need lubrication	Inspect U joints and have replaced if worn; lubricate U joints if necessary (p. 53) ▭●
	Differential oil level low	Check oil level and inspect for leaks; add oil if needed (p. 52) ▭●
Gears do not engage	Gearshift linkage bent, stuck, or out of adjustment	Take car for service
	Transmission oil level low	Check oil level and add oil if necessary (p. 48) ▭●
Transmission jumps out of gear	Gearshift linkage bent, stuck, or out of adjustment	Take car for service
	Transmission oil level low	Check oil level and add oil if necessary (p. 48) ▭●
Gears locked	Gearshift linkage bent, stuck or out of adjustment	Take car for service
AUTOMATIC TRANSMISSION		
Gears slow to shift; gears slip; gears do not shift up in drive	Automatic transmission fluid level too high or too low	Check fluid level and drain or add fluid (p. 50) ▭●
	Automatic transmission fluid contaminated	Drain, then add new fluid (p. 50) ▭●
	Vacuum modulator faulty	Test modulator; replace if necessary (p. 49) ▢○
	Vacuum modulator hose faulty	Inspect vacuum hose and replace if necessary (p. 49) ▢○
Rough initial gear engagement in drive or reverse	Automatic transmission fluid level too high or too low	Check fluid level and drain or add fluid (p. 50) ▭●
	Automatic transmission fluid contaminated	Drain, then add new fluid (p. 50) ▭●
	Universal (U) joints worn or need lubrication	Inspect U joints and have replaced if worn; lubricate U joints if necessary (p. 53) ▭●
Gears do not shift at correct speeds; shifting delayed	Automatic transmission fluid level too high or too low	Check fluid level and drain or add fluid (p. 50) ▭●
	Vacuum modulator hose faulty	Inspect vacuum hose and replace if necessary (p. 49) ▢○
Vibration, grinding or clunking sounds from under car	Constant velocity (CV) joints dirty or worn; CV boots worn	Inspect CV joints and boots (p. 53) ▢○; have replaced if necessary
	Universal (U) joints worn or need lubrication	Inspect U joints and have replaced if worn; lubricate U joints if necessary (p. 53) ▭●
	Differential oil level low	Check oil level and inspect for leaks; add oil if needed (p. 52) ▭●

DEGREE OF DIFFICULTY: ▢ Easy ▭ Moderate ■ Complex
ESTIMATED TIME: ○ Less than 1 hour ● 1 to 3 hours ● Over 3 hours

CHECKING AND ADJUSTING A CABLE-OPERATED CLUTCH (Manual transmission)

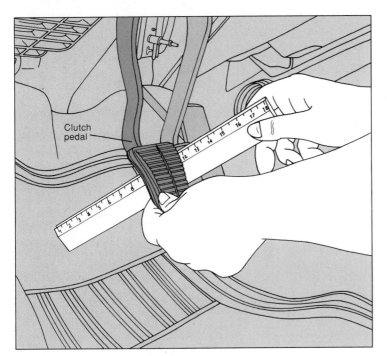

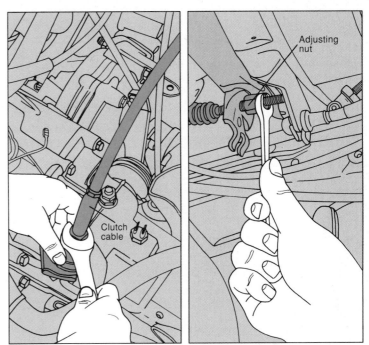

1 **Measuring clutch pedal free play.** The clutch pedal should have approximately one inch of free play—the distance that you can depress the pedal before resistance is felt. The service manual will specify the free play distance for your car. To measure free play, hold a ruler beside the pedal and move the pedal by hand *(above)*. If the amount of free play is greater or less than that specified in the service manual, adjust the clutch cable *(step 2)*.

2 **Adjusting the cable nut.** On a front-wheel-drive car, locate the clutch fork under the hood on the driver's side, toward the front of the car *(above, left)*. On a rear-wheel-drive car *(above, right)*, raise the car on jack stands *(page 137)* and locate the clutch fork near the transmission housing. With an open end wrench, loosen the locknut where the clutch cable joins the clutch fork, then turn the adjusting nut. Steady the cable with locking pliers to keep it from twisting.

CHECKING THE FLUID IN A HYDRAULIC CLUTCH (Manual transmission)

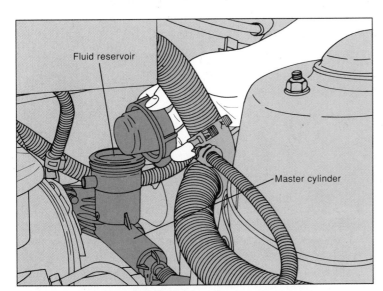

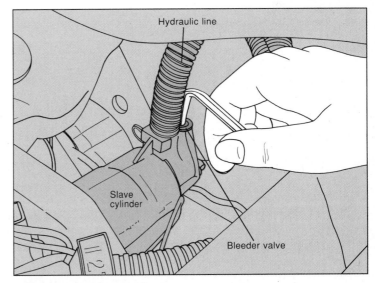

1 **Checking the fluid level.** Locate the hydraulic fluid reservoir on top of the clutch master cylinder, close to the fire wall on the driver's side. Twist off the top of the reservoir *(above)* and place it upside down on a clean surface. The fluid level should reach the FULL mark, if there is one, or come within 1/4 inch of the top. If the reservoir is nearly empty, bleed the system of air before new fluid is added *(step 2)*. To top up the fluid, go to step 4.

2 **Servicing the hydraulic line and fittings.** Inspect the hydraulic line leading from the master cylinder to the slave cylinder and have it replaced if you spot leaks or damage. Examine all fittings on the master and slave cylinders and tighten any loose ones with a hex wrench, combination wrench or tubing wrench, as needed. To bleed the system *(step 3)*, first use a wrench to open the bleeder valve on top of the slave cylinder *(above)*.

CHECKING THE FLUID IN A HYDRAULIC CLUTCH (Manual transmission, continued)

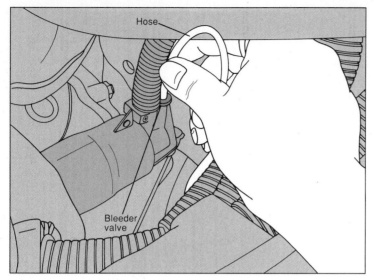

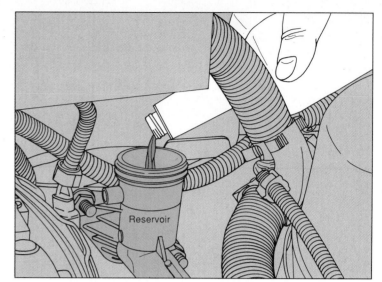

3 **Bleeding the system.** Attach one end of a piece of hose to the opened bleeder valve *(above)*, and submerge the other end in a jar of brake fluid. Have a helper depress the clutch pedal while you open and close the bleeder valve, until no more air bubbles appear in the jar. Periodically check the fluid level in the reservoir as you bleed, and top it up, if necessary. Remove the hose and close the bleeder valve.

4 **Adding fluid.** Avoid contamination of the hydraulic fluid by carefully wiping debris from the rubber liner in the top and from the reservoir surface. Fill the reservoir with brake fluid from a sealed container to the FULL mark, if there is one, or until the fluid comes to 1/4 inch from the top edge *(above)*. Twist on the top and clean up any spills. Check the level again after driving the car; if it has dropped significantly, a leak in the system has gone undetected.

CHECKING TRANSMISSION OIL IN A FRONT-WHEEL-DRIVE CAR (Manual transmission)

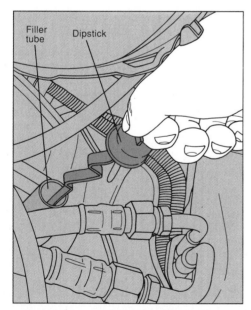

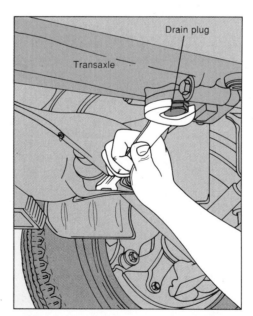

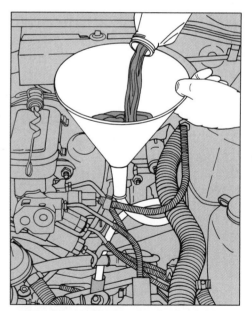

1 **Checking the oil level.** Some transaxles have a dipstick on top; others have a filler plug at the end. Park the car on a level surface, and wipe the dipstick or filler plug clean. Pull a dipstick out of its filler tube *(above)*, wipe it, reinsert it fully and remove it again to read the oil level. If the car has a filler plug, unscrew it and insert your finger in the hole; the oil level should nearly reach the hole.

2 **Draining the oil.** Only drain the oil if it is contaminated or if directed by the owner's manual. Raise the front of the car on jack stands *(page 137)*. Set a basin under the transaxle. On the bottom of the transaxle are one or two drain plugs; the one farthest from the engine is for draining the oil. Unscrew the plug *(above)*, allow the oil to drain, then replace the plug. If the oil contains metal shards, take the car for service.

3 **Adding oil.** If the car has a dipstick, insert a funnel with a flexible neck or a length of hose attached to a funnel into the filler tube, and slowly pour in the oil recommended by the manufacturer *(above)*. If the car has a filler plug, add oil at the filler plug hole with a syringe, squeeze bottle or funnel up to the level of the hole. Replace the dipstick or filler plug.

CHECKING TRANSMISSION OIL IN A REAR-WHEEL-DRIVE CAR (Manual transmission)

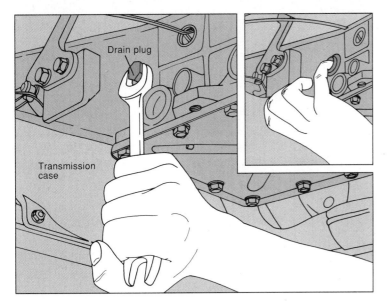

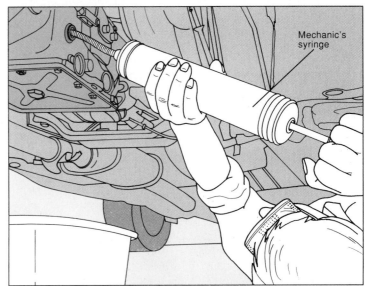

1 **Removing the filler plug.** Raise the car on jack stands *(page 137)* so that it is level. Wipe clean the filler plug on the side of the transmission case and use a wrench to unscrew the plug *(above)*. Insert your finger in the hole *(inset)*; the oil level should almost reach the hole. If not, add more oil *(step 2)*. If the oil contains metal shards, take the car for service.

2 **Adding oil.** Using the oil specified by the owner's manual, insert a hose and funnel or a mechanic's syringe *(above)* into the filler plug hole and add oil up to the level of the hole. Replace the plug and wipe off any spills. To drain the oil, follow the procedure for a front-wheel-drive car *(page 48)*, unfastening the drain plug at the bottom of the transmission case.

INSPECTING AND REPLACING THE VACUUM MODULATOR (Automatic transmission)

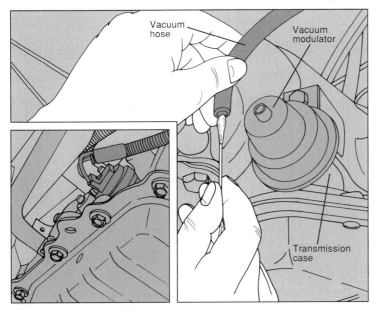

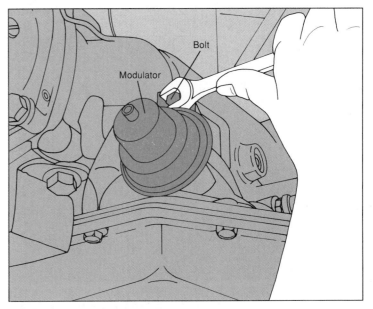

1 **Checking for vacuum.** An electronic vacuum modulator *(inset)* must be professionally serviced. To check a mechanical vacuum modulator, first inspect the modulator's vacuum hose and replace it if damaged. Then pull the hose off the modulator nipple and insert a cotton swab into the hose *(above)*. Transmission fluid on the swab indicates that the modulator leaks; replace it *(step 2)*. Next check that the modulator is receiving vacuum from the engine. Turn on the engine. **Caution:** Do not wear loose clothes or jewelry and keep hands away from engine parts. Rest a small piece of paper against the modulator nipple. If the vacuum cannot hold the paper in place, the vacuum lines or engine may be faulty; take the car for service.

2 **Removing the modulator.** With the vacuum hose disconnected from the modulator, unscrew the bolt on the bracket that holds the modulator to the transmission case *(above)*. If there is no bracket, the modulator itself is screwed into the case; insert a thin wrench or a special tool behind the modulator and unscrew it. Save the center pin and O ring from the old modulator in case these parts are not supplied with the replacement. To install a new modulator, reverse the steps you took to remove it.

CHECKING AND CHANGING TRANSMISSION FLUID (Automatic transmission)

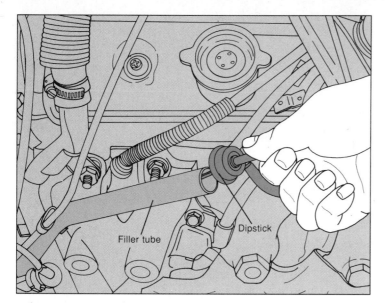

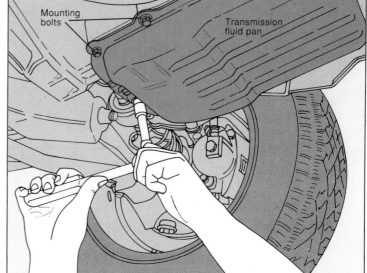

1 Checking the fluid level. Drive for 20 minutes to warm the engine. Then stop the car, engage the parking brake and quickly move through each gear, ending at PARK or NEUTRAL, as directed by the owner's manual; this forces the automatic transmission fluid (ATF) through the system. Let the engine idle and locate the ATF dipstick between the engine and the firewall. Do not mistake the engine oil dipstick for it. Wipe the filler tube, then pull out the dipstick, wipe and reinsert it, and pull it out again to read the fluid level *(above)*. If the ATF level is low, add more fluid *(step 8)*. If the ATF is not pinkish red, or it has a strong burnt odor, or the owner's manual recommends you change the ATF, drain and add new fluid *(steps 2 through 8)*. If the ATF contains metal shards, take the car for service.

2 Loosening the transmission fluid pan. Let the engine cool. Raise the car on jack stands *(page 137)*, and place a basin under the transmission pan. If the pan has a drain plug, unscrew it with a wrench to release the fluid first, then remove the pan to change the filter *(step 4)*. If the pan has no drain plug, use a socket wrench to unscrew all but two of the transmission pan bolts *(above)*. Loosen, but do not remove, the two bolts closest to the front of the car.

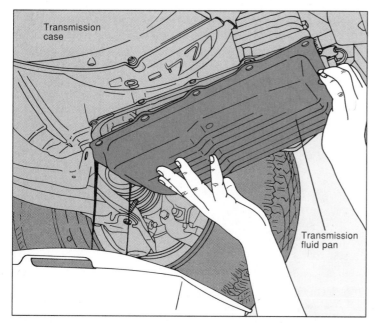

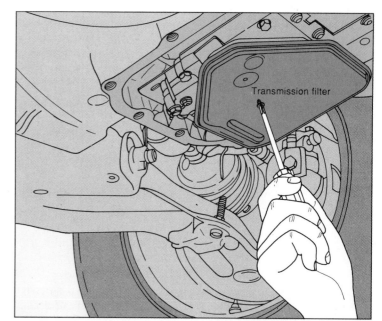

3 Draining the fluid. Support the pan with both hands as the fluid flows out of it *(above)*. If the pan adheres to the transmission and impedes the flow, gently insert a putty knife in the joint to separate them. The fluid may gush out; hold onto the pan. Remove the last two bolts. If there is a magnet in the pan's base, check it for metal particles drawn from the fluid; these indicate a serious transmission problem requiring professional repair. Store drained fluid in a sealed container for recycling.

4 Removing the filter. Always clean or change the filter when changing the ATF. The filter may be held in place by mounting screws *(above)*, by clips or by retainers on the back of the filter. If you must remove an O ring, or gasket, note its location to ensure correct reassembly. Wash a mesh-screen filter in solvent and reinstall it. A filter made of paper must be replaced; install the new filter, noting any "This side up" markings, and do not overtighten the screws.

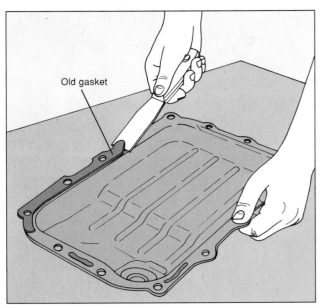

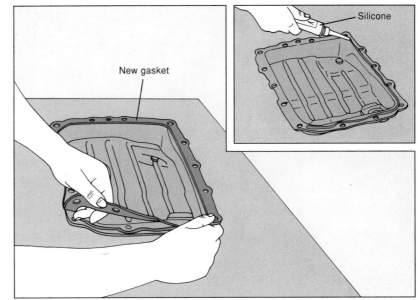

Silicone

Old gasket

New gasket

5 **Removing the gasket from the pan.** With a putty knife, scrape off the old gasket from both the pan *(above)* and the transmission. If a silicone gasket compound was used instead of a preformed gasket, remove it the same way. Then clean the pan thoroughly with a solvent and dry it with a lint-free rag.

6 **Replacing the gasket.** A preformed rubber or cork gasket is easier than silicone for a beginner to install. Apply a thin layer of automatic transmission fluid to the rim of the pan to seat the gasket. Align the new gasket on top *(above)*, and reinstall the pan *(step 7)*. To replace a silicone gasket compound, first clean and dry the mating surfaces of the pan and the transmission. Apply a 1/8-inch bead of silicone to the pan's rim *(inset)* and reinstall the pan loosely, hand-tightening the bolts in the order shown in step 7 to squeeze the silicone against the transmission. Allow the silicone to set for 30 minutes before tightening the bolts securely *(step 7)*.

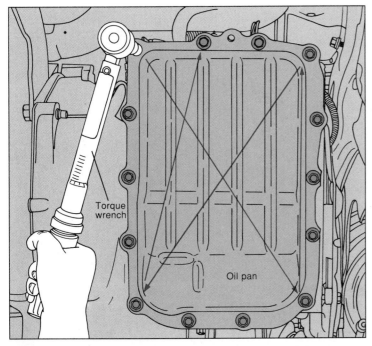

Torque wrench

Oil pan

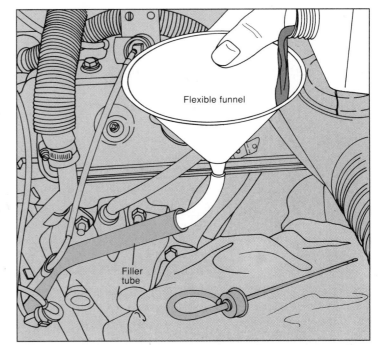

Flexible funnel

Filler tube

7 **Torquing the mounting bolts.** Wipe the mounting bolts clean, then hand-tighten each bolt into position following the crisscross pattern shown above. Take care not to strip the threads. The pattern ensures that equal pressure is applied to all points on the pan. Use a torque wrench *(above)* to tighten the bolts again in the same sequence, this time to the car manufacturer's specifications.

8 **Adding automatic transmission fluid.** Pull out the dipstick and insert a funnel into the filler tube. Slowly pour in the automatic transmission fluid recommended by your owner's manual *(above)*, checking its level, until the dipstick reads FULL. Do not overfill. Start the engine and circulate the fluid through the system by shifting through all the gears, stopping at PARK or NEUTRAL as in step 1. Check the fluid level again and top it up, if necessary. Check the level once more after driving the car.

CHECKING AND ADDING DIFFERENTIAL OIL (Rear-wheel-drive cars)

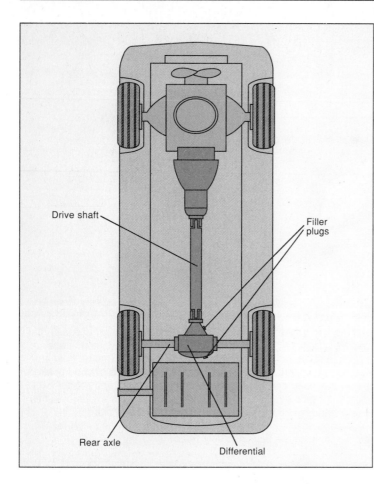

Drive shaft

Filler plugs

Rear axle

Differential

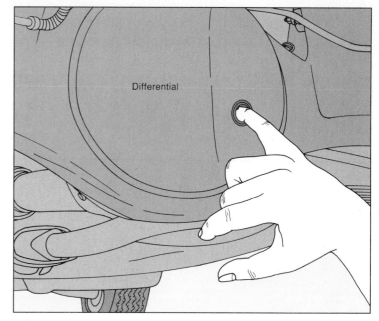

Differential

1 **Checking the differential oil.** Raise the car on jack stands *(page 137)* if necessary, making sure the car is level. Locate the filler plug either at the side or on the rear of the differential housing *(left)*. If there are two plugs, use a wrench to unscrew the higher one of the two (the other is the drain plug). Insert a finger into the hole *(above)*; if you cannot feel the oil with your fingertip, the level is low and more oil is needed *(step 3)*. First, though, check for leaks from the differential and have the car professionally inspected if you find any. Before adding oil, determine whether your car has a limited-slip differential *(step 2)*; such a differential requires a special lubricant.

Jack

2 **Checking for a limited-slip differential.** Look for a tag on the differential. If there is no tag, conduct the following test: Leave the car in position if you raised it in step 1. If you did not, jack up just its rear wheels *(page 136)*. With the brake off and the transmission in neutral, turn one rear wheel by hand *(above)*. If it turns easily and its partner on the same axle rotates in the opposite direction, the differential is conventional. If the wheel does not turn easily, and its partner rotates in the same direction, your car has a limited-slip differential.

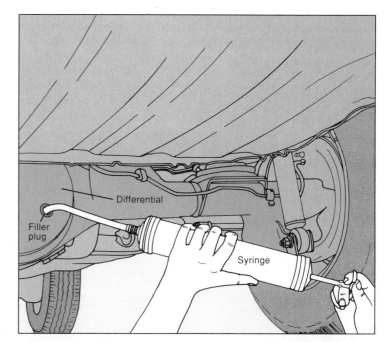

Differential

Filler plug

Syringe

3 **Adding differential oil.** Make sure that you have the differential lubricant recommended by your owner's manual. Insert the new oil through the filler hole on the differential housing using a mechanic's syringe *(above)*, a squeeze bottle, or a hose and funnel. Add just a little at a time to ensure you don't overfill. Then replace the plug and wipe away any spills.

INSPECTING THE CONSTANT VELOCITY (CV) JOINTS

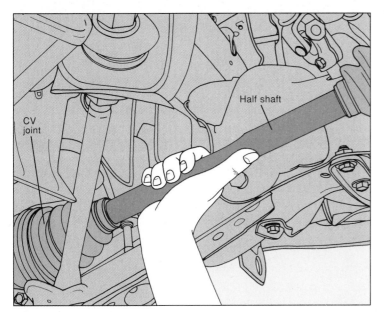

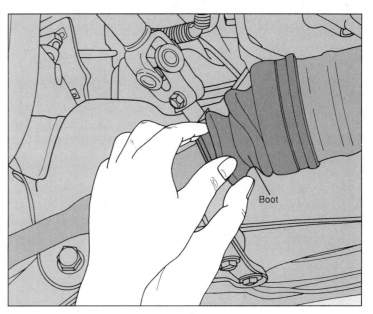

1 **Testing for joint free play.** Front-wheel-drive and some rear-wheel-drive cars have constant velocity (CV) joints at each end of the front and rear axles. With one hand, grip one half shaft firmly and push it up and down *(above)*; similarly test the other side. If free play exists at the CV joints and along the shaft, take the car for service; the joints are worn. Also have the car inspected if you feel vibrations or hear clicking, clunking or chattering from the front axle.

2 **Examining the joint boot.** The key to a CV joint's longevity lies in the sealing ability of its protective rubber boot. A damaged boot allows vital joint lubricant to escape and lets contaminants enter. Inspect each boot for cracks or signs of deterioration in the folds *(above)*. If the boot is split or torn, have the joint inspected and lubricated, and have the boot replaced.

INSPECTING THE UNIVERSAL (U) JOINTS (Rear-wheel-drive cars)

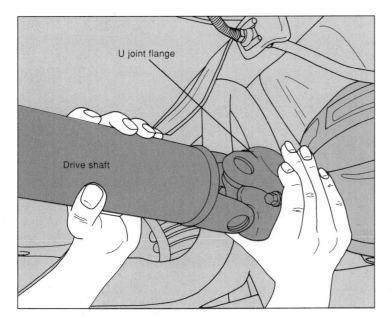

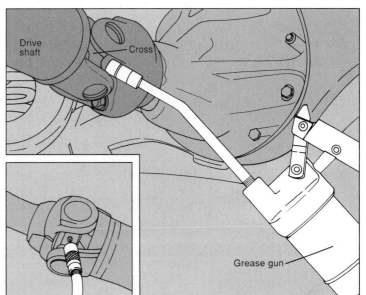

1 **Testing the drive shaft U joints.** The drive shaft may have just one U joint, a double U joint, or two U joints; inspect each one. Raise the car *(page 137)* so that the rear wheels hang free. Then grip the drive shaft with one hand, and hold the U joint flange with the other *(above)*. Try to move the driveshaft up and down and side to side. If there is movement at the flange, the U joint is worn and should be professionally serviced.

2 **Lubricating the drive shaft U joint.** Clean grease and dirt from the nipple-type or plug-type grease fitting on the U joint cross. To insert lubricant, press the nozzle of a grease gun onto the nipple *(above)* and pump the gun's handle a couple of times. If the cross has a plug instead of a nipple, remove the plug and screw in a flexible fitting *(inset)*; attach the grease gun hose to it. Be sure to lubricate all U joints, if there are more than one. A U joint that has no grease fitting is permanently lubricated and cannot be greased.

ENGINE

The modern gasoline engine is the product of 100 years of tinkering, experimentation and refinement. Yet it still operates according to many of the same principles as gasoline engines built in the 1880s.

Like its predecessor, the modern engine is powered by the combustion of gasoline mixed with air. This mixture is drawn into a combustion chamber at the top of a hollow cylinder. A cylindrical metal plug, the piston, is housed in the cylinder with just enough room to move up and down. A rod swings from below the piston, so that the whole piston-rod-cylinder assembly resembles a fist and forearm enclosed in a sleeve. When the air/fuel mixture at the top of the cylinder is ignited by a spark plug, it explodes, forcing the piston down the cylinder, which makes the rod turn the crankshaft. Other pistons move up and down their cylinders, in turn. The resulting rota-

tion of the crankshaft is transmitted by a series of gears through the drive train to the wheels.

Attempts to make the car engine smaller and more fuel-efficient have led to a number of variations, and no one engine can now be described as standard. To save space, smaller, more compact engine blocks can be mounted across the engine compartment, perpendicular to the wheels. This is known as transverse mounting, common on small economy cars. A still more important innovation is fuel injection, discussed in the Fuel System chapter *(page 62)*.

The inner workings of the modern engine have become increasingly complex and precise, and many fuel and exhaust functions are now computer controlled. For this reason it is not advisable for a beginner to undertake most repairs. However, learning to recognize and diagnose potential problems is

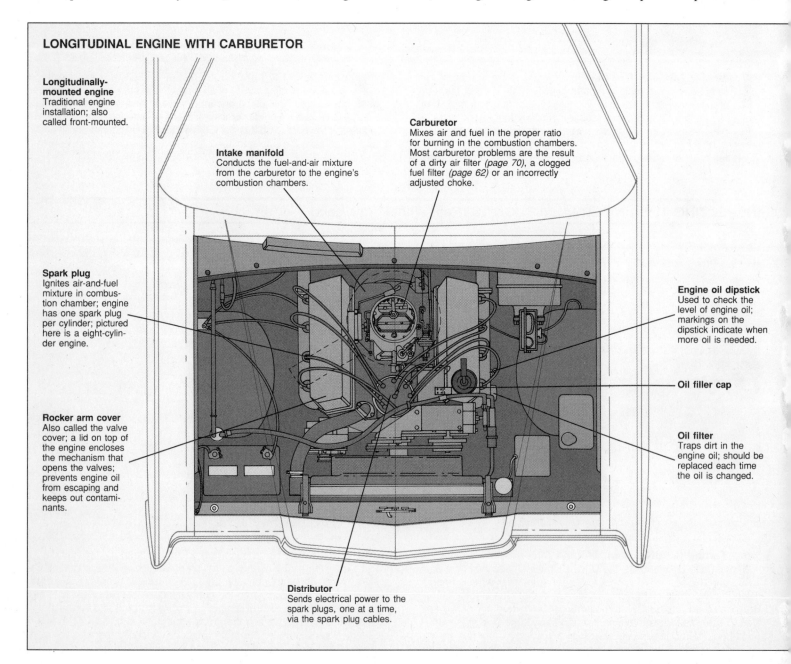

LONGITUDINAL ENGINE WITH CARBURETOR

Longitudinally-mounted engine
Traditional engine installation; also called front-mounted.

Intake manifold
Conducts the fuel-and-air mixture from the carburetor to the engine's combustion chambers.

Carburetor
Mixes air and fuel in the proper ratio for burning in the combustion chambers. Most carburetor problems are the result of a dirty air filter *(page 70)*, a clogged fuel filter *(page 62)* or an incorrectly adjusted choke.

Spark plug
Ignites air-and-fuel mixture in combustion chamber; engine has one spark plug per cylinder; pictured here is a eight-cylinder engine.

Engine oil dipstick
Used to check the level of engine oil; markings on the dipstick indicate when more oil is needed.

Oil filler cap

Rocker arm cover
Also called the valve cover; a lid on top of the engine encloses the mechanism that opens the valves; prevents engine oil from escaping and keeps out contaminants.

Oil filter
Traps dirt in the engine oil; should be replaced each time the oil is changed.

Distributor
Sends electrical power to the spark plugs, one at a time, via the spark plug cables.

invaluable, since the more information you can give to your mechanic, the more likely he is to make the correct repair. Simple testing devices—such as the vacuum gauge described in this chapter—are available at auto supply stores.

The engine rotates one thousand times each minute on average, generating a tremendous amount of heat and friction. Without lubrication the engine would soon overheat, seize or crack. Engine oil pumped throughout the engine coats its moving parts, reducing friction. At the same time oil cools, cleans and helps to seal the combustion chambers. As oil circulates through the engine, it picks up dirt and carbon residue. Changing the oil and oil filter frequently *(page 58)* is one of the simplest and most useful things you can do to prolong the life of your engine. Store the waste oil for recycling; do not flush it down the sewer.

If properly maintained, your engine will last well beyond the life of its warranty. Rubber, plastic and fiber components, such as belts and gaskets, will begin to deteriorate before the metal parts of the engine and will then have to be replaced with increasing frequency. You will be able to change some accessible gaskets *(page 60)*, but in many cases you will have to leave the work to a mechanic.

Keep in mind that many problems with engine performance are not engine problems at all. A glance at the Troubleshooting Guide on the next page will reveal that many engine-related symptoms have their source in other car components, especially in the electrical and fuel systems. Sounds and smells also point to specific problems *(page 141)*, from leaking coolant to a pinhole puncture in the exhaust system. Refer to other chapters for additional symptoms.

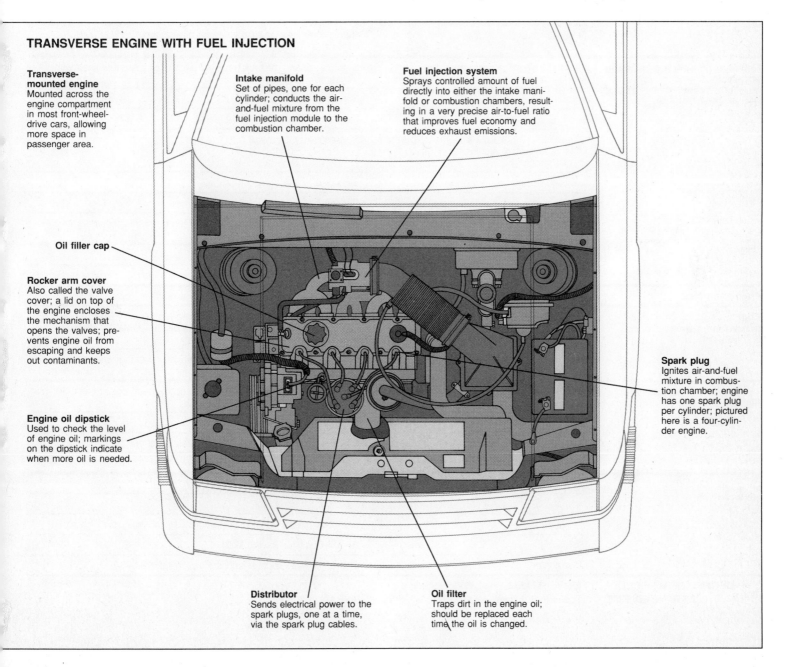

TRANSVERSE ENGINE WITH FUEL INJECTION

Transverse-mounted engine
Mounted across the engine compartment in most front-wheel-drive cars, allowing more space in passenger area.

Intake manifold
Set of pipes, one for each cylinder; conducts the air-and-fuel mixture from the fuel injection module to the combustion chamber.

Fuel injection system
Sprays controlled amount of fuel directly into either the intake manifold or combustion chambers, resulting in a very precise air-to-fuel ratio that improves fuel economy and reduces exhaust emissions.

Oil filler cap

Rocker arm cover
Also called the valve cover; a lid on top of the engine encloses the mechanism that opens the valves; prevents engine oil from escaping and keeps out contaminants.

Spark plug
Ignites air-and-fuel mixture in combustion chamber; engine has one spark plug per cylinder; pictured here is a four-cylinder engine.

Engine oil dipstick
Used to check the level of engine oil; markings on the dipstick indicate when more oil is needed.

Distributor
Sends electrical power to the spark plugs, one at a time, via the spark plug cables.

Oil filter
Traps dirt in the engine oil; should be replaced each time the oil is changed.

TROUBLESHOOTING GUIDE

SYMPTOM	POSSIBLE CAUSE	PROCEDURE
No sound at all when ignition key is turned	Battery or ignition system faulty	Service battery or ignition system (p. 96)
	Transmission in gear	Shift into PARK or NEUTRAL
Engine cranks but doesn't start	Car out of gas	Gently rock car; if you hear a sloshing sound, fuel gauge may be faulty. Otherwise, add at least 1 gallon of gas
	Engine flooded	Press accelerator to the floor and release. Try to start car. If unsuccessful, wait 10 minutes and try again.
	Battery weak	Service the battery (p. 96); jump-start car if necessary (p. 17)
	Ignition system faulty; or distributor, ignition coil or spark plug cables wet	Service ignition system (p. 96)
	Fuel filter clogged or fuel pump faulty	Service fuel system (p. 62)
	Engine too cold	Install a block heater (p. 61) ▭●
Engine runs poorly or stalls in cold weather	Carburetor icing	Add "dry gas" (isopropyl alcohol) to the gas tank
	Oil viscosity too heavy	Check owner's manual for recommended oil rating; change oil and filter if necessary (p. 58) ▭●
	Poor fuel vaporization (carbureted engine)	Remove air cleaner (p. 70); spray aerosol starting fluid into carburetor
Engine runs poorly or stalls in hot weather	Vapor lock (engine heat vaporizing gas in fuel line or pump)	Stop car, open hood and let engine cool, or wrap fuel lines with wet rags
Engine runs roughly	Ignition system faulty	Service ignition system (p. 96)
	Spark plugs or cables faulty	Service spark plugs and cables (p. 96)
	Carburetor or choke plate faulty (carbureted engine); cold-start injector faulty (fuel-injection engine)	Service fuel system (p. 62)
	Gasoline octane rating too low	Switch to higher-octane gasoline
	Fuel filter clogged or fuel pump faulty	Service fuel system (p. 62)
	Water or dirt in gas	Add "dry gas" (isopropyl alcohol) to the gas tank; replace fuel filter (p. 62)
	Idle speed set improperly	Take car for service
	Emission control system faulty	Take car for service
Engine is noisy	Sound may point to specific problem	Listen carefully to diagnose source of problem (p. 141)
Engine uses too much oil (more than 1 quart every 500 miles)	Gasket or seals leaking; piston rings or valves worn; carburetor dirty	Locate source of leak using vacuum gauge (p. 57) ▭○; if problem is a leaky gasket, replace it if accessible (p. 60) ▭●; otherwise, take car for service
	Oil viscosity too light	Check owner's manual for recommended oil rating; change oil and filter if necessary (p. 58) ▭●
Temperature indicator light flashes on while driving; engine may stall	Hot weather or high altitude; prolonged stop-and-go driving	Stop car, open hood and let engine cool; check coolant level in radiator and add if necessary (p. 80)
	Oil level too low	Check oil level and add if necessary (p. 58) ▭○
	Coolant level too low	Check coolant level and add if necessary; check for leaks (p. 80)
	Cooling system faulty; thermostat stuck	Service cooling system (p. 80)
Oil gauge light flashes on while driving	Oil level too low	Check oil level and add if necessary (p. 58) ▭○
	Oil pump or pressure-relief valve worn	Take car for service
	Oil gauge faulty	Check oil gauge sending unit and wiring (p. 96)
	Oil filter clogged	Replace oil filter (p. 58) ▭○
	Oil leaking	Check gaskets, oil filter and drain plug (p. 58) ▭○

DEGREE OF DIFFICULTY: ▭ Easy ▬ Moderate ■ Complex
ESTIMATED TIME: ○ Less than 1 hour ◖ 1 to 3 hours ● Over 3 hours

DIAGNOSING ENGINE PROBLEMS WITH A VACUUM GAUGE

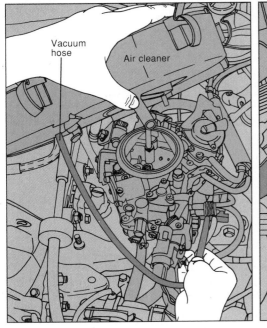

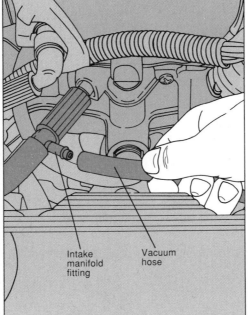

Vacuum hose

Air cleaner

Intake manifold fitting

Vacuum hose

1 **Disconnecting the vacuum hose.** A vacuum gauge *(page 132)* measures the vacuum in the intake manifold produced by the pistons. If your car has a fuel economy gauge on the dash you can check vacuum readings regularly. Otherwise, use a hand-held vacuum gauge to diagnose engine problems. First locate a vacuum hose on your car's intake manifold. On a carbureted engine *(far left)*, remove the air cleaner *(page 70)* to reach it. One end of the vacuum hose is attached to the air cleaner; the other is connected to a fitting on the intake manifold, located just below the carburetor. Pull the hose off the fitting, leaving the other end attached to the air cleaner. On a fuel-injection engine *(near left)*, the intake manifold feeds into the head of the engine and is generally located near the valve cover or rocker arm cover. On V-type engines, it may be mounted between the two covers. Pull the hose off the intake manifold fitting, leaving the other end attached to the engine.

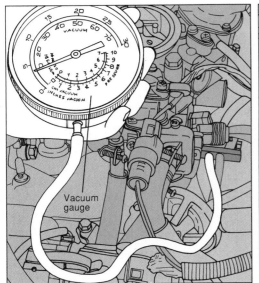

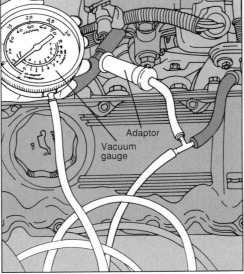

Vacuum gauge

Adaptor
Vacuum gauge

2 **Checking the vacuum.** Attach the vacuum gauge to the intake manifold vacuum source. Use the hoses and adaptors provided with the gauge in the combination necessary to reach the components and take the reading. On the carbureted engine *(far left)* one hose reaches the fitting on the manifold. On the fuel-injection engine *(near left)* a fitting adaptor, two hoses and a T connector are combined, both to reach the manifold (or the throttle body) and to seal the disconnected vacuum hose. Make sure all fittings and hoses are plugged air tight. Start the engine and let it run for 15 minutes, or until the automatic choke slows the idle. The vacuum gauge reading *(below)* will diagnose an engine malfunction; observe both the needle's position and its motion.

(For gauges marked in kilopascals, multiply these readings by 3.386.) Steady reading between 15 and 22 in. Hg is normal. Check service manual for exact specs. Depress and release accelerator quickly. The needle should drop to 5 in. Hg, then climb to 25 in. Hg before stabilizing at normal.

Steady high reading above normal indicates restricted air intake. Check for clogged air filter *(page 74)* or stuck choke *(page 68)*.

Steady low reading of 5 in. Hg indicates a vacuum leak at intake manifold, carburetor gaskets or engine vacuum hose. Check to see that hoses are properly connected. Steady low reading between 8 and 14 in. Hg suggests ignition timing is off or piston ring leaks.

If needle drops to near zero when the engine accelerates and climbs back to a lower than normal reading, the exhaust system may be blocked *(page 70)*.

Fluctuating reading: If the needle swings or vibrates between 10 and 20 in. Hg or 15 and 19 in. Hg the problem may be the valves. If the needle fluctuates regularly between 5 and 20 in. Hg a leaking head gasket is indicated. If the needle floats between 14 and 16 in. Hg, spark plugs may be gapped too close *(page 113)*.

CHECKING THE OIL LEVEL

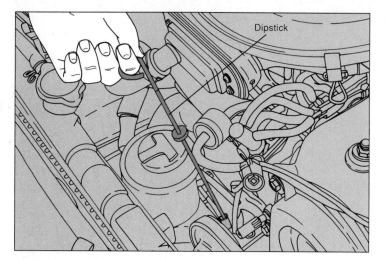

Dipstick

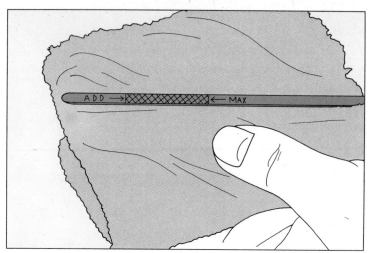

1 **Removing the dipstick.** For an accurate reading, check the engine oil level when the engine is cool. Make sure the car is parked on a level surface. The location of the dipstick varies from car to car. Check the front and sides of the engine block—the dipstick has a small curled handle and runs down into the block. Remove the dipstick and wipe it clean with a dry rag. Reinsert it completely and pull it out again.

2 **Reading the dipstick.** Dipsticks are marked to indicate whether the engine has enough oil or whether you need to add oil. If the oil coats the stick below the ADD mark or just up to it, add one quart of oil *(page 59)* of the proper rating and viscosity *(below)*. Do not add oil unless the level indicated on the dipstick is at or below the add level. Overfilling can make the oil spill over or foam, or even damage the engine.

CHANGING THE OIL AND FILTER

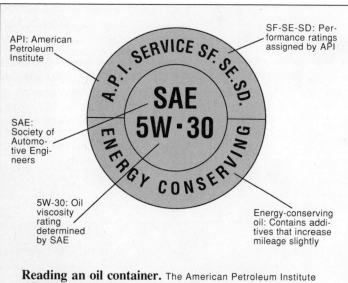

API: American Petroleum Institute

SF-SE-SD: Performance ratings assigned by API

A.P.I. SERVICE SF-SE-SD.

SAE 5W-30

ENERGY CONSERVING

SAE: Society of Automotive Engineers

5W-30: Oil viscosity rating determined by SAE

Energy-conserving oil: Contains additives that increase mileage slightly

Reading an oil container. The American Petroleum Institute (API) licenses its symbol to oil manufacturers who meet its standards, and assigns oil performance ratings. The first letter of the rating, S, means that the oil is suitable for gasoline engines (C indicates a diesel engine oil). The second letter indicates the type of blend. F is the most recent rating category and indicates the latest blend available. It contains many beneficial additives. Cars made after 1982 should use only SF oil. SAE viscosity ratings are a measure of the oil's weight, or thickness. For warm weather driving, an engine needs a heavier oil to compensate for the thinning effects of heat; in cool weather it needs a lighter oil to balance the thickening effects of cold. In the example above, the 5W-30 rating indicates a multiviscosity oil. This is a blended oil with additives that allow it to work well in both hot and cold weather. The weight of oil you should use depends on the climate in your region and the size of your engine. Consult the owner's manual to determine which ratings are specified for your car, or check with a mechanic.

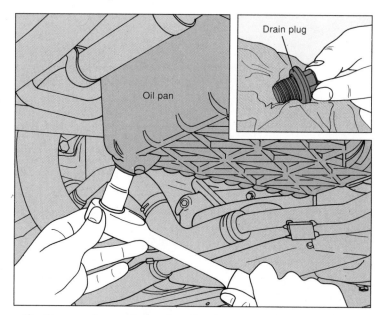

Drain plug

Oil pan

1 **Unscrewing and cleaning the drain plug.** Before changing the oil, run the car for a few minutes—oil flows more quickly when it is warm. Be aware that the engine may be hot to the touch. Oil may be changed when the engine is cold but it will drain much more slowly. Raise the car on jack stands *(page 137)* and place a basin large enough to hold six or seven quarts beneath the drain plug, located on the oil pan. Loosen the plug with a wrench *(above)*, then unscrew it by hand. To avoid contact with the hot oil, let the drain plug fall into the basin and retrieve it after the oil has cooled. Clean the drain plug with a dry cloth *(inset)*. Pieces of the old gasket (a ring sometimes fitted between the plug and the oil pan to provide a tight seal) may adhere to the plug. If so, sand lightly to remove remnants. If the plug threads are worn or stripped, replace it using a drain-plug kit.

CHANGING THE OIL AND FILTER (continued)

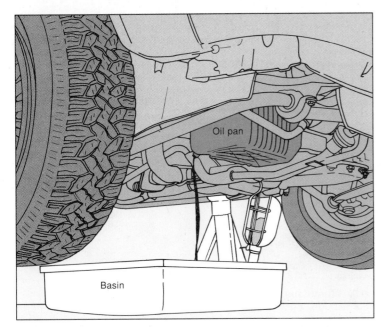

Basin

Oil pan

2 **Draining the oil.** Allow the oil to flow into the basin. If the engine is cold, this will take 30 minutes. When the oil has drained completely, wipe the plug fitting and make sure no pieces of gasket have adhered to it; if so, sand lightly to remove them. The gasket should be replaced if damaged. Reinsert the drain plug and new gasket, tightening by hand. When the plug is hand tight, give it a quarter turn with a wrench. Be careful not to overtighten the plug; you may strip the threads.

Strap wrench

Filter

Filter   Strap

3 **Removing the oil filter.** Replace the old filter each time you change the oil. Otherwise, the old oil inside it will circulate with the new oil once you start the engine. Move the draining basin under the filter, a metal cylinder at the bottom or side of the engine block. Sometimes it can be reached easily through the hood of the car. If this is the case, or if you have enough room to maneuver under the car, loosen it with a strap wrench *(above, left)*. The strap tightens to grip the filter as the wrench is turned counterclockwise. For hard-to-reach filters, straps that fit a socket wrench and extension are available *(above, right)*. Some cars require a cap wrench. Loosen the filter with the wrench, then unscrew and remove it by hand.

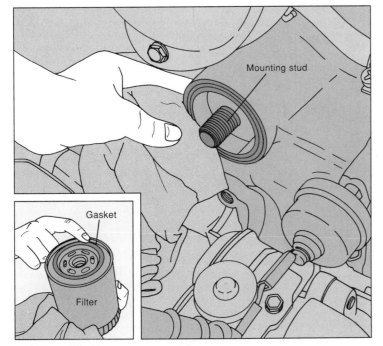

Mounting stud

Gasket

Filter

4 **Cleaning the mounting stud.** Wipe the mounting stud with a cloth *(above)* and check that pieces of the rubber filter gasket have not adhered to the surface of the engine. Lightly scrape or sand any pieces that remain. Insert the new gasket in the groove on the new oil filter and coat the gasket with fresh engine oil *(inset)*. Thread the filter clockwise onto the mounting stud and tighten it by hand; tighten with a wrench only if indicated in the service manual.

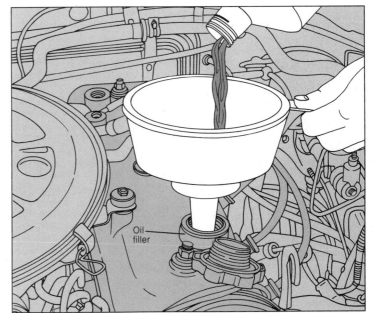

Oil filler

5 **Adding fresh oil.** Find the cap covering the oil filler—usually on or beside the engine valve cover, or rocker arm cover. Check the owner's manual to determine how much oil to add, and pour the oil into the filler using a funnel *(above)* or an oil-can spout. Replace the filler cap and start the car; the oil warning light may stay on for a few seconds. Check the drain plug and filter for leaks, then turn off the engine and remove the jack stands. Check the oil level with the dipstick and add more oil if needed. Pour the old oil into sealable containers, and find a service station that will recycle it.

REPLACING THE ROCKER ARM COVER GASKET

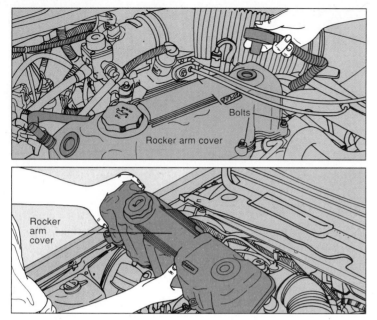

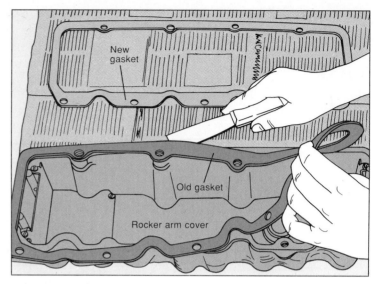

1 Removing the rocker arm cover. The joint between the engine and rocker arm cover is sealed by a gasket made of rubber or cork. The gasket is not as heat-resistant as the metal parts of the engine and may leak before the engine itself shows wear. To replace the gasket, use masking tape to label the positions of hoses and wires fitted to the cover, as well as the position of each bolt holding the cover in place. Detach the hoses and wires *(above, top)*; then loosen the rocker arm cover bolts with a socket wrench and remove them by hand, keeping the bolts in order so you can replace them in their original fittings. Lift off the cover *(above, bottom)*; the gasket will usually come with it.

2 Removing the old gasket. Pull the gasket off the cover. Use a flexible putty knife to scrape it free if it adheres *(above)*. Lightly sand away any old bits of stuck gasket from both the edge of the cover and the mating surface of the engine, and wipe them with alcohol. Hold a straightedge along the edges of the cover to check if it has become warped. If the warpage is more than just very minor, have the cover replaced.

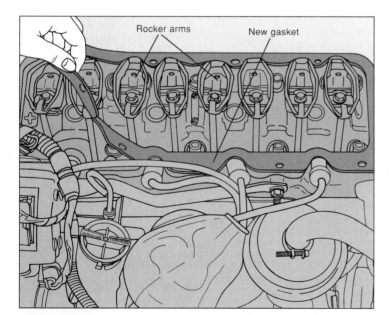

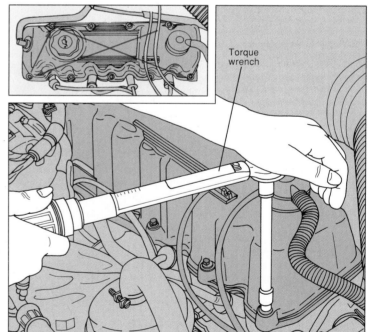

3 Putting on the new gasket. Apply a thin bead of gasket sealant to the cover side of the new gasket and the mating surface of the engine. Smear the sealant with your fingers so that both surfaces are lightly but evenly coated. Place the new gasket, dry side down, on the mating surface of the engine *(above)*. Make sure that the gasket is correctly aligned and that none of the bolt holes are covered.

4 Replacing the cover. Carefully replace the rocker arm cover. The sealant on the new gasket is sticky, so be sure to align the cover correctly before applying pressure to it. Replace each bolt in its original fitting and tighten them by hand. Check the service manual to find the correct torque for the bolts, or phone the dealership for the specifications. Set an adjustable torque wrench to the correct pressure and tighten the bolts *(above)*. Do not tighten beyond the point at which the wrench slips. Tighten the bolts in a crisscross pattern *(inset)* to even the stress on the cover. Reattach the hoses and wires to the rocker arm cover.

INSTALLING A BLOCK HEATER

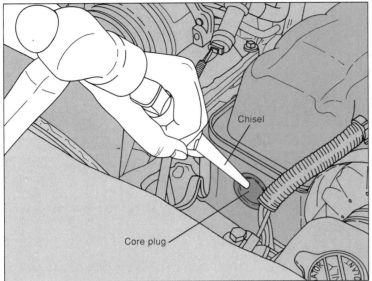

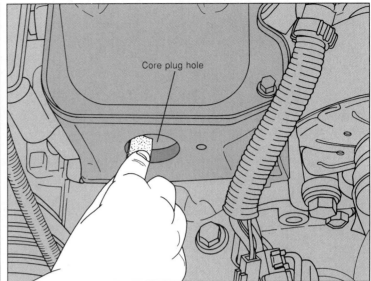

1 Removing the core plug. A block heater is an electrical heating element installed in the engine block. The element is plugged into a household outlet; by keeping the engine warm, it makes winter starts easier when the temperature falls below freezing. The inaccessibility of the core plugs on some models can make this a difficult repair for a beginner. Check the core plug locations on your car's engine. Begin by draining the coolant from the cooling system *(page 84)*.

Check the instructions with the block heater kit to determine where it should be placed on the engine. Next, locate the correct core plug—a flat, round piece of metal the same diameter as the block heater. Loosen the plug by knocking it carefully with a hammer and chisel *(above, left)*. Do not gouge the engine block. When you have loosened the plug, pry it out. Sand the edges of the hole to remove rust and burrs *(above, right)* and wipe it clean. Lubricate the hole with a few drops of engine oil.

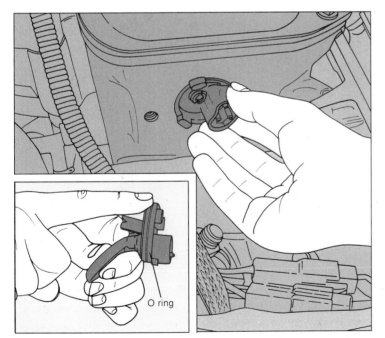

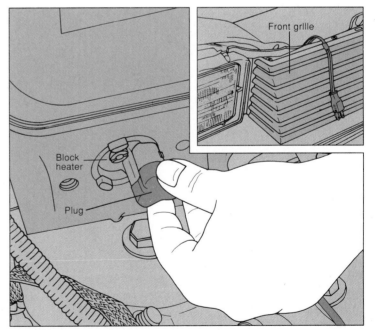

2 Inserting the block heater. Lubricate the rubber O ring, or gasket, on the heating element as recommended by the manufacturer *(inset)*. Do not use oil or a sealant; it will damage the rubber ring. Check the kit instructions to determine how the block heater should sit in the hole; this position is listed as a clock-face number. In the example above, the head of the ground terminal faces three o'clock. Insert the heater, push it tight against the engine block and tighten the screw just until snug.

3 Attaching the electrical plug. Attach the plug and cord assembly to the plug face on the block heater *(above)*. Route the cord through the front grille *(inset)*. The cord should not touch any of the car's hot or moving parts. Secure the cord to the grille with electrician's tape or plastic twist-ties. Replace the coolant before starting the car.

FUEL SYSTEM

The fuel system of most modern cars consists of the fuel tank, fuel pump, filter and carburetor, and the lines that connect them. When the engine is running, gasoline is drawn from the fuel tank by the fuel pump and delivered through the fuel filter to the carburetor. Since liquid fuel will not burn, it must be mixed with air in the carburetor and vaporized as much as possible before entering the combustion chambers. Inside the chambers, the air/fuel mixture is ignited by spark plugs (in carbureted and fuel-injected engines), or combusted through pressure (in diesel engines).

The carburetor must mix air and fuel in varying proportions to suit different driving conditions. Cold-weather starts require a "rich" fuel mixture of about 7 parts air to 1 part gasoline; highway driving may call for mixture as "lean" as 18 parts air to 1 part gasoline. The amount of air entering the carburetor is controlled by a pivoting flap called the throttle plate, which is linked to the accelerator pedal by a cable or rod. Most engines also have an automatic choke, which closes during starting to ensure a rich initial air/fuel mixture, then gradually opens as the engine warms up.

On many new gasoline engines (and all diesel engines), electronic fuel injection has replaced the traditional carburetor. In a carbureted engine, fuel is drawn into the engine by vacuum pressure; in a fuel-injected system, it is sprayed or injected into the engine under pressure. The air/fuel ratio in a fuel-injected engine is controlled by a computer and various engine sensors that monitor engine speed and temperature, and open or close the injectors accordingly. Since this system delivers the air/fuel mixture more precisely to the cylinders, the result is better cold-weather starting, improved mileage

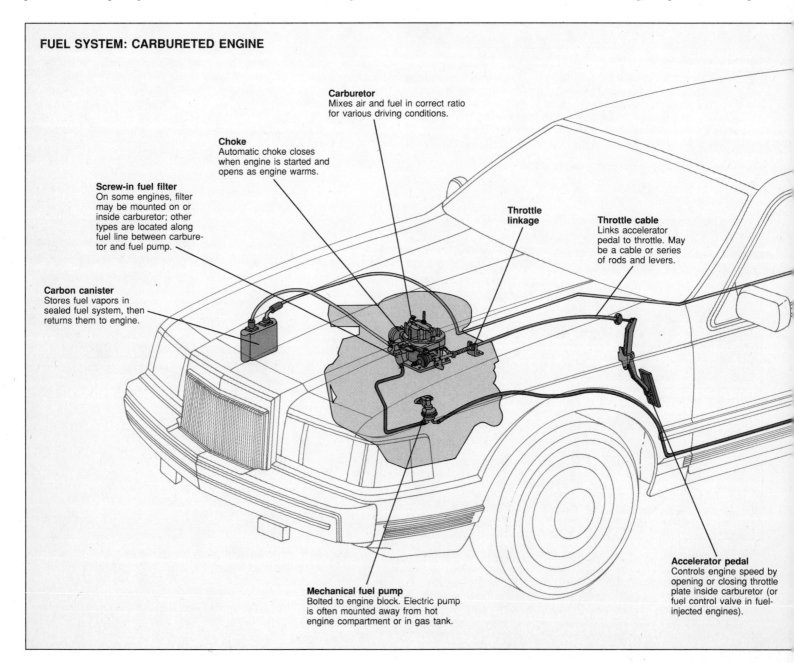

FUEL SYSTEM: CARBURETED ENGINE

Carburetor
Mixes air and fuel in correct ratio for various driving conditions.

Choke
Automatic choke closes when engine is started and opens as engine warms.

Screw-in fuel filter
On some engines, filter may be mounted on or inside carburetor; other types are located along fuel line between carburetor and fuel pump.

Carbon canister
Stores fuel vapors in sealed fuel system, then returns them to engine.

Throttle linkage

Throttle cable
Links accelerator pedal to throttle. May be a cable or series of rods and levers.

Mechanical fuel pump
Bolted to engine block. Electric pump is often mounted away from hot engine compartment or in gas tank.

Accelerator pedal
Controls engine speed by opening or closing throttle plate inside carburetor (or fuel control valve in fuel-injected engines).

and reduced emissions. The disadvantage of fuel injection is that it must be serviced by an expert using special equipment, and so is not covered in this chapter.

Your engine's biggest enemy is dirt, which can enter the fuel system through any of its parts or connections. It's best to keep the fuel tank topped up, for example. Otherwise, condensation can corrode the inside of the tank; this sediment will sink to the bottom of the tank and may enter the system when the gas level is low. To avoid problems with carburetors or fuel injectors, check and replace the fuel filter once a year or when clogged *(pages 65-66)*.

Symptoms of a faulty fuel pump include hard starting, rough running, stalling and backfiring. Mechanical fuel pumps are mounted on the engine block and can be tested and replaced by a do-it-yourselfer *(page 66)*. Electric fuel pumps—often mounted away from the hot engine compartment—are found most often in cars with fuel injection, and should be serviced by a mechanic.

Although the carburetor is a complex mechanism, its parts do not wear out as quickly as those in the electrical system. When the engine refuses to start or runs poorly, begin by troubleshooting the battery, spark plugs, cables and distributor *(page 96)* before tackling the carburetor. A sticking choke plate or linkage is a common cause of hard starting and can be freed with aerosol carburetor cleaner. More complex carburetor repairs—such as setting idle speed and fuel mixture—are best left to a professional.

Weather, too, affects fuel system performance. In extremely cold conditions, condensation in the fuel tank may cause the fuel line to freeze. Carburetor icing occurs when moisture in

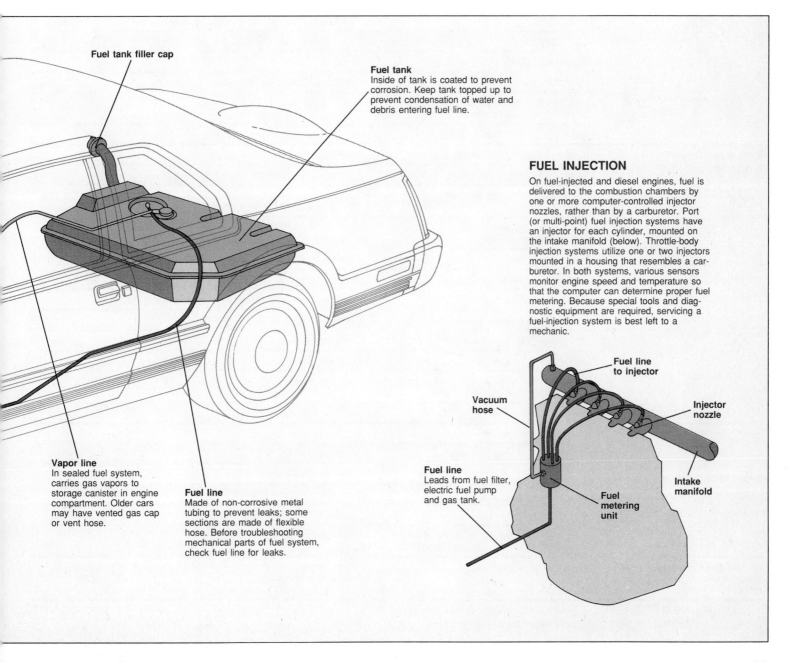

Fuel tank filler cap

Fuel tank
Inside of tank is coated to prevent corrosion. Keep tank topped up to prevent condensation of water and debris entering fuel line.

FUEL INJECTION

On fuel-injected and diesel engines, fuel is delivered to the combustion chambers by one or more computer-controlled injector nozzles, rather than by a carburetor. Port (or multi-point) fuel injection systems have an injector for each cylinder, mounted on the intake manifold (below). Throttle-body injection systems utilize one or two injectors mounted in a housing that resembles a carburetor. In both systems, various sensors monitor engine speed and temperature so that the computer can determine proper fuel metering. Because special tools and diagnostic equipment are required, servicing a fuel-injection system is best left to a mechanic.

Vacuum hose

Fuel line to injector

Injector nozzle

Fuel line
Leads from fuel filter, electric fuel pump and gas tank.

Fuel metering unit

Intake manifold

Vapor line
In sealed fuel system, carries gas vapors to storage canister in engine compartment. Older cars may have vented gas cap or vent hose.

Fuel line
Made of non-corrosive metal tubing to prevent leaks; some sections are made of flexible hose. Before troubleshooting mechanical parts of fuel system, check fuel line for leaks.

the air condenses and freezes the choke or throttle plate. To prevent both conditions, keep your gas tank filled and add a can of "dry gas." A frozen carburetor can be thawed with aerosol de-icer. Hot weather and stop-and-go driving may trigger vapor lock, where gasoline evaporates in the fuel line, pump or carburetor, causing the engine to stall. When this happens, you must let the engine cool, or apply wet rags to the pump and lines until the engine can be started.

Always allow the engine to cool completely before working on the fuel system, and follow all recommended safety guidelines *(page 8)*. Gasoline vapors are extremely explosive; wipe up fuel spills as soon as they occur, and do not smoke or cause an electrical spark. If gasoline gets on your skin, wash it off immediately. Do not spray solvents or starting fluids at a hot engine. Work in a well-ventilated area and store flammable, caustic or poisonous materials properly.

TROUBLESHOOTING GUIDE

SYMPTOM	POSSIBLE CAUSE	PROCEDURE
Engine cranks but doesn't start	Car out of gas	Gently rock car; if you hear a sloshing sound, fuel gauge may be faulty. Otherwise, add at least 1 gallon of gas
	Engine flooded	Press accelerator to the floor and release. Try to start car. If unsuccessful, wait 10 minutes and try again.
	Choke plate stuck	Close choke manually. Clean choke plate and linkage *(p. 68)* □○
	Fuel filter clogged	Replace fuel filter *(p. 65)* □○
	Fuel pump faulty	Service fuel pump *(p. 67)* ◪◑
	Fuel injectors faulty, air flow sensor faulty or vacuum leak (fuel-injected engines)	Take car for service
	Battery or ignition system faulty	Service electrical system *(p. 96)*
Engine runs roughly, accelerates poorly or stalls	Incorrect grade of gasoline	Switch to higher-octane gasoline
	Water or dirt in gas	Fill gas tank and replace fuel filter *(p. 65)* □○
	Carburetor icing (cold weather)	Spray carburetor with aerosol de-icer; add "dry gas" (isopropyl alcohol) to gas tank
	Vapor lock (engine heat vaporizing gas in fuel line or pump)	Stop car, open hood and let engine cool, or wrap fuel lines with wet rags
	Fuel filter clogged	Replace fuel filter *(p. 65)* □○
	Fuel pump faulty	Service fuel pump *(p. 67)* ◪◑
	Choke plate stuck	Clean and lubricate choke plate and linkage *(p. 68)* □○
	Choke vacuum diaphragm faulty	Service vacuum diaphragm *(p. 69)* □○
	Carburetor dirty or out of adjustment	Take car for service
	PCV hose broken or kinked	Check PCV hose *(p. 77)*
	Fuel injectors faulty, air flow sensor faulty or vacuum leak (fuel-injected engines)	Take car for service
	Ignition system faulty	Service electrical system *(p. 96)*
Poor gas mileage	Air filter clogged or dirty	Inspect air filter *(p. 74)*
	Choke faulty	Service choke *(p. 68)* □○
	Carburetor dirty or out of adjustment	Take car for service
	Fuel mixture incorrectly set	Take car for service
	PCV system faulty	Service PCV system *(p. 77)*
	Fuel injectors leaky, air flow sensor faulty or vacuum leak (fuel-injected engines)	Take car for service
Engine does not return to idle speed when accelerator is released	Throttle linkage binding	Check accelerator pedal for binding and lubricate if necessary; service throttle *(p. 68)* □○

DEGREE OF DIFFICULTY: □ Easy ◪ Moderate ■ Complex
ESTIMATED TIME: ○ Less than 1 hour ◑ 1 to 3 hours ● Over 3 hours

REPLACING THE FUEL FILTER

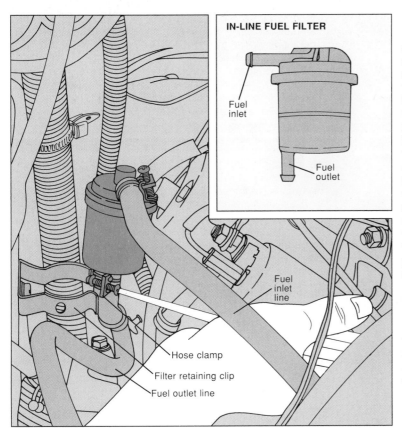

INx-LINE FUEL FILTER

Fuel inlet

Fuel outlet

Fuel inlet line

Hose clamp

Filter retaining clip

Fuel outlet line

Replacing an in-line fuel filter (Chrysler, AMC, most imports). In-line fuel filters are sealed, disposable canisters that should be replaced once a year or when they become clogged. Located on the fuel line between the fuel pump and the carburetor, the filter is held in place by hose clamps. Begin by removing the air cleaner *(page 75)* to expose the carburetor. Locate the fuel line entering the carburetor and trace the line back to the fuel filter. Place a rag underneath the filter to catch any gas that may drip during the repair, then loosen the clamps on both ends of the filter with a screwdriver *(left)* or pliers (spring-type clamps). Note the direction of fuel flow marked on the filter. Slip the hoses off the filter and remove it, then insert a pencil or golf tee in the hose leading from the fuel pump to prevent gas from leaking. If the hoses appear cracked, brittle or soft, replace them, too. (Most replacement filters come with new hoses and clamps.) Install the new filter, noting the direction of fuel flow, and reattach the hoses. Tighten the hose clamps just enough to prevent leakage. Wipe up any spilled gas, start the engine and check for leaks. If necessary, turn off the engine and tighten the clamps slightly. Reinstall the air cleaner.

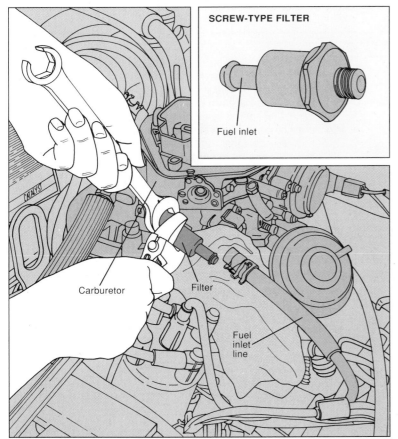

SCREW-TYPE FILTER

Fuel inlet

Carburetor

Filter

Fuel inlet line

Replacing a screw-type fuel filter (Ford). One end of a screw-type filter is threaded directly to the carburetor; the other end is attached to the fuel line with a hose clamp. Remove the air cleaner *(page 75)* to expose the carburetor, then locate the fuel line leading to the fuel filter. Place a rag between the fuel filter and the intake manifold to catch any gas that may drip from the filter, then loosen the hose clamp with a screwdriver (screw-type clamp) or pliers (spring-type clamp). Insert a pencil or golf tee into the end of the disconnected fuel line to prevent gas from leaking. Next, fit an open-end wrench on the housing to which the filter is screwed, hold it steady, and loosen the filter by turning it counterclockwise with a second wrench. Screw the new filter in place by hand, then tighten with the same double-wrench technique *(left)*. If the fuel line appears damaged, replace it. Otherwise, reconnect the fuel line, wipe away any spilled gas and start the engine. If there are any leaks, turn off the engine and tighten the filter and clamp. Reinstall the air cleaner.

REPLACING THE FUEL FILTER (continued)

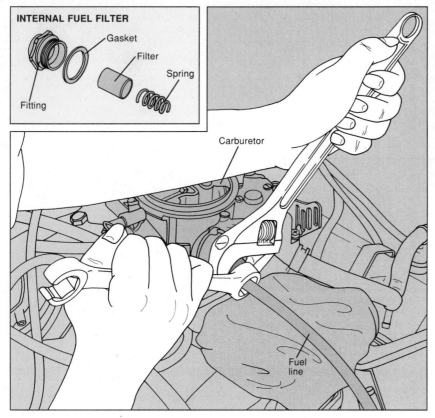

INTERNAL FUEL FILTER

Gasket

Filter

Spring

Fitting

Carburetor

Fuel line

Removing an internal fuel filter (GM). Internal filters are housed inside the carburetor. The filter has several parts *(inset)*, but only the paper or bronze filter and the gasket are replaced. First remove the air cleaner *(page 75)* to expose the carburetor, then locate the fuel line. Place a rag beneath this point to collect gas that may leak during the repair. Hold the filter fitting steady with one wrench and carefully loosen the fuel line by turning it counterclockwise with a second wrench *(left)*. Insert a pencil or golf tee into the disconnected fuel line to prevent gas from leaking during the repair. Next, remove the filter fitting by turning it counterclockwise with a wrench. As the fitting comes off, catch the nylon gasket, filter and spring. Insert the new filter and gasket (and new spring, if necessary) into the carburetor in their proper order. Screw on the fitting by hand, then tighten with a wrench. Reconnect the fuel line with the same double-wrench technique, clean up any spilled gas and start the engine to check your work. If there are any leaks, turn off the engine and tighten the connections.

SERVICING A MECHANICAL FUEL PUMP

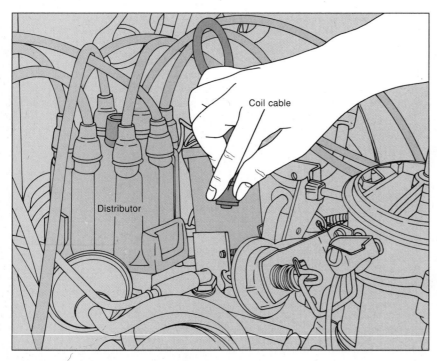

Coil cable

Distributor

1 **Troubleshooting the fuel pump.** Before working on the fuel pump, carefully inspect the gas tank, fuel line, pump and carburetor with a flashlight. If there are no apparent leaks, begin servicing the fuel pump by grounding the ignition system to prevent the car from starting during the repair. Disconnect the cable that runs between the coil and the distributor cap from the distributor *(left)*. Attach one end of a jumper wire to the cable. Attach the other end of the jumper to the engine block. (But do not attach the jumper to the carburetor or air cleaner stud.) On high-energy ignition (GM) distributors, disconnect the ignition lead from the distributor cap instead. Next, disconnect the fuel line from the fuel filter *(page 65)* or carburetor *(above)*. Place the end of the line into a container and have an assistant crank the engine a few times. If gas spurts from the line, the fuel pump is not broken. (However, if the engine runs roughly, lacks power or stalls at high speeds, the pump may be worn; have it checked more precisely by a mechanic.) If no fuel spurts through the line, either the fuel tank is blocked or the fuel pump itself is faulty. If you suspect the fuel tank, take your car for professional service. If not, reconnect the fuel line and replace the faulty pump *(next step)*.

SERVICING A MECHANICAL FUEL PUMP (continued)

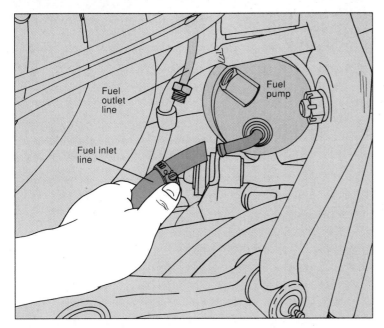

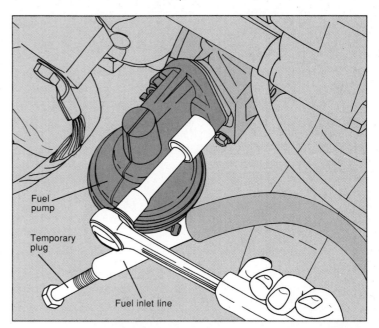

2 Disconnecting the fuel pump. Trace the fuel line from the filter or carburetor to the fuel pump, which is usually accessible from the top of the engine compartment. Disconnect the fuel inlet and outlet lines from the pump using a screwdriver (screw-type clamps) or pliers (spring-type clamps). If the fuel lines are secured with metal fittings instead of clamps, use one wrench to steady the fuel pump and another to loosen the fittings. Pull the fuel lines off the pump *(above)*.

3 Freeing the the fuel pump. Since the end of the incoming line is below the level of the fuel tank, gas will leak through the line if it is not blocked. Temporarily plug the end with a pencil, golf tee or bolt, as shown. Use a socket wrench to loosen and remove the bolts holding the fuel pump to the engine block *(above)*. As you pull the pump free, its rocker arm will slide out of the engine block. Stuff a clean rag into the opening on the engine, and use a putty knife to scrape away old gasket cement from the mounting surface. Wipe the surface clean, then remove the rag. If the new pump does not have fuel line fittings, reuse the fittings from the old pump. Be sure to place the fittings on the new pump in the same direction.

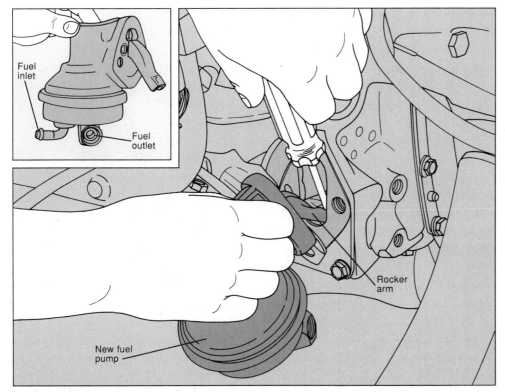

4 Installing the new fuel pump. Apply an even coat of gasket sealer to both sides of the gasket, then place it on the fuel pump. The rocker arm on some types of pumps is actuated by a pushrod in the engine. Look inside the engine block where the fuel pump was mounted. If there is a pushrod, carefully use a screwdriver to pry it up while you place the pump in position, making sure that the rocker arm fits beneath the pushrod. Insert and tighten the mounting bolts by hand until the pump is seated against the gasket. Finish tightening with a socket wrench. Reconnect the fuel inlet and outlet lines to the pump and reattach the ignition cable. Start the engine and check your work. If there are any leaks, turn off the engine and tighten the connections.

SERVICING THE CHOKE

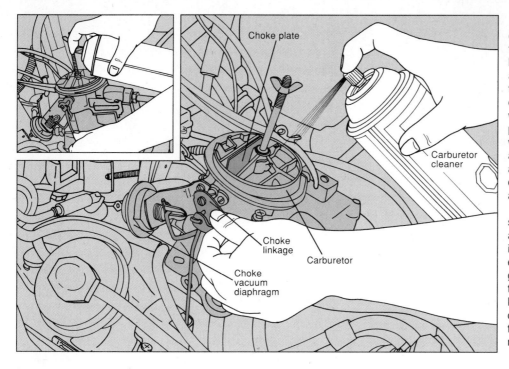

Choke plate

Carburetor cleaner

Choke linkage

Carburetor

Choke vacuum diaphragm

Cleaning the choke plate. With the engine off and cold, remove the air cleaner *(page 75)* to expose the carburetor and its choke assembly. Have an assistant press and release the accelerator pedal. The choke plate (also called the butterfly) should snap almost completely closed. If not, lubricate the plate and its hinges with aerosol carburetor cleaner *(left)*. Dry the parts with a clean rag, then move the plate with your fingers. To prevent further sticking, apply a drop of silicone-based lubricant to all accessible moving parts. Have your assistant depress and release the accelerator pedal again; the choke plate should pivot freely.

On models with a linkage from the thermostatic coil, check for a bent or damaged linkage. Move the choke linkage manually to see if it binds anywhere. Using aerosol carburetor cleaner and a clean rag, wipe off any dirt or grease and work the linkage manually a few times *(inset)*. Apply a drop of silicone-based lubricant to all accessible moving parts. If the choke butterfly still doesn't close properly, the thermostatic coil may be damaged—see a mechanic.

SERVICING THE THROTTLE

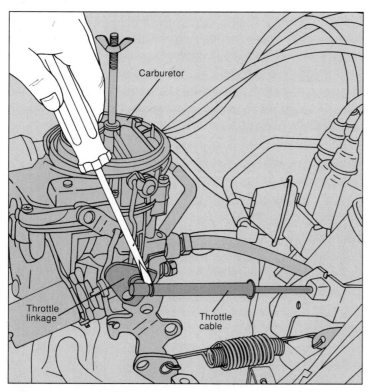

Carburetor

Throttle linkage

Throttle cable

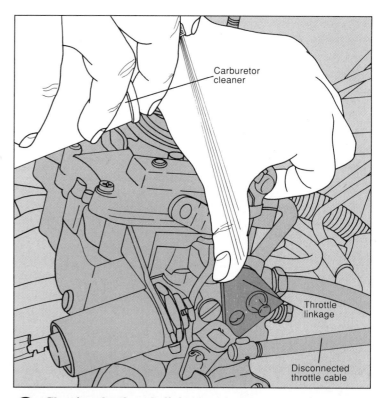

Carburetor cleaner

Throttle linkage

Disconnected throttle cable

1 Disconnecting the throttle cable. Remove the air cleaner *(page 75)* to expose the carburetor, then locate the throttle linkage on the driver's side of the carburetor. The throttle cable (or rod) connects this linkage to the accelerator pedal. To test the assembly, first disconnect the throttle cable from the linkage *(above)*. On most cars the cable is held in place by a cotter pin or clip; remove it with pliers, then pry the cable free with a screwdriver.

2 Cleaning the throttle linkage. Move the throttle linkage by hand. If it binds, spray the linkage with carburetor cleaner *(above)* and wipe with a clean rag. Lubricate the moving parts with silicone-based lubricant. Next, move the accelerator pedal up and down by hand. If there is uneven movement, check for sharp bends in the throttle cable. A kinked cable must be replaced, never straightened. Reattach the cable to the throttle linkage and replace the air cleaner.

SERVICING THE CHOKE VACUUM DIAPHRAGM

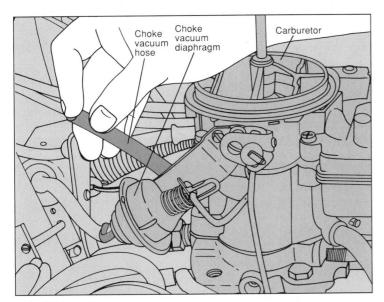

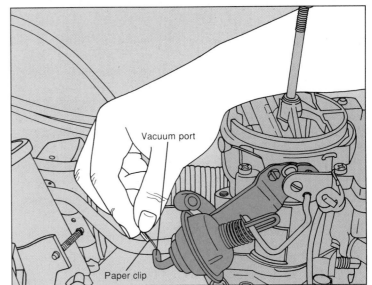

1 **Checking for vacuum.** When the car is started, the vacuum diaphragm pulls the carburetor choke plate open slightly to prevent the engine from receiving too rich an air/fuel mixture. To inspect it, first remove the air cleaner *(page 75)* and examine the vacuum hose connecting the diaphragm and carburetor. Tighten or replace the hose, if necessary. Next, have an assistant start the car. Pull the hose off the vacuum diaphragm and use your finger to feel for suction *(above)*. If there is little or no suction, turn off the car and pull the hose off the carburetor. If the hose is undamaged, check the vacuum ports *(step 2)*; if there is suction, service the vacuum diaphragm *(step 3)*.

2 **Inspecting the vacuum port.** A dirty or damaged vacuum port can reduce or block vacuum pressure. With the car off and the vacuum hose disconnected, inspect the vacuum port for splits or cracks. If the carburetor port is damaged, see a mechanic. If the diaphragm port is cracked, replace the diaphragm. You can clean clogged or dirty ports with a bent paper clip or pin *(above)*. Reconnect the hose to the carburetor, start the car and test for suction as in step 1. If there is still little or no suction, reconnect the hose to the vacuum diaphragm and see a mechanic. If there is suction but the choke plate will not open, go to step 3.

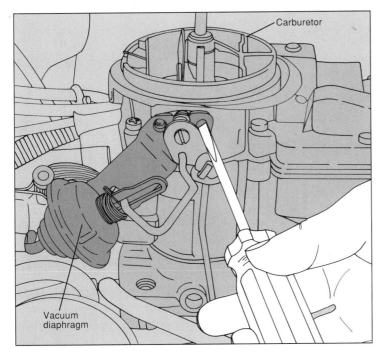

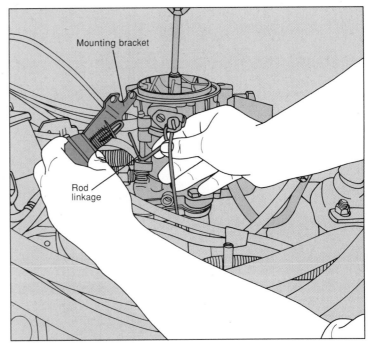

3 **Removing the old vacuum diaphragm.** If there is suction in the vacuum hose but the choke plate will not open properly, the vacuum diaphragm may need servicing. Refer to the service manual for your make and model for adjustment specifications and techniques, or see a mechanic. If the vacuum diaphragm is properly adjusted but the symptoms remain, the diaphragm should be replaced. Disconnect the vacuum hose and remove the screws holding the diaphragm mounting bracket to the carburetor *(above)*.

4 **Installing the new diaphragm.** The rod linkage connects the vacuum diaphragm to the choke plate. To disengage the assembly, twist the vacuum diaphragm sideways until the rod is free *(above)*. Twist the new vacuum diaphragm into the rod linkage and replace the screws. Connect the vacuum hose to the new diaphragm and adjust the diaphragm according to the specifications in your service manual. If the engine still runs poorly, have the choke adjusted professionally.

AIR CLEANER AND EXHAUST

A car's engine consumes a far greater volume of air than fuel—9,000 parts air to one part gasoline. The air cleaner, through which the air is drawn, not only filters out dirt before it can reach the engine and damage it, but also muffles the sound of the air passing into the carburetor (or into the throttle body or intake manifold on fuel injection engines).

A dirty air filter can cause loss of power from the engine and poor fuel economy. Inspect the filter every 12,000 miles; more often if you drive under dusty conditions. The Troubleshooting Guide *(page 72)* lists some of the symptoms of a dirty filter, and directs you to the page in this chapter that describes its removal, cleaning and replacement. Filters and other components of the air cleaner may vary in shape, but not in function. The illustrations on page 73 will help you recognize the parts and locate them in your car.

The air cleaner system has a heat control that keeps the temperature of the air entering the carburetor relatively constant. This enables the carburetor to operate more efficiently and decreases pollution emissions. The damper flap inside the air intake snorkel meters the proportion of heated air and cool outside air entering the air cleaner. The heated air comes from the exhaust manifold via the heat duct; the outside air enters through the air intake duct. A malfunctioning damper flap, which can result in increased pollution emissions, hard starting and rough running, may result from a faulty heat-sensing switch *(page 75)* or vacuum motor *(page 76)*.

Of the many emission control mechanisms on today's cars, two have components serviceable by the do-it-yourselfer: the positive crankcase ventilation (PCV) system and the exhaust gas recirculation (EGR) system. The PCV system reduces

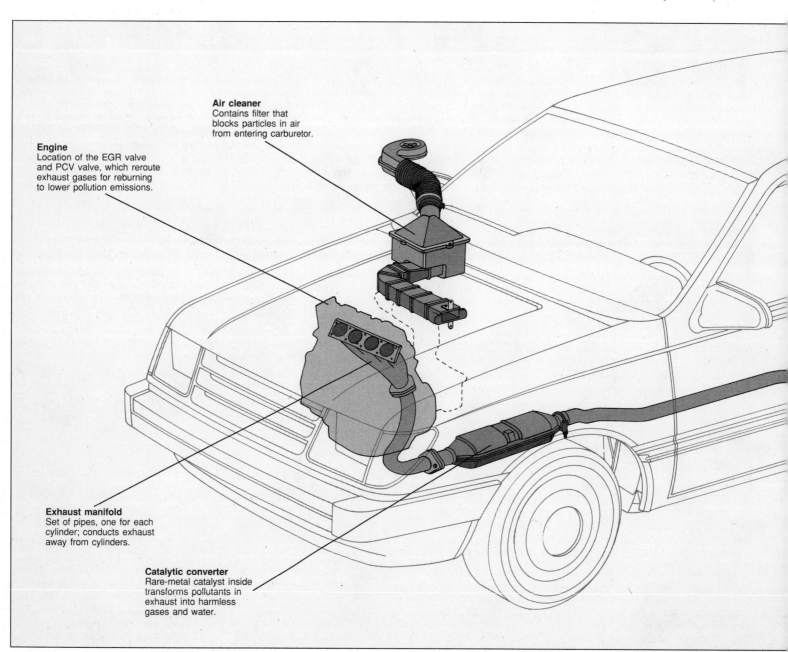

Air cleaner
Contains filter that blocks particles in air from entering carburetor.

Engine
Location of the EGR valve and PCV valve, which reroute exhaust gases for reburning to lower pollution emissions.

Exhaust manifold
Set of pipes, one for each cylinder; conducts exhaust away from cylinders.

Catalytic converter
Rare-metal catalyst inside transforms pollutants in exhaust into harmless gases and water.

pollution by recycling gases that leak from the combustion chambers into the crankcase back into the combustion chambers for reburning. The PCV valve regulates the amount of gases that are recycled. The EGR system lowers the combustion temperature to limit the formation of nitrogen oxides, which form smog. It does this by diverting some of the engine's exhaust gases into the combustion chambers. The EGR valve controls the flow of the exhaust gases. Periodically inspect the PCV and EGR valves; when checking the air filter, also inspect the PCV filter *(page 77)*.

Since 1975, most cars have been manufactured with another emission control device—the catalytic converter. Located on the exhaust pipe near the exhaust manifold, it chemically restructures carbon monoxide and hydrocarbons into carbon dioxide and water. It resembles the muffler, but do not confuse

the two. A muffler can be replaced by the do-it-yourselfer, but do not attempt to replace a catalytic converter yourself.

The exhaust system, pictured below, carries unburned fuel remnants and gases away from the car. The exhaust manifold collects waste gas from each engine cylinder and sends it through the exhaust pipe to the catalytic converter and the muffler. The muffler's interior baffles and tubes quiet the explosive release of exhaust; on some cars a resonator further dampens exhaust noise. Finally, the tailpipe directs the exhaust to the outside air. Do not attempt to remove the muffler or tailpipe from a one-piece welded exhaust system; such a job requires professional equipment. But you can replace a muffler or tailpipe attached by clamps *(page 79)* without using special tools. Work on a cold car, with the engine off, and do not smoke. Wear safety goggles when working under the car.

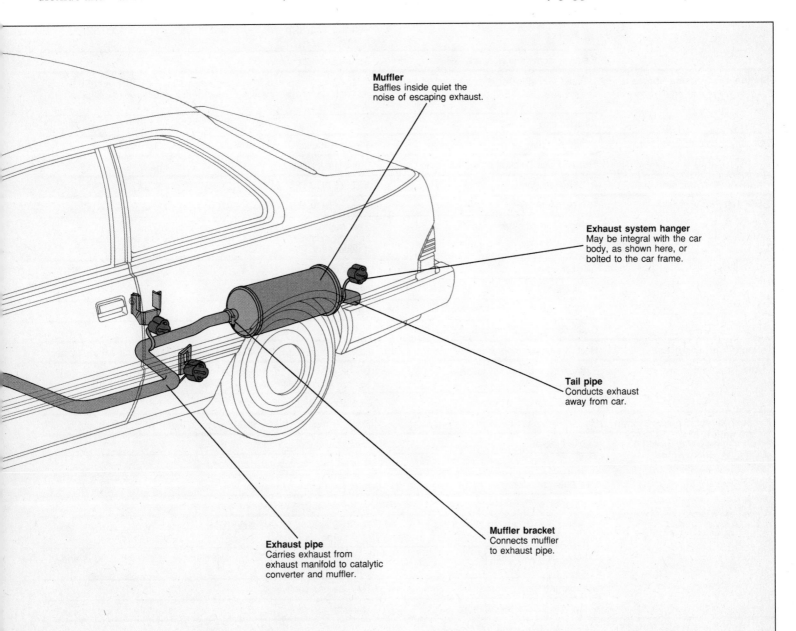

Muffler
Baffles inside quiet the noise of escaping exhaust.

Exhaust system hanger
May be integral with the car body, as shown here, or bolted to the car frame.

Tail pipe
Conducts exhaust away from car.

Exhaust pipe
Carries exhaust from exhaust manifold to catalytic converter and muffler.

Muffler bracket
Connects muffler to exhaust pipe.

TROUBLESHOOTING GUIDE

SYMPTOM	POSSIBLE CAUSE	PROCEDURE
Engine hard to start	EGR valve stuck or opens at wrong time	Test EGR system (p. 78) ▨●
	Air filter dirty	Clean or replace air filter (p. 74) □○; inspect PCV filter (p. 77) □○
Engine sputters when idling	PCV valve faulty	Inspect PCV filter and test PCV valve (p. 77) ▨○
	Damper flap stuck or opens at wrong time	Test damper flap and check for vacuum (p. 75) □○; test heat-sensing switch (p. 75) ▨●; replace vacuum motor (p. 76) ▨●, if necessary
	EGR valve stuck or opens at wrong time	Test EGR system (p. 78) ▨●
	Air filter dirty	Clean or replace air filter (p. 74) □○; inspect PCV filter (p. 77) □○
	Intake manifold leaks	Take car for service
Engine stalls or lacks power	EGR valve stuck or opens at wrong time	Test EGR system (p. 78) ▨●
	Air filter dirty	Clean or replace air filter (p. 74) □○; inspect PCV filter (p. 77) □○
	PCV valve faulty	Inspect PCV filter and test PCV valve (p. 77) ▨○
	Damper flap stuck or opens at wrong time	Test damper flap and check for vacuum (p. 75) □○; test heat-sensing switch (p. 75) ▨●; replace vacuum motor (p. 76) ▨●, if necessary
	Catalytic converter clogged	Take car for service
Engine misfires and surges	Damper flap stuck or opens at wrong time	Test damper flap and check for vacuum (p. 75) □○; test heat-sensing switch (p. 75) ▨●; replace vacuum motor (p. 76) ▨●, if necessary
	Air filter dirty	Clean or replace air filter (p. 74) □○; inspect PCV filter (p. 77) □○
Popping noise at carburetor	Inner chambers or muffler collapsed	Replace muffler (p. 79) ■●
	Exhaust pipe blocked or kinked	Take car for service
Oil in air filter housing	PCV valve faulty	Inspect PCV filter and test PCV valve (p. 77) ▨○
Poor fuel economy	PCV valve faulty	Inspect PCV filter and test PCV valve (p. 77) ▨○
	Damper flap stuck or opens at wrong time	Test damper flap and check for vacuum (p. 75) □○; test heat-sensing switch (p. 75) ▨●; replace vacuum motor (p. 76) ▨●, if necessary
	Air filter dirty	Clean or replace air filter (p. 74) □○; inspect PCV filter (p. 77) □○
	Inner chambers of muffler collapsed	Replace muffler (p. 79) ■●
	Exhaust pipe blocked or kinked	Take car for service
	Catalytic converter clogged	Take car for service
Rumble from under car	Hole in exhaust pipe or muffler	Replace muffler (p. 79) ■●; have mechanic replace exhaust pipe
Rattle from under car	Exhaust pipe or muffler loose	Check exhaust system joints and clamps; tighten loose bolts and replace broken clamps (p. 79) ■●
	Tube inside muffler loose	Replace muffler (p. 79) ■●
Exhaust louder on acceleration	Hole in exhaust pipe or muffler	Replace muffler (p. 79) ■●; have mechanic replace exhaust pipe
Black exhaust smoke when starting engine; engine sputters when idling	Choke blocked	Clean and lubricate choke (p. 68) ▨○
	Spark plug cables faulty	Replace spark plug cables (p. 114) ▨●
	Distributor cap cracked	Replace distributor cap (p. 116) □○
	Air filter dirty	Clean or replace air filter (p. 74) □○; inspect PCV filter (p. 77) □○
Exhaust smell in car	Hole in exhaust pipe, muffler or tail pipe	Replace muffler (p. 79) ■●; have mechanic replace exhaust pipe or tail pipe
	Exhaust pipe joints loose	Check exhaust system joints and clamps; tighten loose bolts and replace broken clamps (p. 79) ■●
	Exhaust manifold cracked	Take car for service
	Exhaust manifold gasket leaks	Take car for service

DEGREE OF DIFFICULTY: □ Easy ▨ Moderate ■ Complex
ESTIMATED TIME: ○ Less than 1 hour ◑ 1 to 3 hours ● Over 3 hours

TWO TYPES OF AIR CLEANERS

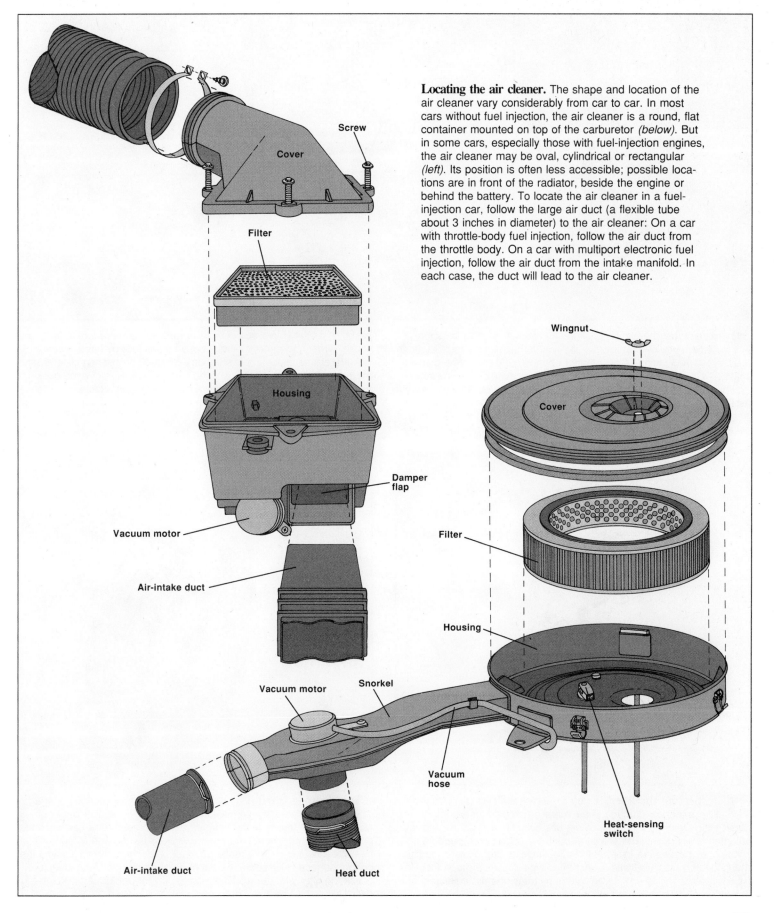

Screw

Cover

Filter

Housing

Damper flap

Vacuum motor

Air-intake duct

Vacuum motor

Snorkel

Air-intake duct

Heat duct

Wingnut

Cover

Filter

Housing

Vacuum hose

Heat-sensing switch

Locating the air cleaner. The shape and location of the air cleaner vary considerably from car to car. In most cars without fuel injection, the air cleaner is a round, flat container mounted on top of the carburetor *(below)*. But in some cars, especially those with fuel-injection engines, the air cleaner may be oval, cylindrical or rectangular *(left)*. Its position is often less accessible; possible locations are in front of the radiator, beside the engine or behind the battery. To locate the air cleaner in a fuel-injection car, follow the large air duct (a flexible tube about 3 inches in diameter) to the air cleaner: On a car with throttle-body fuel injection, follow the air duct from the throttle body. On a car with multiport electronic fuel injection, follow the air duct from the intake manifold. In each case, the duct will lead to the air cleaner.

INSPECTING AND CLEANING THE AIR FILTER

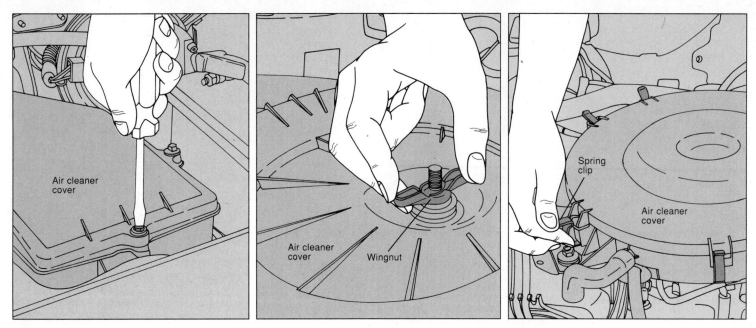

1 Accessing the air filter. If the air cleaner housing is factory sealed, you cannot remove the filter for inspection; instead, have your mechanic examine it after about 50,000 miles (the owner's manual will specify exactly how often), or whenever the engine's behavior indicates a dirty air filter. Examine an accessible air filter every 12,000 miles or as specified by the owner's manual, or whenever engine operation indicates a dirty air filter. The air cleaner cover may be attached by a wingnut, bolts, screws or spring clips, or by a combi-

nation of these. Use a screwdriver to remove screws *(above, left)*, or a socket wrench to remove bolts. Loosen a wingnut by hand *(above, center)*, or use pliers, if it is stubborn. Snap off any spring clips around the edge of the cover *(above, right)* and lift it off. Remove the gasket, if any. Use masking tape to label any hoses or ducts attached to the air cleaner cover and disconnect them if necessary. Lift the air filter out of the air cleaner housing.

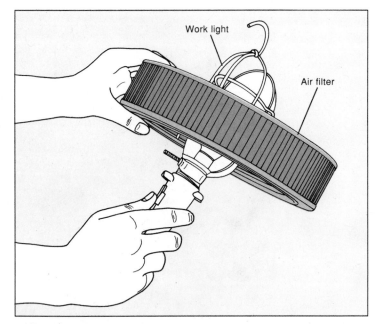

2 Inspecting the filter. If you see oil on the filter, tears in the filter paper, or damage to the metal or plastic frame, replace the filter. Determine how much dirt has accumulated on the filter by inserting a work light or flashlight through the center of a round filter *(above)*, or holding the light behind a rectangular filter. Rotate the filter to inspect the entire surface for dirt. If no light passes through the paper, replace the filter; if some light penetrates, the dirt buildup is not excessive and it can be dislodged *(step 3)*.

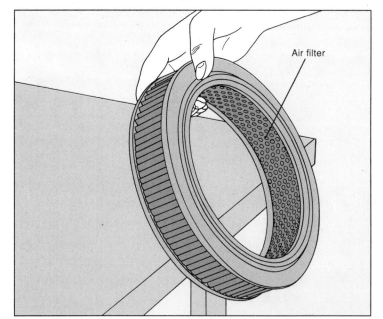

3 Cleaning the filter. Strike the filter frame sharply against a hard surface *(above)*, taking care not to rip the filter paper or dent the frame. If you have an air compressor or a can of compressed air handy, direct the air at low pressure through a round filter from the inside out. On a rectangular air filter, direct the air against the bottom surface to disperse the debris through the top. After cleaning, check the filter with the work light again. If light penetrates through the entire filter, reinstall it; if it does not, replace the filter.

SERVICING THE AIR CLEANER DAMPER FLAP

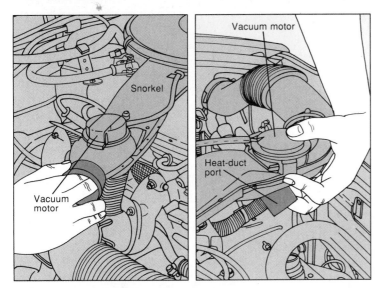

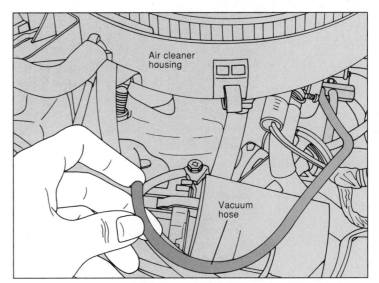

1 **Testing the damper flap for movement.** The damper flap is inside the air cleaner snorkel, near the vacuum motor. To reach it, remove either the air intake duct or the heat duct. The air intake duct is attached to the end of the snorkel with a spring clip. Release the fastener and remove the duct, then reach inside the snorkel and feel whether the flap moves freely *(above, left)*. The heat duct joins the snorkel near the vacuum motor. Undo the retaining clip and pull the duct off its port to inspect the flap *(above, right)*. If the ducts are inaccessible, take out the air filter *(page 74)* to reach the damper flap. The spring-operated flap should open freely; if it sticks, clean the inner walls of the snorkel with a cloth. If the flap still sticks, install a new snorkel or replace the entire air cleaner assembly *(page 76)*.

2 **Testing the vacuum.** Lift out the air filter *(page 74)* if necessary, to locate the heat-sensing switch—a small box inside the air cleaner housing. Find the two narrow rubber vacuum hoses connected to the bottom of the heat-sensing switch; one leads to the vacuum motor, the other to the carburetor or intake manifold. Disconnect the hose leading to the carburetor or intake manifold from the heat-sensing switch. Start the engine. **Caution:** Do not wear loose clothing, hair or jewelry, and keep hands clear of engine parts. Place a fingertip over the end of the hose and feel for suction *(above)*. If there is no suction, check both vacuum hoses for damage and replace them if necessary. If you feel suction, the problem is with the heat-sensing switch *(below)*. Turn off the engine and reconnect the vacuum hose.

TESTING AND REPLACING THE HEAT-SENSING SWITCH

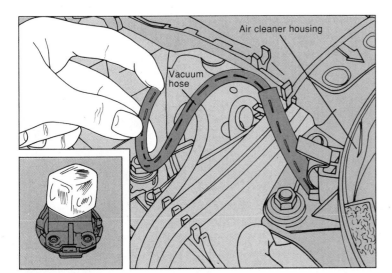

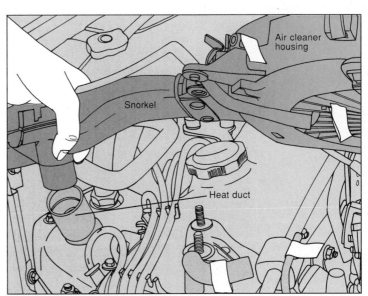

1 **Testing the heat-sensing switch.** Disconnect the vacuum hose between the heat-sensing switch and the vacuum motor at the vacuum motor. Rest an ice cube on the heat-sensing switch *(inset)* and turn on the engine. **Caution:** Do not wear loose clothing, hair or jewelry, and keep hands clear of engine parts. Place a fingertip over the end of the hose *(above)*. As the switch cools, feel for suction in the hose. If suction develops, the heat-sensing switch is good, but the vacuum motor is faulty; replace it *(page 76)*. If no suction exists after 5 to 10 minutes, replace the heat-sensing switch *(steps following)*.

2 **Removing the air cleaner.** Lift the air filter out of the housing *(page 74)* and disconnect the heat duct and air intake duct from the snorkel *(step 1, above)*. Use tape to label the hoses and their connection points on the air cleaner for correct replacement, then pull off the hoses. With a socket wrench, remove the nuts or bolts that secure the air cleaner housing and lift out the air cleaner *(above)*.

TESTING AND REPLACING THE HEAT-SENSING SWITCH (continued)

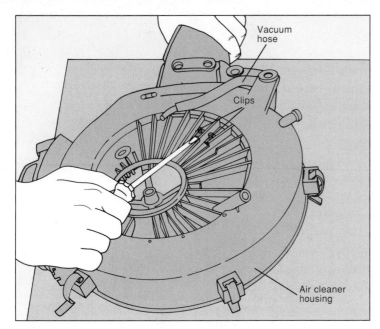

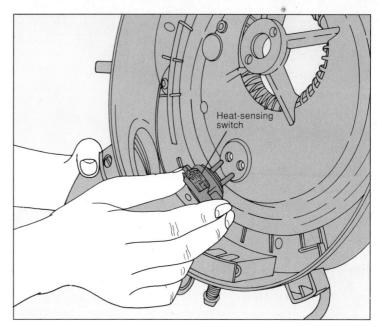

3 **Removing the heat-sensing switch.** Turn the housing upside down on a firm, flat surface. Disconnect the vacuum hoses from the heat-sensing switch. The switch has two short nipples that protrude through the air cleaner housing. A small metal clip on each fastens the switch tightly to the housing. Insert a screwdriver under each clip and gently pry it off *(above)*. Do not use excessive force; the clips are made of pliable aluminum and can easily break or bend.

4 **Replacing the heat-sensing switch.** Turn the air cleaner over and slip the heat-sensing switch out of the air cleaner housing. If the switch has a gasket remove it, too. Fit the new gasket over the nipples of the new switch and slide them through the housing *(above)*. Turn over the housing, place the clips on the nipples and push them down firmly to attach the switch. Reattach the vacuum hose between the heat-sensing switch and the vacuum motor.

REPLACING THE VACUUM MOTOR

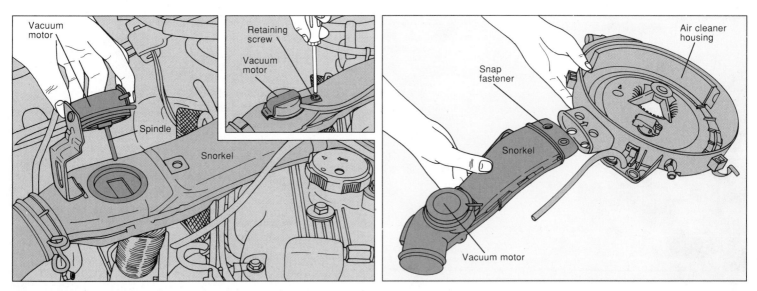

Unscrewing the vacuum motor. Depending on the model of the car, a vacuum motor is removed in one of three ways: It is unscrewed from the snorkel; the snorkel itself is detached from the air cleaner; or the entire air cleaner assembly is removed. If screws secure the vacuum motor to the snorkel, pull the vacuum hose off the vacuum motor and unscrew the motor's retaining screws *(inset)*. The vacuum motor has a spindle hooked to the damper flap inside the snorkel; tip the motor forward and wiggle it to disconnect the spindle *(above, left)*. Install a new vacuum motor by hooking its spindle to the damper flap and replacing the screws. If the motor is welded, riveted, or molded to the snorkel *(above, right)*, remove any screws holding the snorkel to the air cleaner, or disconnect snap fasteners by hand. Pull the snorkel off the air cleaner and install a new one. If the vacuum motor, snorkel and air cleaner housing are all one piece, remove and replace the entire air cleaner assembly *(page 75)*.

INSPECTING AND REPLACING THE PCV FILTER

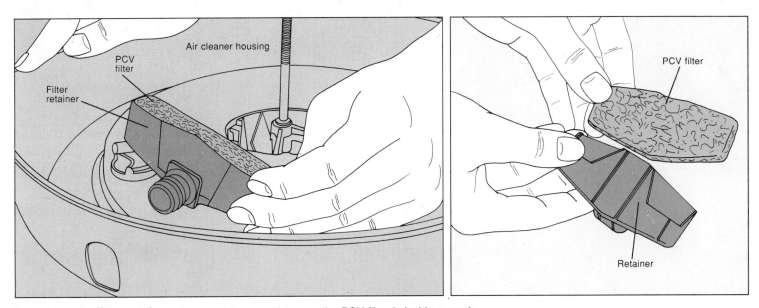

Removing the filter retainer. On some Chrysler V-8 cars, the PCV filter is inside a crank-case inlet air breather; on some American Motors V-8 cars, it is found inside the oil filler cap. These filters can be rinsed with solvent and reused. On most other cars, the PCV filter is housed in a retainer inside the air cleaner housing. Remove the air filter *(page 74)*. Plastic air cleaners may have a retainer molded to the wall of the air cleaner housing; on other models, it will be attached inside the housing with a clip. Pry off the clip, disconnect the PCV hose and remove the retainer *(above, left)*. Slide the filter out of its slot *(above, right)* and inspect it. If the filter looks dirty, insert a new one. Reinstall the retainer and reconnect the PCV hose.

TESTING AND REPLACING THE PCV VALVE

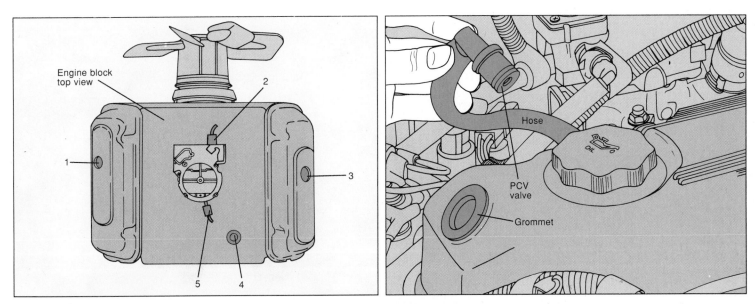

Inspecting the PCV valve. The location of the PCV valve on the engine block varies accord-ing to the model of the car. You may find it at any one of the spots identified in the diagram *(above, left)*. The valve is usually attached to the end of a hose and inserted into a retaining grommet on the engine. Less commonly, it may be "in-line"—within a section of hose connect-ing the air cleaner or intake manifold to the engine block. To test the first type, pull the PCV valve out of its grommet *(above, right)*, and shake it; if it does not rattle, it is damaged. Pull the valve out of the hose, push a matching replacement onto the hose and insert it into the grom-met. To test an in-line PCV valve, pull both ends of the hose off the valve, and shake it. If the valve does not rattle, replace it with a new one.

INSPECTING THE EGR SYSTEM

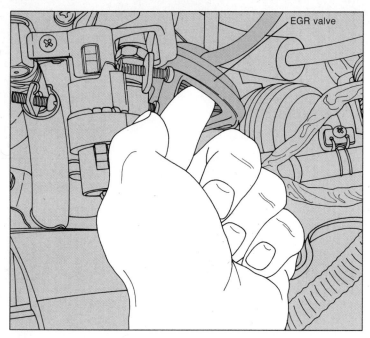

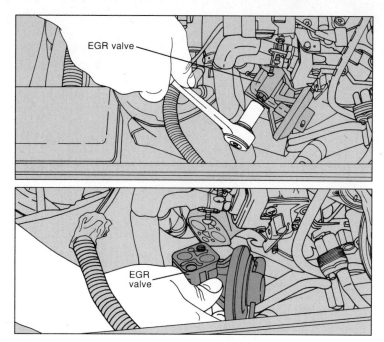

1 **Testing the EGR valve diaphragm.** Locate the EGR valve on the intake manifold. (In some cars, the EGR valve is hidden beneath other parts, making it inaccessible; in this case, have a mechanic test and replace it, if necessary.) The disc-shaped rubber diaphragm mounted on the EGR valve should move in and out easily. Place your finger against the valve diaphragm to feel whether it sticks *(above)*. If the valve diaphragm does not move freely, replace the valve *(step 2)*. If it does move freely, the valve is good; go on to check that vacuum suction is reaching it *(step 3)*.

2 **Removing and replacing the EGR valve.** Detach the vacuum hose from its nipple on the EGR valve. With a socket wrench, remove the bolts holding the valve on the intake manifold *(above, top)*. Lift off the valve *(above, bottom)* and remove its gasket, if it has one. The intense heat the valve receives when the engine is running will sometimes make the valve stick in place. Wearing work gloves, break the seal using hand pressure. If the valve does not come free, have a mechanic remove and replace it. Install a new gasket when you install the replacement valve. Tighten the retaining bolts and reconnect the vacuum hose.

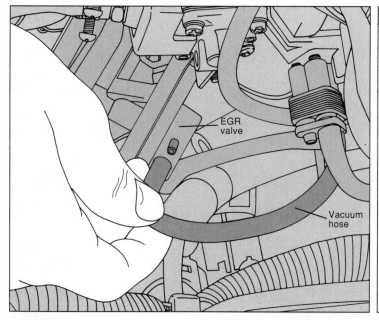

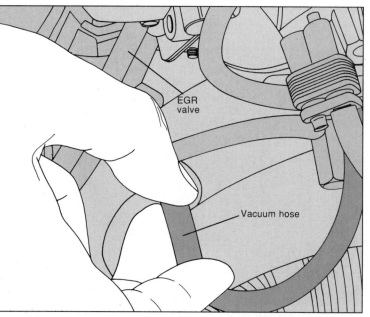

3 **Testing for vacuum in the vacuum hose.** The EGR valve is operated by vacuum suction from the carburetor. If the valve moves freely, but the EGR system seems to malfunction (the engine stalls or hesitates), the vacuum may not be reaching the valve. Slide the hose off its nipple on the EGR valve *(above, left)*. Inspect the hose for leaks or cracks and replace it if damaged. Start the

engine and run it at fast idle. **Caution:** Do not wear loose clothing, hair or jewelry and keep hands clear of engine parts. Place a thumb over the end of the vacuum hose *(above, right)*, and feel for suction, indicating vacuum. If no vacuum exists, take the car for service. On some newer cars, the EGR valve is computer controlled, and will not respond to this test; check the service manual.

INSTALLING A NEW MUFFLER

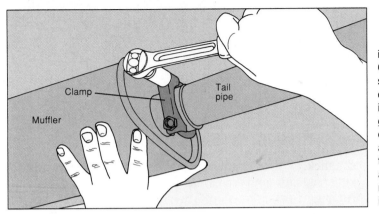

1 **Releasing pipe-to-muffler connections.** If your car has a one-piece exhaust system or a welded exhaust system, do not replace the muffler yourself. Joints that are typically welded include the tail pipe-to-muffler and exhaust pipe-to-muffler connections. Check these areas for metal that has a different sheen from other pipe surfaces; welded repairs appear as a strip of molten metal with no clamps attaching adjoining parts. If the muffler was installed with clamps, it is replaceable. Raise and block the car *(page 137)*. Wear safety goggles to protect against falling rust fragments. Apply penetrating oil to the nuts and bolts securing the front and rear muffler clamps and brackets and to the nuts and bolts on the muffler hanger and the tail pipe hanger. Let the oil penetrate for a few minutes. Then, with a socket wrench, detach the tail pipe hanger from the tail pipe (do not remove the tail pipe hanger from the frame), and unbolt the clamp joining the muffler to the tail pipe *(left)*.

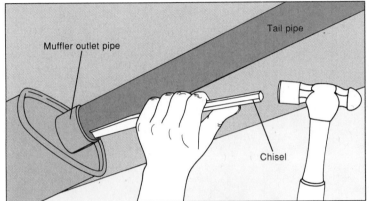

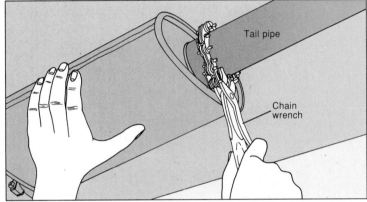

2 **Removing the tail pipe.** To separate the tail pipe and muffler, try wiggling the pipe up and down until it pulls free. If the tail pipe is not dislodged, and it fits inside the muffler outlet pipe, use a ball-peen hammer and a cold chisel or pipe slitter to peel away the muffler outlet pipe *(above, left)*. Ease out the tail pipe. If the tail pipe fits over the muffler outlet pipe, use a chain wrench to free the

tail pipe *(above, right)*. Tighten the chain around the pipe (about 3 inches from a joint, never directly over it), and twist off the pipe. Release the clamp holding the muffler to the exhaust pipe. If the pipe ends are deformed in the process, reshape them with locking pliers or with a pipe expander, available from an auto parts store. Rub the pipe ends with coarse sandpaper until shiny.

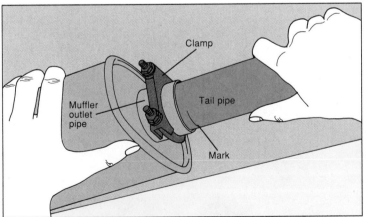

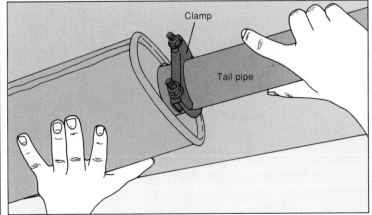

3 **Installing the new muffler.** Buy an identical replacement muffler from a muffler shop. Apply exhaust system sealer to the surfaces where pipes and muffler meet. Slip a new clamp loosely over the exhaust pipe and connect the two parts by hand. Follow the same procedure to attach the tail pipe to the muffler *(above, left)*. The pipes should overlap 1 to 2 inches; if a pipe fits inside the muffler draw a mark on the pipe defining the overlap point so you do not insert it too far. Check that the muffler and tail pipe clear the bottom of the car;

there should be at least a 1-inch gap between them and all body parts. Tighten the clamps with a socket wrench and reconnect the hangers. Shake the exhaust system parts to ensure that the joints are secure. Remove the jack stands from the car. In an open space, run the engine and check that no exhaust escapes from the connections. Then drive the car and listen for noises and vibrations in the system; check and retighten the fasteners if necessary. Tighten all fasteners again after two weeks of driving.

COOLING SYSTEM

The combustion temperature inside the engine can reach 4,500°F; without a cooling system to absorb this heat, the engine's oil would evaporate and its metal parts melt. The cooling system also stabilizes the engine's operating temperature and heats the passenger compartment. Most cars have a liquid cooling system like one of those pictured below.

The liquid coolant is a mixture of water and ethylene glycol, commonly called antifreeze. Mixed in the proper proportion (usually 50/50) the antifreeze both lowers the coolant's freezing temperature and raises its boiling point. A water pump draws the coolant via a hose from the bottom of the radiator through passages in the engine block, where it picks up heat. The heated coolant exits the engine via an upper hose and enters the top of the radiator, where it surrenders its heat as it flows through rows of tubes connected to metal cooling fins.

A fan attached to the water pump pulley helps dissipate the coolant's heat by pulling air through the radiator fins. Some of the coolant warmed by the engine is routed through the heater supply hose to the heater core; a fan blows air across the core to warm it for the passenger compartment. Thus, the heater can't heat the car until the engine is warm; conversely, running the heater in very hot weather can help cool an overheated engine.

The cooling system thermostat is a valve housed where the upper radiator hose joins the engine. It helps the engine warm up quickly when started by blocking the flow of coolant back to the radiator until the engine reaches operating temperature. An engine that warms up slowly or overheats in hot weather may suffer from a stuck thermostat. The radiator cap keeps the coolant under pressure to raise its boiling point, and allows

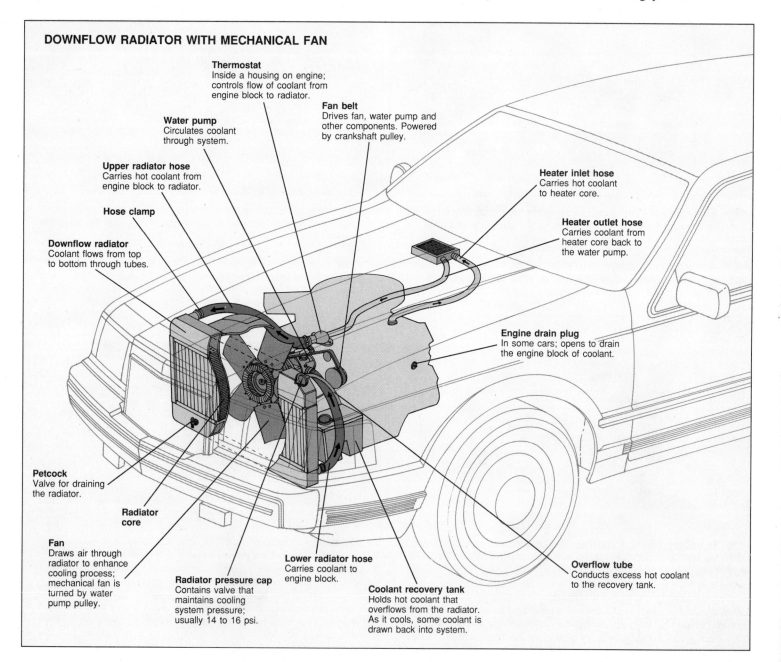

DOWNFLOW RADIATOR WITH MECHANICAL FAN

Thermostat
Inside a housing on engine; controls flow of coolant from engine block to radiator.

Fan belt
Drives fan, water pump and other components. Powered by crankshaft pulley.

Water pump
Circulates coolant through system.

Upper radiator hose
Carries hot coolant from engine block to radiator.

Hose clamp

Heater inlet hose
Carries hot coolant to heater core.

Heater outlet hose
Carries coolant from heater core back to the water pump.

Downflow radiator
Coolant flows from top to bottom through tubes.

Engine drain plug
In some cars; opens to drain the engine block of coolant.

Petcock
Valve for draining the radiator.

Radiator core

Fan
Draws air through radiator to enhance cooling process; mechanical fan is turned by water pump pulley.

Radiator pressure cap
Contains valve that maintains cooling system pressure; usually 14 to 16 psi.

Lower radiator hose
Carries coolant to engine block.

Coolant recovery tank
Holds hot coolant that overflows from the radiator. As it cools, some coolant is drawn back into system.

Overflow tube
Conducts excess hot coolant to the recovery tank.

excess coolant to escape in a controlled manner in case of boil-over. Replace the cap only with one of the right size and pressure rating for your car.

The car's cooling system is one of the simplest to work on yourself, and its routine maintenance will improve the performance and longevity of the engine. Regularly check the coolant level and test its proportion of antifreeze with a hydrometer *(page 85)*. Let a hot engine cool at least 20 minutes before removing the radiator pressure cap, or the liquid may spurt and scald you. Antifreeze is sweet-tasting and poisonous. Store it away from children and pets, and clean up spills.

Coolant deteriorates over time as the rust and corrosion inhibitors added to the ethylene glycol break down. Drain and replace the coolant *(page 84)* once a year, preferably in autumn, and add a rust inhibitor. Flushing expels rust and scale (mineral deposits) by reversing the flow of liquid through the system. Professionals use special pressure hoses to do the job; the do-it-yourself techniques described on pages 84 and 85, though not as powerful, are still very effective.

The Troubleshooting Guide on page 82 lists common cooling system problems. Since the system operates under pressure, it is especially important to check for leaks: Look for holes in the radiator, soft or damaged hoses or loose hose clamps, or a leaky water pump. You can plug a small leak in the radiator by adding a chemical sealant to the coolant. When replacing a hose, or repairing a cooling system component, drain the coolant to just below the level of the part being worked on. Do not remove air conditioning hoses *(page 92)*. Only inspect the fan *(page 90)* when the engine is cold; an electric fan can go on after the engine is turned off.

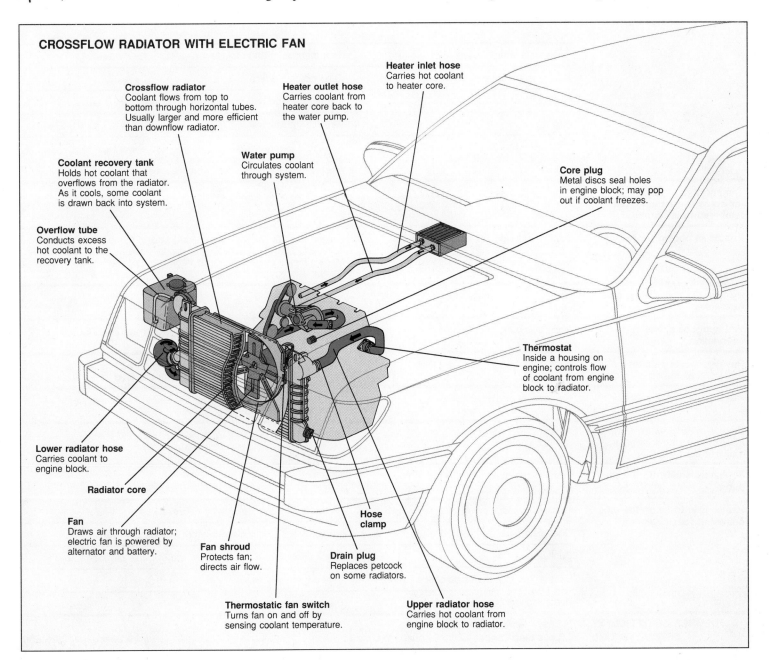

CROSSFLOW RADIATOR WITH ELECTRIC FAN

Crossflow radiator
Coolant flows from top to bottom through horizontal tubes. Usually larger and more efficient than downflow radiator.

Heater outlet hose
Carries coolant from heater core back to the water pump.

Heater inlet hose
Carries hot coolant to heater core.

Coolant recovery tank
Holds hot coolant that overflows from the radiator. As it cools, some coolant is drawn back into system.

Water pump
Circulates coolant through system.

Core plug
Metal discs seal holes in engine block; may pop out if coolant freezes.

Overflow tube
Conducts excess hot coolant to the recovery tank.

Thermostat
Inside a housing on engine; controls flow of coolant from engine block to radiator.

Lower radiator hose
Carries coolant to engine block.

Radiator core

Fan
Draws air through radiator; electric fan is powered by alternator and battery.

Fan shroud
Protects fan; directs air flow.

Hose clamp

Drain plug
Replaces petcock on some radiators.

Thermostatic fan switch
Turns fan on and off by sensing coolant temperature.

Upper radiator hose
Carries hot coolant from engine block to radiator.

TROUBLESHOOTING GUIDE

SYMPTOM	POSSIBLE CAUSE	PROCEDURE
Dashboard temperature warning light comes on after driving for some time; steam under hood	Weather too hot for cooling system capacity; car under heavy load; stop-and-go driving	Pull over and let engine cool; have large-capacity radiator installed
	Coolant level low	Check coolant level (p. 83) □○; add coolant (p. 85) □○▲
	Leak in cooling system hose	Inspect hoses and replace if damaged (p. 86) □◐; inspect hose clamps and tighten, if loose or replace, if broken (p. 86) □○
	Low antifreeze level in coolant	Test coolant freezing point; add antifreeze (p. 85) □○▲
	Coolant old or contaminated	Drain radiator (p. 84) □○ and replace coolant (p. 85) □◐▲
	Radiator clogged or damaged	Inspect radiator and remove debris (p. 83) □○; flush radiator (p. 84) ◼◐ and refill system (p. 85) □◐▲; or have radiator serviced
	Fan belt loose or broken	Inspect belt and tighten if loose (p. 89) □○ or replace, if broken (p. 138) ◼◐
	Radiator pressure cap faulty	Inspect cap (p. 83) □○ and replace if damaged
Immediate overheating; steam under hood	Leak in cooling system hose	Inspect hoses and replace if damaged (p. 86) □◐; inspect hose clamps and tighten, if loose or replace, if broken (p. 86) □○
	Thermostat stuck closed	Test thermostat and replace if necessary (p. 88) ◼◐
	Water pump faulty	Take car for service
	Exhaust system blocked	Inspect tail pipe and remove debris; or take car for service
	Fan faulty	Replace mechanical fan (p. 90) □◐ or electric fan (p. 91) ◼◐
	Coolant frozen (hoses feel hard)	Put car in garage to warm. Test and add coolant (p. 85) □○▲ and replace any damaged hoses or clamps (p. 86) □◐. Have mechanic check for cracks in engine block or radiator
Temperature warning light indicates overheating, but temperature is normal	Warning light sending unit faulty	Replace sending unit (p. 96)
Puddle of coolant under car	Leak in cooling system	Inspect radiator (p. 83) □○; if small leak is found, add radiator sealant to coolant; if large leak is found, have radiator serviced. Inspect hoses and replace if damaged (p. 86) □◐; inspect hose clamps and tighten, if loose or replace, if broken (p. 86) □○
Hose is bulging, brittle, soft or cracked	Hose old or deteriorating	Replace hose (p. 86) □◐
Wet spots or stains at hose connection	Hose clamp loose or broken	Tighten clamp, if loose or replace, if broken (p. 86) □○
Powdery white patches or rust-colored stains on radiator	Leak in radiator	Inspect radiator (p. 83) □○; if leak is small, add radiator sealant to coolant. If leak is large, have radiator serviced
Rust flakes inside radiator	Coolant old or contaminated	Drain, flush and refill system (p. 84) ◼◐▲; or have system professionally flushed
Engine slow to warm to operating temperature; engine stalls in cold weather	Thermostat opens too soon or is stuck open	Test thermostat and replace if necessary (p. 88) ◼◐
Squealing sound from water pump	Water pump faulty	Take car for service
Heater fails to warm the car; defroster doesn't work	Thermostat stuck open	Test thermostat and replace if necessary (p. 88) ◼◐
	One or both heater hoses blocked	Inspect hoses and replace if necessary (p. 86) □◐
	Coolant level low	Check coolant level (p. 83) □○; add coolant (p. 85) □○▲
	Heater core clogged or damaged	Take car for service
	Heater control components faulty	Take car for service

DEGREE OF DIFFICULTY: □ **Easy** ◼ **Moderate** ◼ **Complex**
ESTIMATED TIME: ○ **Less than 1 hour** ◐ **1 to 3 hours** ● **Over 3 hours**

▲ **Special tool required**

CHECKING THE COOLANT

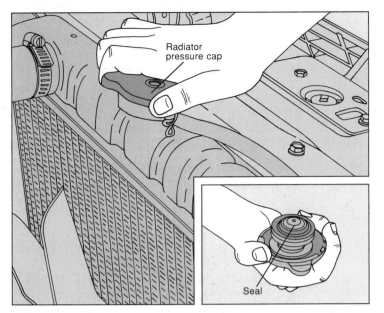

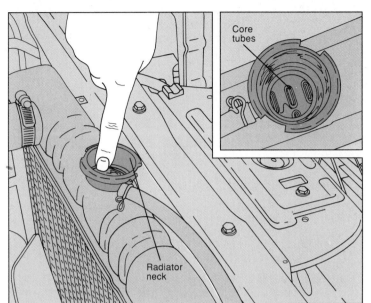

1 **Checking the coolant level.** On a car with a coolant recovery system, check the coolant level against the recovery tank markings; if it is below the level mark, add coolant. If the recovery tank was dry, or to check the coolant in a system without a recovery tank, allow the engine to cool and remove the radiator cap by pushing down and twisting with the heel of your hand *(above)*. Inspect the cap *(inset)* for cracks in the seals and replace it if damaged. Check the coolant quality *(step 2)*; if OK, top up the radiator with coolant *(page 85)* to 2 inches below the filler neck in a crossflow radiator and 1 inch below in a downflow radiator.

2 **Evaluating the coolant.** If the coolant is dark or rusty, drain *(page 84)* and replace it *(page 85)*. Foaming or bubbles indicate air in the system; check for leaks, and replace damaged hoses or hose clamps *(page 86)*. Oil in the coolant can stem from a leak in the engine block or transmission; have the car professionally serviced. Feel for rust in the radiator neck *(above)* and flush the system *(page 84)* if you find any. If the coolant level is low enough, or if you drained some coolant to perform a repair, examine the radiator core tubes *(inset)*; look for white deposits (scale) that can impede coolant flow, and flush the system or have the radiator serviced.

MAINTAINING AND INSPECTING THE RADIATOR

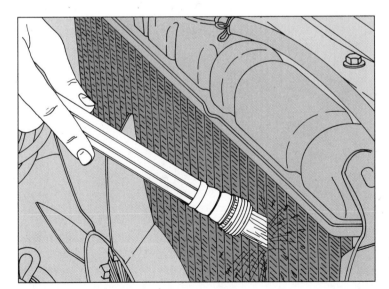

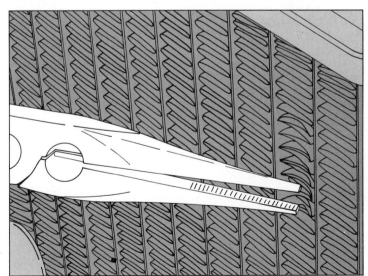

1 **Cleaning the exterior of the radiator.** A radiator free of debris ensures an unobstructed flow of air through its metal fins. Gently pluck out leaves and insects from the fins with your fingers or with long-nose pliers; take care not to damage the delicate metal. Next, use water from a garden hose at low pressure to wash the radiator *(above)*. If space allows, spray water through both sides; if space is limited, try to spray the inside surface of the radiator to push debris through the front.

2 **Examining the fins.** Run a finger across the fins. If they collapse when touched lightly, the metal is deteriorating; have the radiator checked professionally. With long-nose pliers, gently straighten bent fins *(above)*. Patches of white powder or rust indicate a leak. Temporarily seal a small leak by adding a radiator sealant, sold at auto parts stores, to the coolant; a professional should repair a large leak. White powder along the joints where the fins meet the expansion tanks mean that the solder is weakening; have the radiator serviced.

DRAINING THE RADIATOR

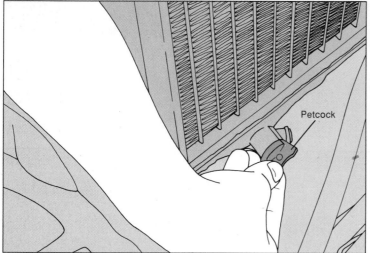

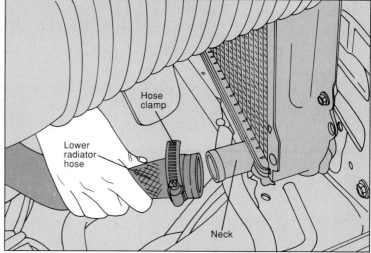

Petcock

Hose clamp

Lower radiator hose

Neck

Draining the coolant. Let the engine cool and remove the radiator cap. Place a basin under the radiator to catch escaping coolant. If the radiator has a petcock at its base, turn it counterclockwise to open it *(above, left)*. Spray a stubborn petcock with penetrating oil and turn it with pliers, using great care not to break it. Some radiators have a drain plug; unscrew it with a wrench. If the car has neither of these,

or if they are corroded shut, disconnect the lower radiator hose. Release the hose clamp *(page 86)* and wiggle the hose off the neck of the radiator *(above, right)*. Once the radiator has drained completely, or to the level required for the repair, close the petcock or replace the plug or hose. To flush the radiator, go to the step below or on page 85.

FLUSHING THE COOLING SYSTEM WITH A FLUSHING T

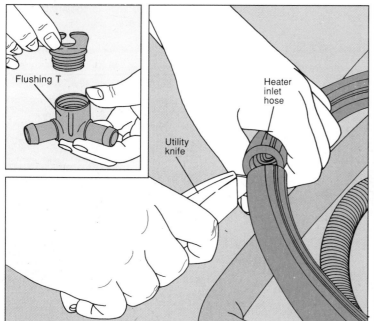

Flushing T

Heater inlet hose

Utility knife

Garden hose

Hose clamp

Deflector

Installing a flushing T. Drain the radiator *(step above)* and locate the heater inlet hose leading from the engine block to the firewall. (Do not confuse it with the heater outlet hose, which leads from the water pump to the firewall.) Purchase a kit with a flushing T *(left, inset)* of the right size to fit the heater inlet hose. Cut through the hose in a convenient spot with a utility knife *(above, left)* and put the clamps supplied in the kit over each hose end. Push the flushing T into both ends of the hose, slide the clamps over it and tighten them with a screwdriver. Remove the cap from the T and screw on a garden hose *(above, right)*. (If the kit has a garden hose adaptor, install it first.) On a downflow radiator,

insert the deflector in the neck of the radiator *(right, inset)*, and point it away from the engine. On a crossflow radiator, disconnect the upper radiator hose from the engine and direct it away from the engine. With the parking brake on and the car in park or neutral, start the car and set the heater control on high. Then turn on the garden hose to medium pressure. The force of the water will expel old coolant through the deflector or upper radiator hose. When the flow is clean, turn off the engine and then the hose, and remove the deflector or reattach the radiator hose. Detach the garden hose and adaptor, and replace the flushing T cap. Top up the system with water before refilling with coolant *(page 85)*.

FLUSHING THE COOLING SYSTEM THROUGH THE RADIATOR

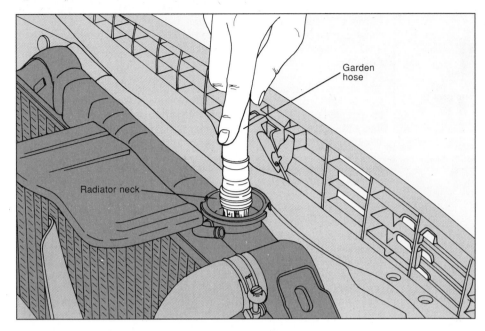

Flushing via the radiator. Drain the radiator *(page 84)*. Insert a garden hose into the neck of the radiator, fill the radiator with clean water and replace the pressure cap. With the brake on and the car in park or neutral, start the engine and set the heater control on high. Wait 5 minutes, then, being extremely careful not to touch the fan, place your hand on the radiator where the upper radiator hose joins it. When the radiator feels warm, you know the thermostat has opened, allowing heated coolant to flow back from the engine. Let the engine run another 5 minutes, then turn it off. Drain the radiator again. Add clean water to refill it and turn on the engine to circulate the liquid. Repeat this process three or four times, until the water draining from the radiator is clear. Top up the system with water before refilling with coolant *(below)*.

REPLACING THE COOLANT

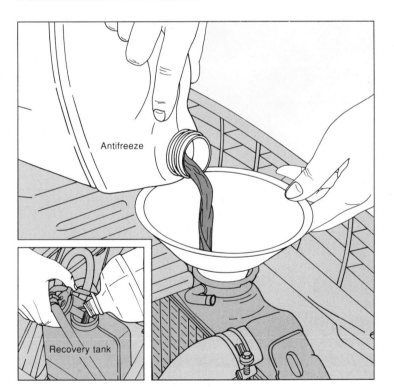

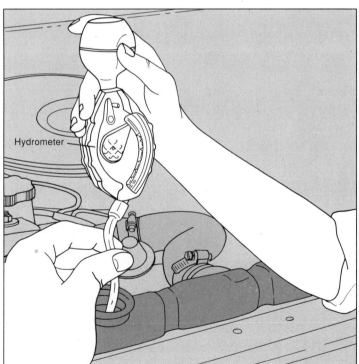

1 **Adding coolant.** To top up the cooling system, add antifreeze to the radiator or recovery tank, as shown. To replace the coolant, flush the system first *(step above)*. Find the cooling system's capacity in the owner's manual. Drain half this amount of water out of the radiator *(page 84)* and replace it with an equal amount of antifreeze. This provides a 50/50 coolant mixture, the proportion recommended for most cars. You can vary the proportion by draining more or less water out of the radiator, but do not exceed 70 percent antifreeze. Idle the engine to circulate the coolant; if the level drops, top up with water and antifreeze. Test and adjust the coolant mixture *(step 2)*.

2 **Testing the coolant.** Insert the tip of a hydrometer into the coolant *(above)*. Squeeze, then release the bulb to suck in liquid. On the hydrometer shown here, a needle will float up to indicate a temperature reading on a chart printed on the hydrometer. This reading is the freezing temperature of the coolant, below which it cannot protect the engine. (Other hydrometers may use floating balls or a scale.) If the reading is too high or too low, partially drain the radiator and add more water or antifreeze, as needed. Repeat until the hydrometer reading is correct. Retest the coolant after driving the car.

INSPECTING AND REPLACING HOSES AND CLAMPS

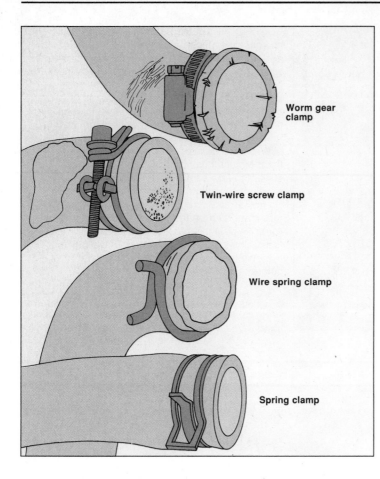

Worm gear clamp

Twin-wire screw clamp

Wire spring clamp

Spring clamp

Hoses and clamps. Coolant circulates through the engine, radiator, water pump and heater core via hoses made of rubber or a rubberlike synthetic. Each hose end fits snugly over a metal neck on the cooling system component, and is secured by a hose clamp. The force of hot coolant circulating under pressure causes quick deterioration of hoses and clamps. Check them every six months for signs of wear that can lead to leaks and loss of pressure. When replacing a hose or a clamp, take the old part with you to buy a matching replacement. Keep in mind that a hose is usually measured by its inside diameter. Some hoses— the lower radiator hose, for example—are molded with curves to fit in the engine compartment; when removing a hose, note the direction of its curves for correct reassembly. Car manufacturers install many different types of clamps. Pictured at left are four of the most common styles. Of the four, the worm gear clamp *(left, top)* makes the strongest and most reliable replacement.

The hoses pictured at left show four types of damage commonly suffered by cooling system hoses. A hose may become hard, brittle and cracked *(top)*, the result of heat and age. Soft, spongy patches, where swelling can occur *(second)* are due to a thinning of the interior wall of the hose caused by oil, rust or other debris in the coolant. Fraying and weakening around the end of a hose *(third)* can be caused by leaking coolant, allowed to escape by a weak or loose clamp. A shiny portion of hose *(bottom)* indicates an oil leak that has soaked into the hose, possibly weakening it. Replace all damaged hoses and ineffective clamps.

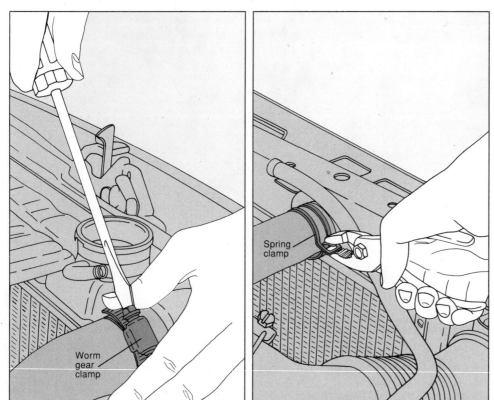

Worm gear clamp

Spring clamp

1 **Removing clamps.** Drain the radiator *(page 84)* below the level of the hose being disconnected or replaced. To remove most types of clamps, including the worm gear clamp shown here, use a screwdriver to loosen its bolt *(far left)*. If the clamp is corroded, spray it with penetrating oil. Push the clamp down the hose, and remove the clamp at the other end the same way. To release a spring clamp *(near left)*, squeeze its two ends together with pliers and push the clamp down the hose. If any clamp is so corroded that it will not loosen, even after penetrating oil has been applied, cut it off *(step 2)*.

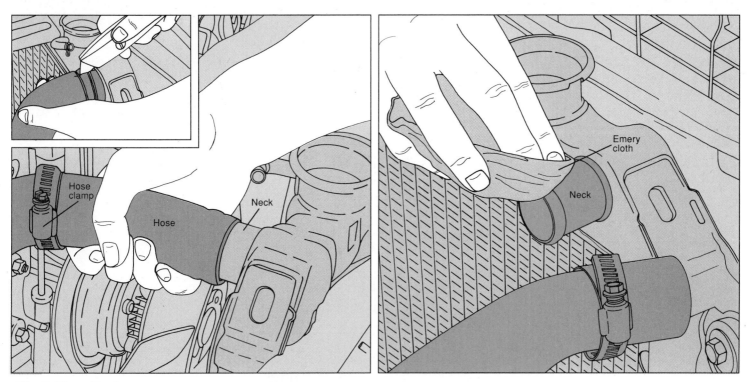

2 **Pulling off a hose.** Gently twist the hose off its neck to free it *(above, left)*. If the hose does not detach easily, do not pry it off with a screwdriver or other tool; the neck, particularly the soft metal of a radiator neck, is easily dented. Instead, use a utility knife to cut a lengthwise slit in the hose *(inset)*, then peel the hose back. If you accidentally bend a neck, straighten it by applying pressure to the inside surface using the rounded handle of a screwdriver or other tool. Use an emery cloth *(above, right)* to clean off rust, dirt or old pieces of hose that may have stuck to the neck.

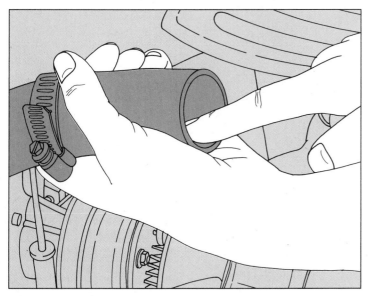

3 **Preparing the replacement hose.** Slide a new clamp onto each end of the hose. Then smear a light coat of silicone lubricant inside the hose ends *(above)* to help ease the hose onto the necks. A little antifreeze will do the same job, but because it is poisonous, wear gloves when using it. Push the hose into position on the neck; up to the installation mark, if there is one, or snugly up against the base of the neck.

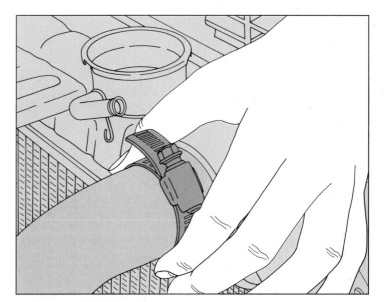

4 **Positioning the clamp.** Work the clamp down the hose and over the neck, leaving 1/4 inch between the end of the hose and the clamp *(above)*. Tighten the clamp. Repeat the procedure at the other end of the hose, and top up the coolant *(page 85)*. With the parking brake on and the car in neutral or park, start the engine and let it idle for 15 minutes. Turn off the engine and check the new hose and clamps for leaks; retighten loose clamps. Check the coolant level and top it up again, if necessary.

TESTING AND REPLACING THE THERMOSTAT

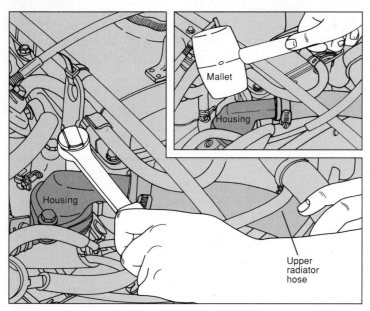

Mallet

Housing

Housing

Upper
radiator
hose

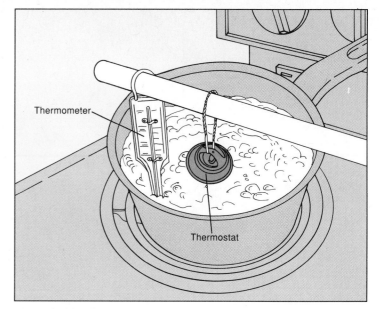

Thermometer

Thermostat

1 **Removing the thermostat.** The thermostat is enclosed by a housing where the upper radiator hose joins the engine block. Detach the air filter *(page 70)* if it blocks access. Remove the negative battery cable *(page 96)* if your car has an electric fan, and disconnect electrical wires leading to the thermostat. Drain the coolant *(page 85)* to below the thermostat and, with a socket wrench, unscrew the housing bolts *(above)*. If necessary, tap the housing lightly with a rubber mallet *(inset)* to separate it from its base. Then lift it off and pull out the thermostat, noting its position.

2 **Testing the thermostat.** Inspect the thermostat and discard it if stuck open or damaged. Note the maximum temperature marked on the rim of the thermostat—the point at which it fully opens to let coolant pass through the system. Hang the thermostat and a cooking thermometer in a pan of cold water, without letting either touch the base or sides *(above)*. Heat the water slowly; the thermostat should begin to open before the water reaches the maximum temperature, and should be fully open at its maximum temperature. As the water cools, the thermostat should close. Replace the thermostat if faulty.

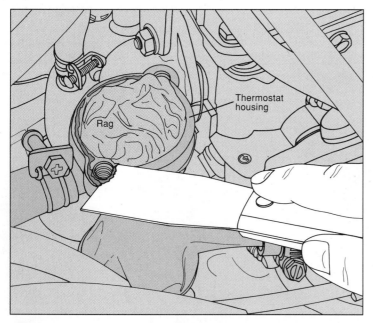

Thermostat
housing

Rag

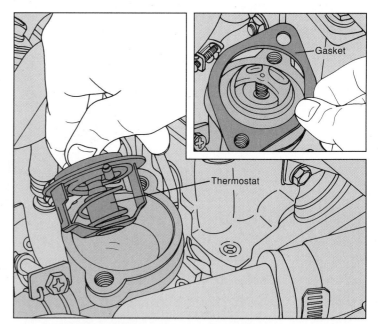

Gasket

Thermostat

3 **Preparing the housing surfaces.** With a clean rag, stop the opening of the lower section of the thermostat housing. Use a putty knife to scrape remnants of gasket and sealant off the rim *(above)*, taking care not to gouge the metal. Remove the rag and repeat the procedure on the upper section of the housing.

4 **Installing the thermostat.** Insert the thermostat in the housing, spring end down *(above)*. Position a new gasket on the edge of the housing *(inset)*; if it requires a sealant, apply the sealant to the edge first. Reinstall the upper section of the housing, screwing the bolts hand-tight. Reconnect any components and wires removed in step 1, and refill the radiator with coolant *(page 85)*. With the parking brake on and the car in park or neutral, idle the engine for 15 minutes. Check the housing joint. If it leaks, tighten the bolts, or allow the engine to cool and reopen the housing to verify that the thermostat and gasket are correctly installed. Top up the coolant.

INSPECTING THE DRIVE BELTS

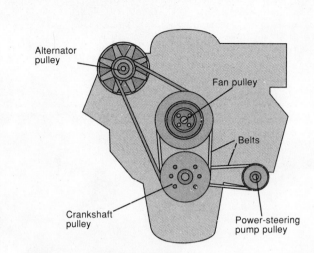

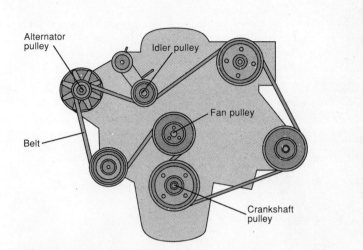

THE MULTIPLE BELT SYSTEM

Older cars had only one drive belt; driven by the crankshaft pulley and commonly called the fan belt, it turned not only the fan, but also the water pump and the generator. Today, many cars use the same basic fan belt system, yet have additional belts to drive optional accessories, such as the air conditioning compressor and the power steering pump. Performance of all belt-driven components depends on the condition and tension of the belts. Inspect the belts *(below)* every three months. If a belt is damaged, replace it, and tighten any belts that are loose *(page 138)*.

THE SERPENTINE BELT SYSTEM

In some late-model cars the fan, water pump, alternator and all the accessories are driven by one long belt that winds around a series of pulleys. An idler pulley, which may be spring operated as shown here, controls its tension. Every three months, inspect the belt for cracks, glazing and other signs of deterioration *(step 1, below)*. Replace the belt immediately if damaged or worn *(page 139)*; when a serpentine belt breaks, all the components it drives will stop functioning. Also check the belt's tension *(step 2, below)*, and adjust it if necessary *(page 139)*.

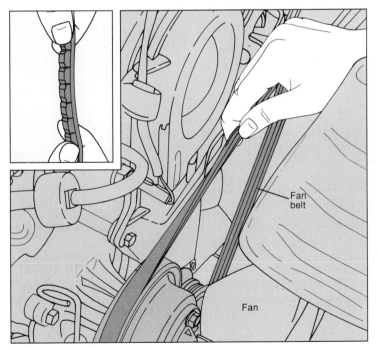

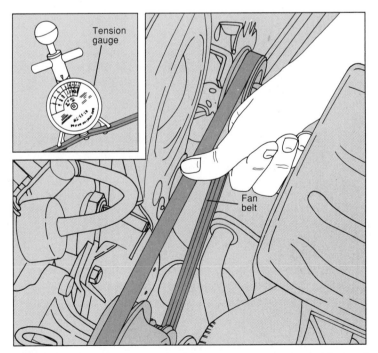

1 **Inspecting a belt for damage.** If the car has an electric fan, disconnect the negative battery cable *(page 96)*. Turn the belt to inspect its underside *(above)*. An oil-soaked or glazed belt can slip in the pulleys; a dry, cracked one *(inset)* will not run smoothly and can break without warning; a belt with unevenly worn edges can lead to improper pulley alignment. If you spot any of these symptoms, change the belt *(page 138 or 139)*. If the belt is undamaged, check its tension *(step 2)*.

2 **Checking a belt's tension.** Place your thumb at the midpoint of the belt and press down *(above)*. You should be able to deflect the belt 1/2 inch with moderately strong pressure; more or less movement means the belt needs adjusting. For a more precise reading, use a tension gauge *(inset)* and refer to the car's service manual for the recommended tension of each of the car's belts. Tighten or loosen the belt as required *(page 138)*.

REPLACING A MECHANICAL FAN BLADE

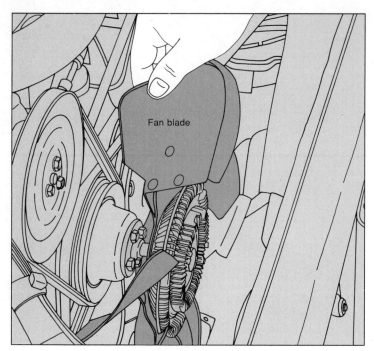

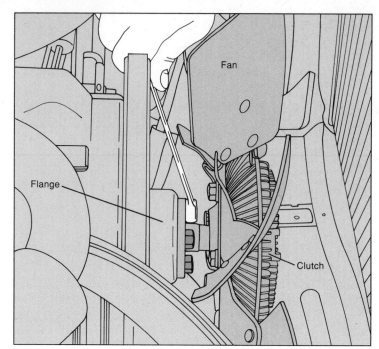

1 **Inspecting the blades.** Rotate the fan *(above)* and check for loose, bent or broken blades. Because the blades are carefully balanced during the manufacturing process, they cannot be repaired or bent back into alignment. If any blade is damaged replace the whole blade unit *(steps 2 and 3)*. The two types of mechanical fans—clutch and direct drive—are both driven by a V-belt from the crankshaft pulley. Distinguish a clutch fan from a direct-drive by locating its clutch, a finned metal plate bolted to its center.

2 **Loosening the blade unit's retaining bolts.** With a socket wrench, unbolt the fan's protective shroud, if it has one, and then remove the bolts holding the fan blade unit to its flange *(above)*; the clutch will come off with it. If, as on some models, the fan belt pulley is between the fan and the flange, remove the fan belt *(page 138)*, then detach the fan from the pulley and flange. Similarly, loosen and remove the retaining bolts of a direct-drive fan. On some direct-drive models, the pulley and a spacer come between the fan and its flange; remove the fan belt first, before detaching the other components.

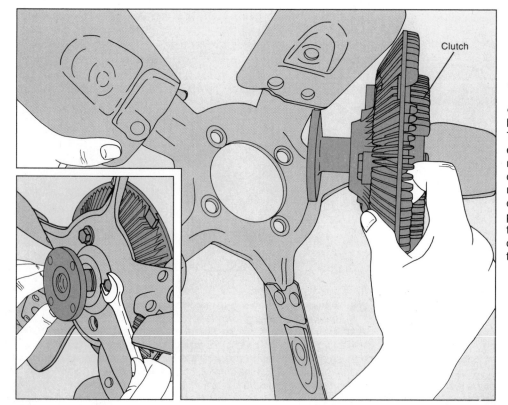

3 **Replacing the blade unit.** On a clutch fan, use a wrench to remove the bolts that secure the clutch to the blade unit *(inset)*, and pull the clutch free *(left)*. To install a new blade unit on a clutch fan or direct-drive fan, reverse the removal procedure, making sure that the blades are positioned correctly; they should face the radiator and not the engine. Tighten all bolts evenly, taking care to reinstall any shims or spacers in their proper positions. Start the engine and check that the fan runs smoothly, without vibrating or striking other components. Adjust its position if necessary.

REPLACING AN ELECTRIC FAN

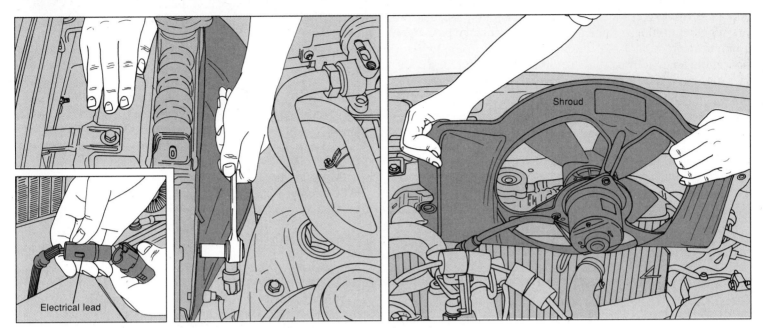

Electrical lead

Shroud

1 **Freeing the fan.** Be sure the engine is off and cold before working on an electric fan. Then remove the negative battery cable *(page 96)*. On some cars, you may have to remove both battery cables and the battery itself to access the fan *(page 102)*. On others, it may be necessary to detach the upper radiator hose *(page 86)*. Disconnect the electrical lead from the motor *(inset)* and, with a socket wrench, release the shroud holding the fan unit *(above, left)* to the radiator. Carefully pull out the shroud and fan unit *(above, right)*.

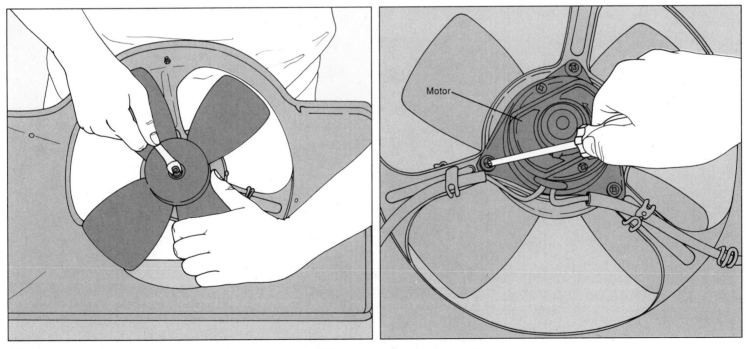

Motor

2 **Removing the fan.** Electric motors vary in their construction, and the steps in separating the shroud, blade unit and motor difffer from model to model. Inspect your fan unit and unfasten each part in logical sequence. Here, the blade unit is attached to the shaft of the fan with a bolt at the center *(above, left)*; on some models, it is held by a clip; remove the bolt or clip to release the blade unit. To free the motor, unscrew the screws that hold it to the shroud *(above, right)*. To reinstall the electric fan or a matching replacement, reverse the procedure, making sure that the blades do not touch the radiator when you put the shroud back in place. Reconnect the electrical lead and the battery. Start the car and let it run for about ten minutes until the coolant heats, starting the fan. If the fan vibrates or strikes other components, adjust it.

AIR CONDITIONING

A boon to drivers on hot and humid summer days, the automobile air conditioning system not only cools air in the passenger compartment, but also dehumidifies it. In common with household air conditioners, its key components include a compressor, an expansion valve, a receiver-drier, a condenser and an evaporator. Flowing through the system is a pressurized refrigerant, alternately in gas and liquid form. The anatomy below shows where the components are located in a car with a longitudinally-mounted engine, how they interconnect, and the route of the refrigerant. Air conditioners vary somewhat in their parts and locations. But the positions of the condenser and evaporator remain the same; use them as reference points for tracing the other components in your system.

When the air conditioner is switched on, the compressor sucks refrigerant gas out of the evaporator and pressurizes it,

raising its temperature in the process. The hot, high-pressure gas then travels to the condenser, located in front of the radiator, where it gives off its heat to the surrounding cooler air as it condenses into a liquid. The liquid refrigerant next passes to the receiver-drier, which holds surplus refrigerant and extracts water from it. From there it flows to the expansion valve and back to the evaporator. Under reduced pressure, the refrigerant vaporizes into a gas, absorbing heat from air that circulates past the evaporator from the adjacent passenger compartment. A fan blows the cooled air back into the car through a system of vents, and the air conditioning cycle begins again.

Moisture that collects on the evaporator drains onto the ground, and on a humid day it is common to find a puddle of water under the car. But verify that the liquid is only water and not a fluid leak *(page 140).*

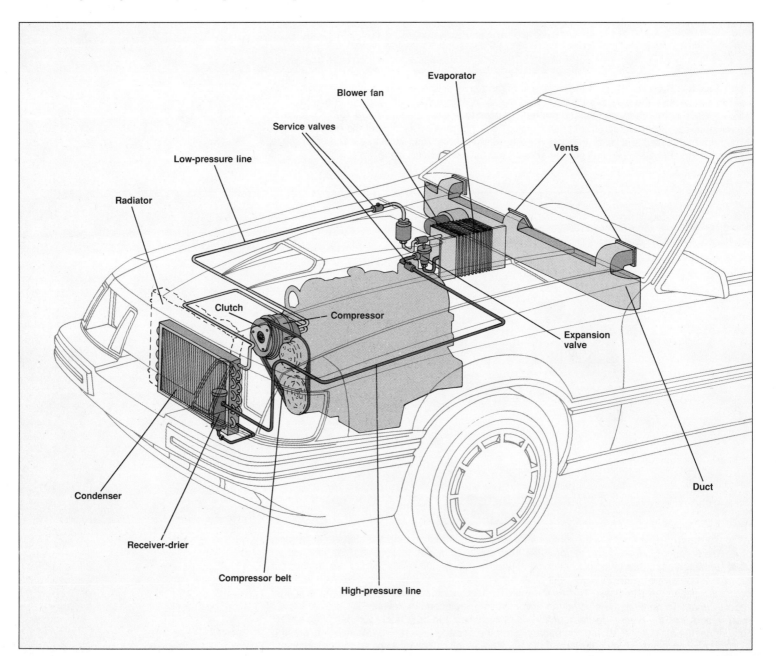

Because the air conditioner is a sealed system containing pressurized refrigerant, there are limits to the number of jobs that a do-it-yourselfer can tackle. Repairs to the evaporator, compressor, condenser or high-pressure hoses, for example, require specialized skills or tools and should be left to a professional. But some common problems can easily be diagnosed and corrected without special equipment; these are listed in the Troubleshooting Guide below.

Before attempting any repair or maintenance, be aware of the hazards associated with refrigerant. Never let it touch your skin or eyes; refrigerant will instantly freeze any surface it contacts. Refrigerant gas emits toxic fumes when ignited, so keep cigarettes, flames and sparks well at bay.

Operate the air conditioner for five minutes at least once a week, even in winter. This will circulate the refrigerant through the system and keep seals, hoses and joints pliable and free from cracks. You can check for escaped refrigerant by running a gloved hand along each hose and fitting; leaks will appear as greasy spots on the surface. Or, spread a soap-and-water solution over hoses and fittings; where the solution bubbles, there is a leak.

To maintain the air conditioner's cooling efficiency, regularly clean the condenser fins *(page 94)*. These are made of delicate metal so should be handled with care. Wear safety goggles to protect your eyes from falling debris and, from underneath the car, pluck out tiny bugs or leaves with your fingers or sweep dirt away with a soft brush.

If the air conditioning system fails to cool adequately, the cause may be a loose or slipping compressor belt. You can test the belt's tension with your thumb as a rough indicator *(page 94)*, but you will obtain a more accurate reading with a tension gauge *(page 94)*. Retighten the belt *(page 94)* or replace it *(page 138)* as necessary.

Regularly check the refrigerant charge, or level *(page 95)*, especially after long periods of driving when the air conditioner has been constantly in use. If your air conditioner has a sight glass, you can view the refrigerant directly; otherwise, read the charge by attaching pressure gauges to the service valves. If the refrigerant charge is too high, there may be a fault in one of the components of the system; if the level is too low, there could be a leak.

Take your car to a professional for inspection and repair, or to recharge the air conditioner with refrigerant, if necessary. Do not try to recharge the system yourself. Even though cans of refrigerant are readily available at auto-parts stores, the procedure can be dangerous if refrigerant should escape accidentally, or if faulty connections are made between the refrigerant dispenser and the air conditioner.

TROUBLESHOOTING GUIDE

SYMPTOM	POSSIBLE CAUSE	PROCEDURE
Air conditioner does not blow air from vents	Blower fuse blown; circuit breaker tripped	Check fuses or circuit breakers; replace or reset *(p. 106)* □○
	Blower fan motor defective	Take car for service
Air conditioner circulates air, but does not cool at all	Compressor magnetic clutch faulty	Listen for a clicking sound as magnetic clutch engages *(p. 95)* □○; if no sound, take car for service
	Compressor belt broken, worn or slipping	Check and tighten compressor belt *(p. 94)* □○; replace belt if necessary *(p. 138)* ◪○
	Refrigerant charge low	Check refrigerant charge *(p. 95)* □○▲; take car for service
Air conditioner does not cool air adequately	Air leaking from doors, windows or vents	Close doors, windows and vents tightly
	Weather stripping damaged	Check weather stripping *(p. 125)* □○
	Condenser fins dirty, clogged or bent	Clean condenser fins *(p. 94)* □○
	Compressor belt worn or slipping	Test belt tension *(p. 94)* □○; replace belt if necessary *(p. 138)* ◪○
	Compressor magnetic clutch faulty	Listen for a clicking sound as magnetic clutch engages *(p. 95)* □○; if no sound, take car for service
	Refrigerant charge low	Check refrigerant charge *(p. 95)* □○▲; take car for service
	Coolant level in radiator low	Check radiator coolant level *(p. 80)* □○; add coolant if necessary *(p. 85)* □○
	Cooling system thermostat defective	Test thermostat *(p. 88)* □○; replace it if necessary *(p. 88)* ◪○
	Fan belt worn or slipping	Test fan belt tension *(p. 89)* □○; replace if necessary *(p. 138)* ◪○
	Radiator clogged or coolant dirty	Flush radiator *(p. 84)* ◪●

DEGREE OF DIFFICULTY: □ Easy ◪ Moderate ■ Complex
ESTIMATED TIME: ○ Less than 1 hour ◖ 1 to 3 hours ● Over 3 hours ▲ Special tool required

CLEANING THE CONDENSER

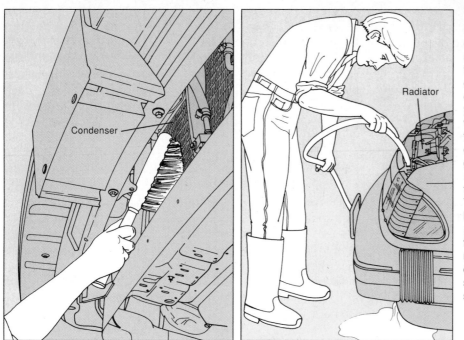

Removing debris from the condenser.
Because of the condenser's location in front of the radiator and behind the grille, dirt, bugs and leaves accumulate on its front cooling fins. These wavy strips of aluminum are delicate and easily damaged, so clean them with caution. Depending on the model of your car, you may be able to dislodge foreign matter with a soft brush inserted from below. Raise the car on ramps or jack stands *(page 137)*, or roll under it on a dolly. Wearing safety goggles, gently stroke the fins with the brush *(far left)*; rough brushing or hard blows can bend them, impeding the condenser's efficiency. To clean the fins from above, insert a garden hose between the condenser and radiator *(near left)* and direct a stream of water through the fins from back to front. (This may not be possible if your car's radiator is very close to the condenser.) Use low water pressure to prevent damaging the fins. Carefully straighten bent fins with long-nose pliers.

TESTING AND ADJUSTING THE COMPRESSOR BELT

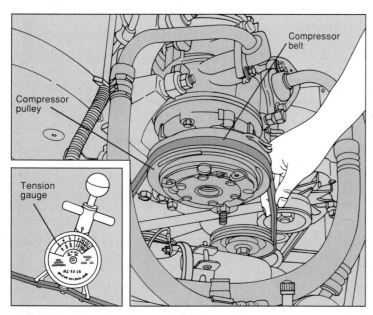

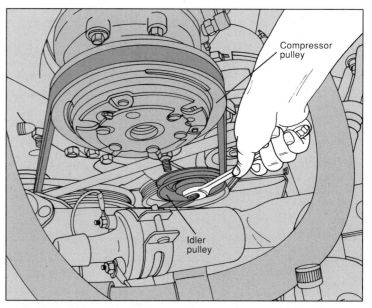

1 **Inspecting the compressor belt.** Examine the belt that wraps around the compressor pulley. If it is cracked or frayed, or its inner surface is shiny—indicating slippage—replace the belt *(page 138)*. If the compressor belt is sound, check its tension. First warm the belt by running the engine and air conditioner for five minutes. Turn off the engine and air conditioner, grasp the belt with thumb and forefinger midway between two pulleys *(above)* and push the belt in with your thumb. You should be able to shift the belt no more than 1/8 inch. (A new belt should be even tighter, to allow for loosening as it breaks in.) If there is enough space in the engine compartment, use a tension gauge *(inset)* to obtain an accurate reading *(page 138)*. Compare this reading to the specifications in your car's service manual.

2 **Adjusting the compressor belt tension.** The make and model of your car determine which component you shift to increase the compressor belt tension; it may be the compressor itself, the alternator *(page 112)*, the power steering pump *(page 38)* or a separate idler pulley. The car's service manual will direct you to the correct component, or you may examine the pulleys within the belt's span to find the one that has an adjustable fastener. To adjust the idler pulley, as shown here, loosen its retaining bolts with a wrench *(above)*, and push the pulley away from the compressor to tighten the belt. Hold the pulley in place while you retighten the bolts. Test the belt's tension again *(step 1)* and readjust it if necessary. Recheck the tension after driving the car with the air conditioner running about an hour.

CHECKING THE REFRIGERANT CHARGE

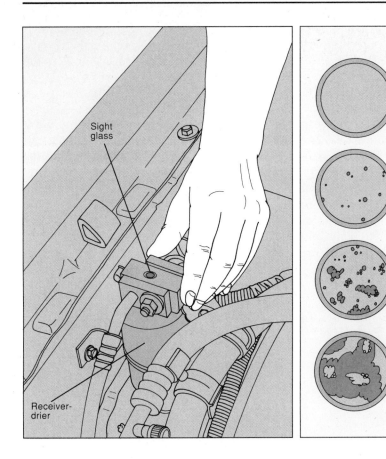

Sight glass

Receiver-drier

Reading the charge through a sight glass. On air conditioners that have one, the sight glass sits on top of the receiver-drier *(far left)*—a cylindrical metal container—or on one of the lines leading from the top of the receiver-drier. Wipe the sight glass clean, turn on the engine and set the air conditioner at maximum cool. Then check that the magnetic drive clutch in the compressor pulley is working: Have a helper turn the air conditioner off, then on, while you listen for a click as the pulley clutch engages and the compressor belt starts to revolve. If you hear no click, and the air conditioner does not cool adequately, have the compressor checked. Let the system run for five minutes, then compare the appearance of the refrigerant to the diagrams at left:

Clear refrigerant *(top)* indicates that the system is either fully charged or empty. If the air conditioner expels cool air at the vents, and bubbles appear when it is turned off and when the clutch disengages, the system is fully charged. If the system is empty, turn it off and have a professional inspect it for leaks or damage before recharging it.

Bubbles *(second from top)* indicate that the system is undercharged (low on refrigerant), or that the magnetic clutch is disengaged. Wait for the clutch to click on, and read the sight glass again. If the bubbles remain, have a professional check the system for leaks or damage before recharging it.

Foamy refrigerant *(third from top)* reveals a system with a very low charge, which could damage the air conditioner. Have a professional check it for leaks or damage before recharging it.

Cloudy refrigerant *(bottom)* indicates that the drying agent in the receiver-drier is disintegrating. Have the air conditioner repaired professionally.

Compressor

Pressure gauge

Low-pressure valve

Reading the charge with air conditioner pressure gauges. Special pressure gauges, which screw onto service valves on the air conditioning system, allow you to determine the exact level of refrigerant charge. The typical air conditioner has two valves; one at the low-pressure side of the system and one at the high-pressure side. The valves, also called ports, may be on the compressor, the receiver-drier or the refrigerant lines. Most valves are of the Schrader type, the same as a tire valve. Some valves are of the more complex Rotalok type; these are always on the compressor and require an adaptor kit to convert them to Schrader valves.

Wearing safety goggles and gloves, and working outdoors, unscrew the valve caps. (If a valve leaks, replace the cap and have the valve repaired professionally.) With the engine and air conditioner off, screw one gauge onto the low-pressure valve *(left)*. The valve shown here is located on the compressor and is marked with an S for suction (low pressure). Then screw the other gauge onto the high-pressure valve. (Another style of air conditioner pressure gauge, which resembles a tire pressure gauge, may also be used.) The two gauge readings, shown in pounds per square inch (psi), should be nearly equal. If one reading is far lower than the other, or if you get a reading of 0 psi, have the system professionally inspected; it may need recharging or repair. If the readings are equal or close to equal, conduct a second, more precise test to rule out a slow leak in the system. This time, turn on the engine and air conditioner and take the readings again; typically, a good low-pressure reading is about 10 to 30 psi and high pressure about 140 psi. Consult your car's service manual for the acceptable range of pressure readings. Unusually low readings may indicate a loss of refrigerant; unusually high readings, damage to the components. Turn off the engine and air conditioner and remove the gauge from the low-pressure valve first. Wait five minutes before removing the gauge from the high-pressure valve to allow the pressure to fall to a safe level and to prevent the discharge of refrigerant.

ELECTRICAL SYSTEM

From a fix-it point of view, the myriad functions and components of the automobile's electrical system can seem daunting. But if you follow all safety tips, work logically, and carry out instructions carefully, you can approach any repair on these pages with confidence.

The electrical system comprises four subsystems. In the *starting system*, the battery provides the initial power to start the engine. Once the engine is running, the *charging system* (alternator) takes over, generating power for the car's electrical system and recharging the battery. In the *ignition system*, high-voltage current flows from the distributor to the spark plugs, where it ignites the air-fuel mixture in the combustion chambers. In the *accessory system*, low-voltage current powers the lights, horn and other electrical devices.

You can identify the components of the ignition, starting, and charging systems by consulting the illustration below; the diagram on the opposite page will help you locate the parts and wiring of the accessory system.

Some of the most common electrical problems, from dim headlights to balky engine starts, can be traced to the battery. Always wear safety goggles and rubber or heavy-duty work gloves when working on the battery. It contains acid that can burn the skin or eyes; it can also explode if exposed to sparks or flame, so never smoke in its vicinity. When disconnecting battery terminals, always detach the negative (ground) cable first; when reattaching, connect the positive (hot) cable first. The Troubleshooting Guide on page 98 lists typical battery problems, pinpoints the symptoms of each, and directs you to

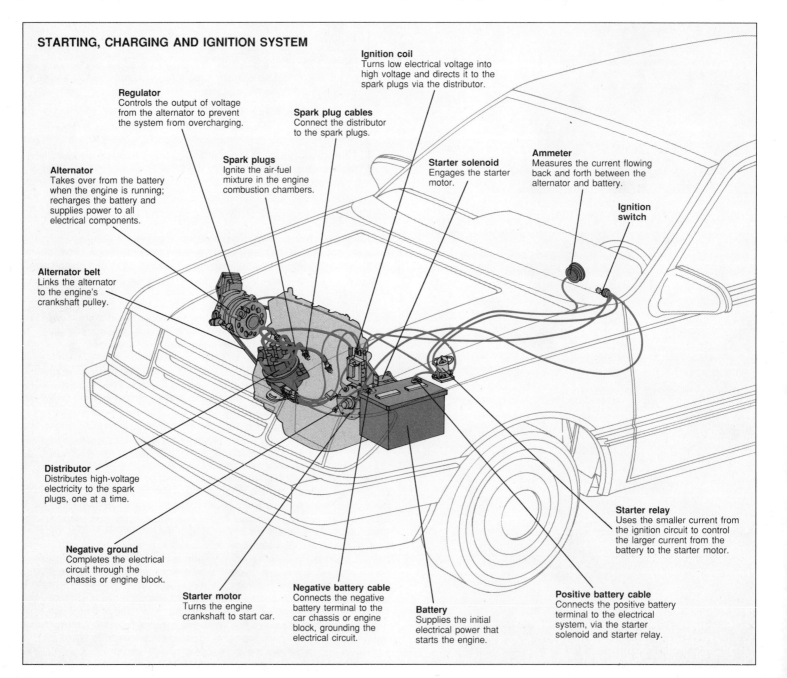

STARTING, CHARGING AND IGNITION SYSTEM

Ignition coil
Turns low electrical voltage into high voltage and directs it to the spark plugs via the distributor.

Regulator
Controls the output of voltage from the alternator to prevent the system from overcharging.

Spark plug cables
Connect the distributor to the spark plugs.

Alternator
Takes over from the battery when the engine is running; recharges the battery and supplies power to all electrical components.

Spark plugs
Ignite the air-fuel mixture in the engine combustion chambers.

Starter solenoid
Engages the starter motor.

Ammeter
Measures the current flowing back and forth between the alternator and battery.

Ignition switch

Alternator belt
Links the alternator to the engine's crankshaft pulley.

Distributor
Distributes high-voltage electricity to the spark plugs, one at a time.

Starter relay
Uses the smaller current from the ignition circuit to control the larger current from the battery to the starter motor.

Negative ground
Completes the electrical circuit through the chassis or engine block.

Starter motor
Turns the engine crankshaft to start car.

Negative battery cable
Connects the negative battery terminal to the car chassis or engine block, grounding the electrical circuit.

Battery
Supplies the initial electrical power that starts the engine.

Positive battery cable
Connects the positive battery terminal to the electrical system, via the starter solenoid and starter relay.

the appropriate test, maintenance procedure or repair. It also describes other common electrical faults.

Electricity flows from the positive post of the battery along its cable, through fuses, breakers, switches and relays, to a ground on the body of the car. The negative battery post, whose cable is also attached to the car body, completes the loop by picking up the returning electricity. Many electrical problems are the result of a break in this wiring circuit. Refer to the wiring diagrams in your car's service manual before conducting circuitry repairs. The windshield washer pump schematic on page l08 is typical of what you will find there; it translates many of the symbols appearing on automobile wiring diagrams. Before disconnecting any electrical part, mark its exact location for correct reassembly. And before discard-

ing a blown fuse, faulty socket or burned-out bulb, be sure the replacement is a perfect match.

Your tool kit for electrical repairs should include an unpowered test light, fitted with a large alligator clip. Never insert the probe in ignition system parts or wires when the ignition switch is on. The kit should also hold a 3- or 4-foot jumper wire with alligator clips at both ends; wire cutting, stripping, crimping and soldering tools; electrical tape and dielectric compound (to prevent corrosion). Include in it, too, a spark plug socket and ratchet, a battery terminal puller, and a wire battery brush. This chapter also demonstrates the use of an automobile voltmeter, an automatic battery charger and, for cars with onboard diagnostic computers, a portable scanner to access the information it contains.

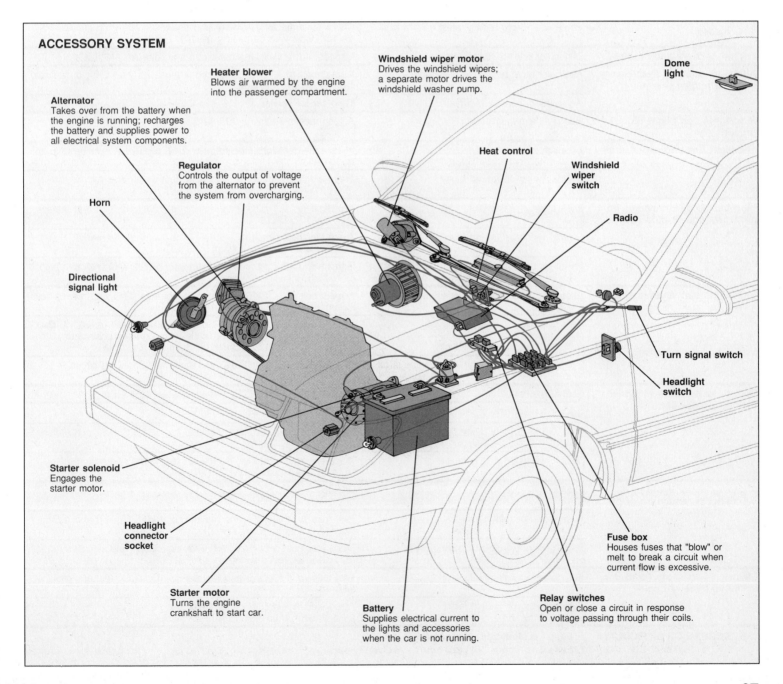

ACCESSORY SYSTEM

Heater blower
Blows air warmed by the engine into the passenger compartment.

Windshield wiper motor
Drives the windshield wipers; a separate motor drives the windshield washer pump.

Dome light

Alternator
Takes over from the battery when the engine is running; recharges the battery and supplies power to all electrical system components.

Regulator
Controls the output of voltage from the alternator to prevent the system from overcharging.

Heat control

Windshield wiper switch

Horn

Radio

Directional signal light

Turn signal switch

Headlight switch

Starter solenoid
Engages the starter motor.

Headlight connector socket

Fuse box
Houses fuses that "blow" or melt to break a circuit when current flow is excessive.

Starter motor
Turns the engine crankshaft to start car.

Battery
Supplies electrical current to the lights and accessories when the car is not running.

Relay switches
Open or close a circuit in response to voltage passing through their coils.

TROUBLESHOOTING GUIDE

SYMPTOM	POSSIBLE CAUSE	PROCEDURE
No sound at all when ignition key is turned	Battery dead	Test battery charge (p. 99) □○; charge weak battery (p. 101) □●▲ or replace battery (p. 102) ▣○; clean and grease posts and terminals (p. 100) □○; check for drain (p. 101) ▣●
	Battery terminal loose or corroded	Clean and grease posts and terminals (p. 100) □○
	Fusible link faulty	Take car for service
	Starter or starter solenoid faulty	Take car for service
	Ignition switch faulty	Wiggle key and retry starter; take car for service
Engine barely turns over, then stops; or only clicking is heard when ignition key is turned	Battery weak	Load test battery (p. 99) □○; charge weak battery (p. 101) □●▲, or replace battery (p. 102) ▣○; clean and grease posts and terminals (p. 100) □○; check for drain (p. 101) ▣●
	Battery terminal loose or corroded	Clean and grease posts and terminals (p. 100) □○
Engine cranks strongly but does not start	No spark from spark plugs	Check and replace spark plugs (p. 113) ▣● and spark plug cables (p. 114) ▣●
Engine starts and runs when jump-started or after battery is charged, but does not start after disuse	Battery deteriorated; will not hold sufficient charge	Charge battery (p. 101) □●▲, then load test it (p. 99) □○; replace battery, if necessary (p. 102) ▣○
	Power drain from battery while engine is off	Check for drain (p. 101) ▣● and determine offending circuit (p. 108) ▣●; charge battery (p. 101) □●▲
Engine sputters and misses	Distributor or rotor faulty	Inspect and replace distributor cap and rotor (p. 116) □○
Alternator warning light comes on while engine is running	Alternator drive belt loose or damaged	Inspect belt (p. 112) □○; tighten, if loose (p. 112) □○, or replace, if damaged (p. 138) ▣●
	Alternator or voltage regulator faulty	Take car for service
Headlights don't light the road properly	Headlight aim inaccurate	Adjust headlight aim (p. 103) ▣○
Headlight does not work at all	Headlight burned out	Install new headlight (sealed-beam unit, p. 102 □○; halogen bulb, p. 104 □○)
	Switch, wiring or ground faulty	Trace electrical circuit (p. 108) ▣●; test wiring and switch (p. 109) ▣●; repair wiring (p. 110) ▣○
High beams or low beams do not work (one or both headlights)	Fuse blown or relay faulty	Test fuse (p. 110) □○ and replace (p. 106) □○; test and replace relay (p. 107) □○
	Switch, wiring or ground faulty	Trace electrical circuit (p. 108) ▣●; test wiring and switch (p. 109) ▣●; repair wiring (p. 110) ▣○
	Headlight burned out	Install new headlight (sealed-beam unit, p. 102 □○; halogen bulb, p. 104 □○)
Headlights dim when engine slows	Alternator drive belt loose or damaged	Inspect belt (p. 112) □○; tighten, if loose (p. 112) □○, or replace, if damaged (p. 138) ▣●
	Battery weak	Load test battery (p. 99) □○; charge weak battery (p. 101) □●▲, or replace battery (p. 102) ▣○; clean and grease posts and terminals (p. 100) □○; check for drain (p. 101) ▣●
	Power drain from battery while engine is off	Check for drain (p.101) ▣● and determine offending circuit (p. 108) ▣●; charge battery (p. 101) □●▲
Bulb does not work in signal light or interior light	Bulb burned out	Access bulb (p. 104) □○ and replace (p. 105) □○
	Socket contact dirty or faulty	Clean or replace socket (p. 106) ▣○
	Fuse blown or relay faulty	Test fuse (p. 110) □○ and replace (p. 106) □○; test and replace relay (p. 107) □○
	Switch, wiring or ground faulty	Trace electrical circuit (p. 108) ▣●; test wiring and switch (p. 109) ▣●; repair wiring (p. 110) ▣○
A pair of signal lights or all signal lights remain on or off	Flasher defective	Replace flasher (p.107) □○
	Fuse blown or relay faulty	Test fuse (p. 110) □○ and replace (p. 106) □○; test and replace relay (p. 107) □○
	Switch, wiring or ground faulty	Trace electrical circuit (p. 108) ▣●; test wiring and switch (p. 109) ▣●; repair wiring (p. 110) ▣○
Electrical accessory (horn, for example) does not work	Fuse blown or relay faulty	Test fuse (p. 110) □○ and replace (p. 106) □○; test and replace relay (p. 107) □○
	Switch, wiring or ground faulty	Trace electrical circuit (p. 108) ▣●; test wiring and switch (p. 109) ▣●; repair wiring (p. 110) ▣○

DEGREE OF DIFFICULTY: □ Easy ▣ Moderate ■ Complex
ESTIMATED TIME: ○ Less than 1 hour ◕ 1 to 3 hours ● Over 3 hours　　　　▲ Special tool required

THE CAR BATTERY

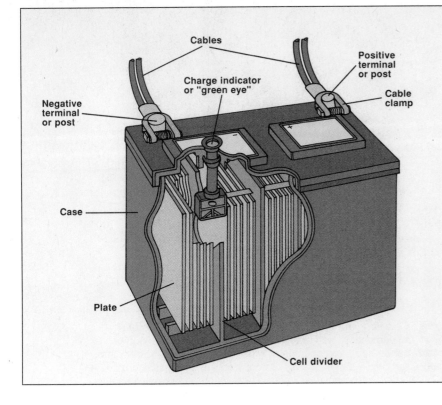

Cables

Positive terminal or post

Charge indicator or "green eye"

Cable clamp

Negative terminal or post

Case

Plate

Cell divider

Maintaining a car battery. The modern battery *(left)* is a plastic box divided into six cells and filled with an electrically conductive sulfuric acid solution called an electrolyte. The electrolyte interacts with the battery's electrodes—metal plates that contain lead—to produce 12 volts of electricity. The power flows in an unbroken loop from the posititve terminal, through the car's wiring, and back to the negative terminal. Most batteries today are of the sealed "maintenance-free" type, with a charge indicator, or "green eye," on top. But still in use are batteries with removable caps sealing the cells; these must be topped up periodically with electrolyte.

Battery acid is toxic, corrosive and explosive. When working on the battery, always wear safety goggles and heavy-duty rubber or leather gloves to avoid burns. To prevent explosion, never smoke or cause sparks near a battery. Routinely clean or replace corroded parts *(page 100)*; corrosion around terminals weakens the electrical connection. Replace the battery if the case is cracked or bulging. Do not twist or pry the cable clamps from the lead terminal posts. If leaving a car parked for 30 days or more, disconnect the negative cable *(page 100)*, so that power cannot drain from the battery.

TESTING THE BATTERY

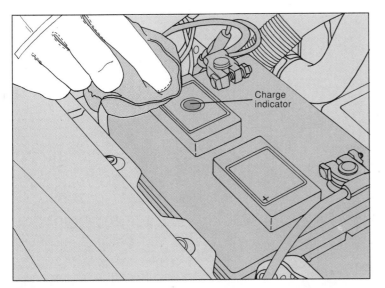

Charge indicator

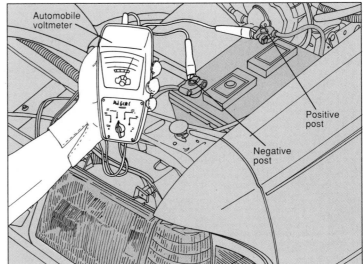

Automobile voltmeter

Positive post

Negative post

1 **Reading the charge indicator.** The green eye, a sight glass on the top of many maintenance-free batteries, provides a first check of the battery's condition. Clean it with a rag to read it clearly *(above)*. The eye is the visible part of a built-in hydrometer, which measures the battery's electrolyte strength. It contains a green ball that floats to the top when the battery is good (more than 75 percent charged). If the starter does not crank and the eye is dark, the battery may be discharged; test it further with a voltmeter *(next step)*. A clear or yellow eye signifies a low electrolyte level; replace the battery. A non-sealed battery with removable caps can be tested with a hand-held hydrometer and refilled if necessary.

2 **Load testing the battery.** Clamp the alligator clips of an automobile voltmeter to the battery terminals; the black lead to the negative (-) post and the red lead to the positive (+) post. If the meter reads less than 12 volts, charge the battery *(page 101)*. If the meter shows 12 volts or higher, perform a load test: Turn on the high beam headlights, the heater and the 4-way flashers for 15 seconds. Switch everything off for 15 seconds, then back on for 15 seconds. With the accessories still on, the meter should read 9.5 volts or more. If not, the battery needs charging *(page 101)*.

SERVICING THE BATTERY

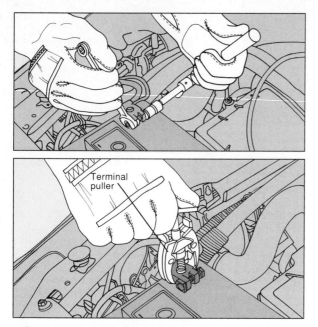

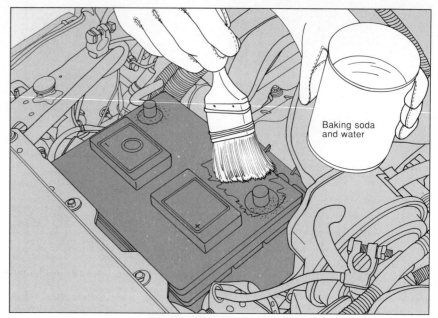

1 **Disconnecting the cables.** To avoid sparks, detach the negative (black) cable first, then the positive (red) cable. To remove the clamp from its post, hold the head of the bolt stationary with an open-end wrench, and loosen the nut with a socket wrench *(above, top)*. Then fit the hooks of a terminal puller under the clamp and tighten the screw of the puller against the center of the post *(above, bottom)*, lifting off the clamp. Remove the clamp from a side-mounted post with a socket wrench, as above, loosening it enough to pull it off by hand.

2 **Cleaning the battery case.** Wash the top and sides of a sealed battery with a solution of one heaping tablespoon of baking soda and one cup of water, applying the mixture with a large, soft-bristle brush *(above)*. Before washing a non-sealed battery, seal the vent caps tightly with plastic tape to keep the cleaning solution from entering the battery. Rinse the battery thoroughly with water from a garden hose; do not allow debris to collect on the battery base and tray. Dry the battery with paper towels.

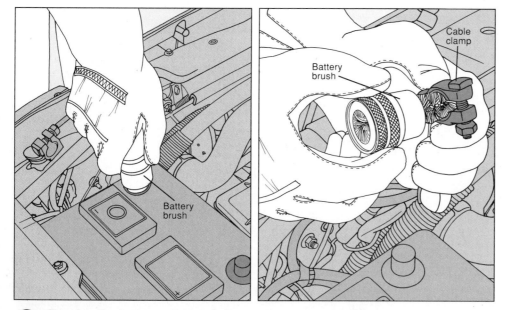

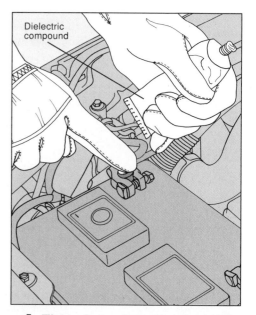

3 **Cleaning the battery posts and clamps.** Place the post end of a wire battery brush over each post and twist it several times *(above, left)* to remove corrosion. Scour the inside of each cable clamp with the other end of the brush *(above, right)*; also use it to remove dirt and corrosion from the outside of the clamps. Brush all surfaces bright and smooth. A smaller wire brush is available for cleaning side-mounted posts.

4 **Tightening and greasing the terminals.** Replace the positive (red) cable, then the negative (black) cable. Tighten the terminal nut and bolt using the same two-wrench technique as in step 1. Smear a dab of dielectric compound, available at auto parts stores, on each post and clamp to repel water and inhibit corrosion *(above)*.

TESTING FOR CURRENT DRAIN

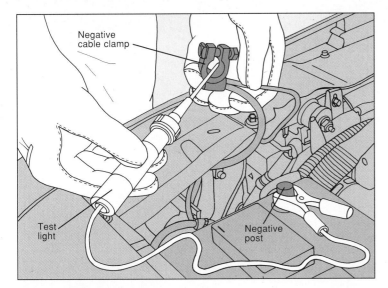

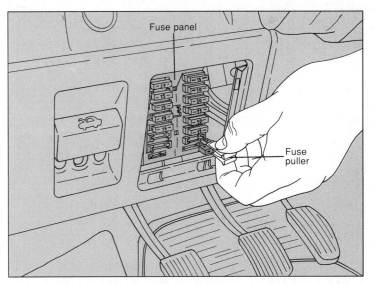

1 **Checking for a current drain.** Begin by closing the doors and turning off all electrical accessories. Check whether a glove box light, trunk light or other accessory remains on due to a faulty switch (a bulb you cannot see will remain warm). If not, you can locate a pinched or broken wire, a hidden cause of current drain, by using an unpowered test light. First check that the battery is charged *(page 99)*, and disconnect the negative battery cable *(page 100)*. Attach the alligator clip of the test light to the negative post and place the probe firmly in contact with the negative cable clamp *(above)*. If the test light glows, the current drain remains; trace the offending circuit *(page 108)*.

2 **Pulling one fuse at a time.** Locate your fuse panel, usually under the dashboard on the driver's side and, with a fuse puller *(page 106)*, systematically remove and replace one fuse at a time *(above)*. When the test light (with its alligator clip and probe still in place) goes out, note which circuits are affected by referring to your owner's manual or the guide on the fuse panel cover. Now reattach the negative cable to the battery. Replace the fuse and examine the bulbs or motors on the fuse's circuits. Also check to see if frayed wires in the circuit are contacting other wires or the car body.

CHARGING THE BATTERY

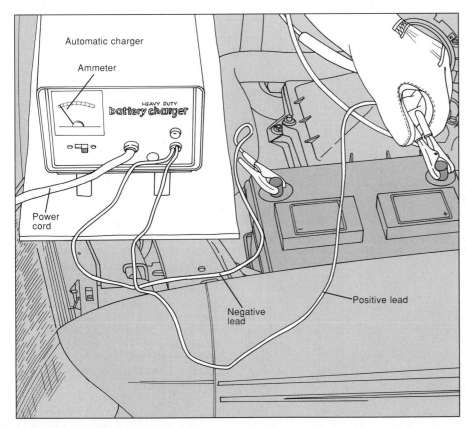

Restoring power with an automatic charger. Designed for home use, a 4-amp, 6-amp or 10-amp battery charger will slowly and safely charge a battery. Depending on the depletion of the battery and the power of the charger, the process may take as little as an hour, or as long as 24 hours. Use the charger in a well-ventilated area. Do not charge a sealed battery if the eye is clear or yellow *(page 99)*. If charging a non-sealed battery, be sure that the electrolyte covers the plates; top it up with distilled water, if necessary.

To use the charger, disconnect the cables from the battery *(page 100)*. Then, with the charger off (or unplugged, if it has no ON/OFF switch), connect the proper alligator clamp to each battery post *(left)*; the red lead to the positive post, and the black lead to the negative post. Turn on or plug in the charger. The charger's ammeter will indicate the number of amps that the battery is drawing, slowly dropping toward zero as the battery reaches full charge and the eye turns green. Leave the charger on until the meter indicates 1 amp, then unplug it, disconnect the clamps and reconnect the cables. An automatic charger can be left on without fear of overcharging. But an older, non-automatic charger should be disconnected as soon as the battery is charged; otherwise, excess current may damage the battery and possibly cause an explosion. When using a non-automatic charger, carefully follow the manufacturer's instructions for correct charging times.

REPLACING THE BATTERY

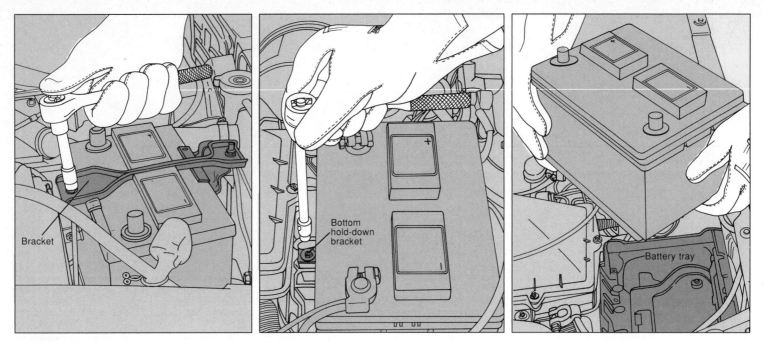

Bracket

Bottom hold-down bracket

Battery tray

Freeing the battery from its hold-down hardware. Disconnect the negative battery cable, then the positive cable *(page 100)*. Locate the hold-down nut, which secures either a bracket across the top of the battery *(above, left)*, or a clamp at the base *(above, center)*. With a socket wrench, remove the nut and lift or turn the bracket out of the way. If the nut is corroded in place, apply penetrating oil to loosen it. If space allows, reach under the battery with both hands and lift it

out *(above, right)*. Alternatively, grip the battery at its corners, where it is strongest. A set of straps specially designed for lifting and carrying batteries may also be used. Before replacing a battery, wash its base and tray with a solution of baking soda and water *(page 100)*. Secure the hold-down hardware hand-tight. Over-tightening may crack the case but, left too loose, a case may wear against adjoining hardware.

REPLACING A SEALED-BEAM HEADLIGHT

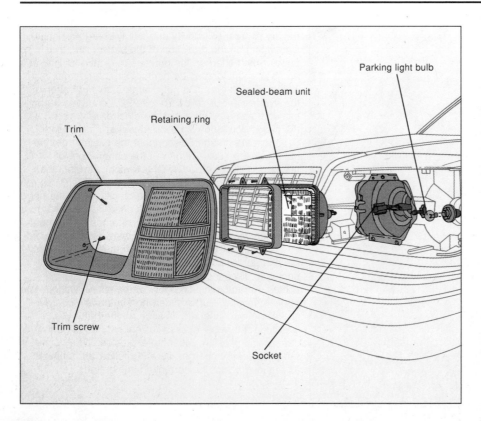

Parking light bulb

Sealed-beam unit

Retaining ring

Trim

Trim screw

Socket

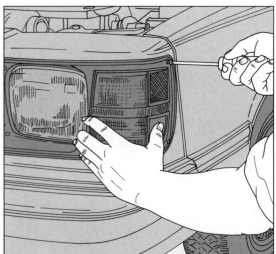

1 **Removing the trim.** Remove the trim screws with a Phillips or Torx-head screwdriver *(above)*, and gently pull the trim free. The trim may surround two sealed beams, or it may include a parking light housing, as shown here. To free the parking light socket from the trim, twist it counter-clockwise one-quarter turn.

REPLACING A SEALED-BEAM HEADLIGHT (continued)

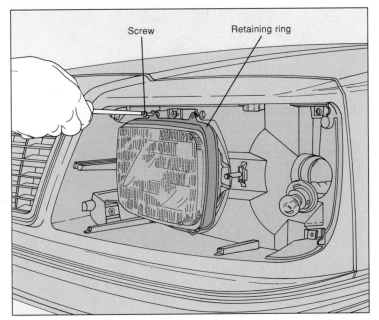

Screw   Retaining ring

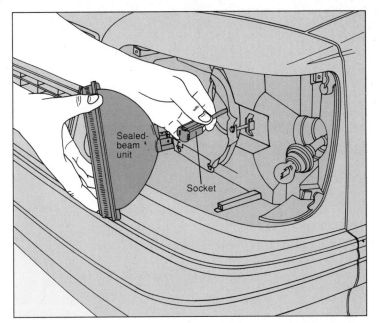

Sealed-beam unit

Socket

2 **Removing the retaining ring.** Remove all but one of the retaining ring screws with the appropriate screwdriver, usually a Phillips type *(above)*. Take care not to disturb the aim-adjusting screws. Hold the sealed-beam unit with one hand to prevent it from falling, then remove the last screw and lift off the retaining ring. If a round retaining ring has slotted screw holes, loosen the screws one or two turns and rotate the ring until the wider ends of the holes sit behind the screw heads; then lift off the ring.

3 **Removing and replacing the sealed-beam unit.** Hold the headlight firmly in one hand. With the other hand, wiggle the socket off the headlight prongs *(above)*. If the socket is hard to reach, grasp the wires leading to it; on some cars, this can be done from inside the engine compartment. When installing a new headlight, push the socket all the way onto the prongs. Apply dielectric compound to the joint between the socket and prongs to prevent corrosion. Replace the retaining ring and trim.

AIMING THE HEADLIGHTS

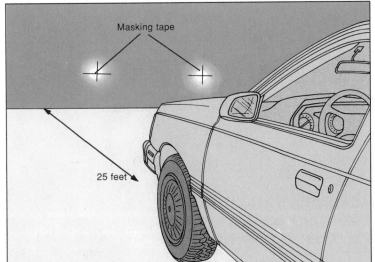

Masking tape

25 feet

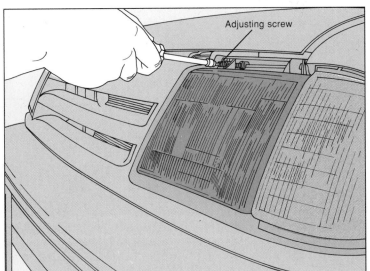

Adjusting screw

Aiming the headlights. The centers of the low beams should land on the road about 100 feet ahead of the car, the left headlight angled straight ahead and the right angled slightly toward the edge of the road: High beams should aim just below the horizon. Headlights are best professionally adjusted, but if you must aim the headlights yourself, first check that the tires are properly inflated *(page 26)* and that the car is carrying its usual load. Park the car on a level surface, the headlights 10 inches from a wall or garage door. Turn on the low beams and draw or tape a cross on the wall to mark the center of

each beam. Back the car, perfectly straight, 25 feet from the wall *(above, left)*. Each headlight has two adjusting screws, one at the top or bottom, and one at the side. To aim the lights, simply tighten or loosen these screws *(above, right)*. Adjust both low beams 2 inches below the horizontal tape lines; adjust the left light even with its vertical line and the right light 2 inches to the right of its vertical line. On a four-light system, adjust the high beams the same way as the low beams; on a two-light system, the high beams are automatically adjusted with the low beams.

REPLACING A HALOGEN HEADLIGHT BULB

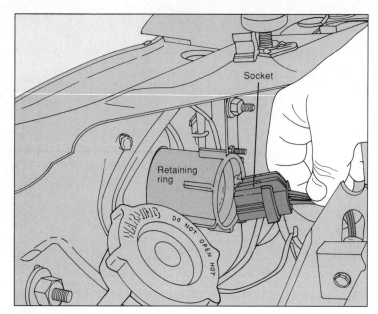

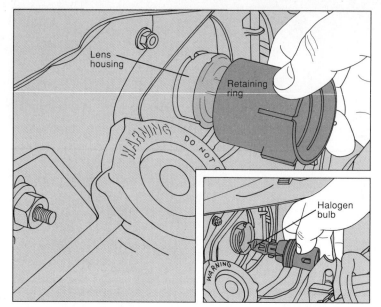

1 Removing the socket. A halogen headlight bulb that is not part of a sealed-beam unit is changed from the back; reach it by opening the hood. The bulb and its base are one unit, held in place inside the lens by a retaining ring. The socket, which plugs into the base of the bulb, is inside the ring. Turn the socket counterclockwise one-quarter turn. If the socket does not turn or is difficult to reach, grasp the wires leading from it and give a sharp tug to remove it *(above)*. On cars in which the socket is easily accessible, grasp the socket itself to pull it free. Where the halogen headlight is part of a sealed-beam unit, replace it like a sealed-beam headlight *(page 102)*.

2 Replacing the bulb. Turn the retaining ring counterclockwise to remove it *(above)*. Grasp the base of the bulb *(inset)* and gently pull it from the lens housing. Take care not to touch the glass globe of the new halogen bulb; oils from your skin left on the surface will react with heat and weaken the glass. If you do touch the glass, sponge it clean with water and dry it thoroughly with a paper towel. Insert the new bulb in the lens, replace the retaining ring and push the socket firmly onto the bulb base. If you twisted the socket to remove it in step 1, line up its slots with those on the bulb base and turn the socket clockwise one-quarter turn.

ACCESSING LIGHTS

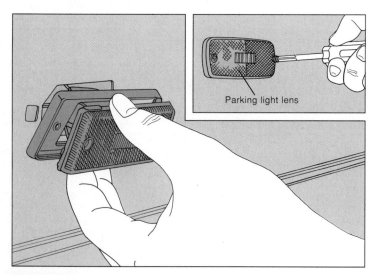

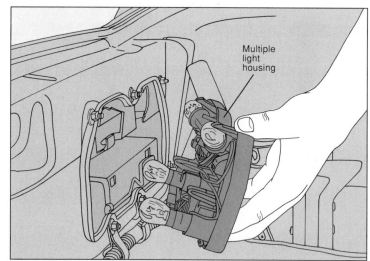

Removing an exterior lens. Use a screwdriver to remove the retaining screws on the lens *(inset)*. Lift off the lens carefully to avoid tearing the rubber gasket behind it *(above)*. Replace a cracked lens or a stiff or damaged gasket with new matching parts. Wash the new lens with soap and water and dry it thoroughly before reassembly. Tighten the retaining screws with light pressure to avoid cracking the lens.

Removing an interior-mounted bulb housing. Manufacturers often group several exterior car lights together in one housing, accessible from inside the trunk or engine compartment and secured with wing nuts, twisting knobs or snaps. Once released, the housing (such as the taillight assembly shown here) can be pulled away from the car body *(above)*. To free the housing from the car entirely, pull off the plastic wiring connector attached to it. On some models, you will have to bend back a tab before pulling off the connector.

ACCESSING LIGHTS (continued)

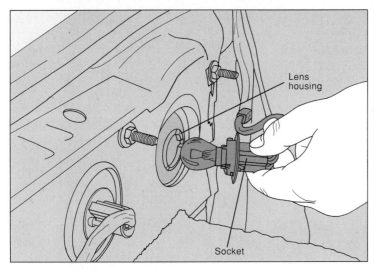

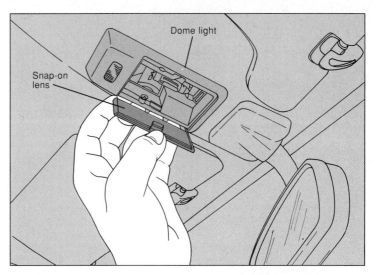

Removing a socket-mounted light. Side-marker lights and turn-signal lights are commonly socket-mounted. Twist the socket no more than one-quarter turn counterclockwise and pull it out *(above)*. To reinstall a socket, twist it clockwise until snug.

Removing a snap-on or twist-on lens. A lens without screws or other exterior retainers is typical of interior dome and map lights. Grip a snap-on lens between your thumb and finger *(above)*, gently squeeze the fragile tabs past the ridges in the base of the light and lift the lens off. Replace the lens by squeezing it a little in order to snap it back in place without bending the tabs. Grasp a round twist-in lens and turn it counterclockwise to unscrew it.

REPLACING BULBS

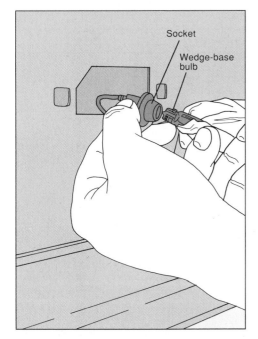

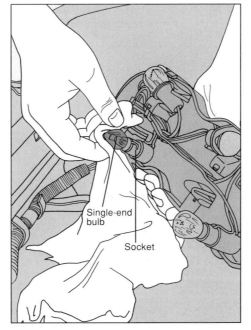

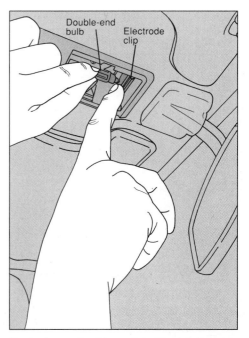

Replacing a wedge-base bulb. This bulb, commonly found in side-marker lights, has a base that sits snugly between the electrical contacts in its socket. Holding the bulb with a cloth to protect your hand in case the glass breaks, pinch the base of the bulb and pull it out *(above)*. Hold the new bulb with a cloth as you push it into place.

Replacing a single-end bulb. A single-end bulb with one or two filaments is commonly found in flashers and taillights. Hold it with a cloth to protect your hand, push it in against its socket spring, and twist it counterclockwise *(above)*. Replace the bulb by turning it clockwise. A two-filament, single-end bulb has two brass-colored alignment pins at its base. To replace it, fit the lower pin into the deeper slot in the socket.

Replacing a double-end bulb. A double-end bulb is found in dome, map and make-up lights. Hold the bulb with one hand and gently pry open one of its electrical contacts *(above)*. Move the clip that holds the electrical contacts in place only as far as necessary; if the clip doesn't spring back to hold the new bulb tightly, bend it in slightly.

CLEANING AND REPLACING SOCKETS

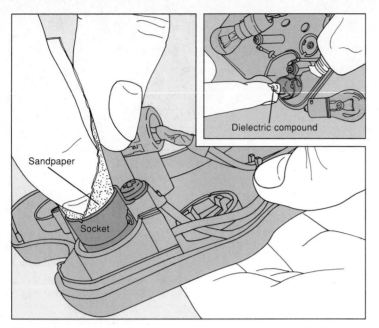

Dielectric compound

Sandpaper

Socket

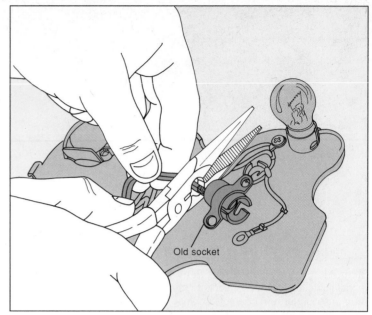

Old socket

Cleaning a socket. To improve its electrical contact with a bulb, polish the inside of a socket with fine sandpaper *(above)* or emery cloth and blow away the dust. Be sure to burnish the electrical contacts at the bottom of the socket as well. Smear dielectric compound inside the socket to protect it against corrosion *(inset).*

Replacing a socket. Using long-nose pliers or wire cutters, snip the wires no more than 4 inches from the old socket, as shown (the wire on a replacement socket is only 4 inches long). Unscrew or loosen any clamps that hold the socket in place, and take the old socket and bulb with you to buy a matching replacement socket. Crimp the wires of the new socket in place and solder the connections *(page 111).*

REPLACING FUSES AND CIRCUIT BREAKERS

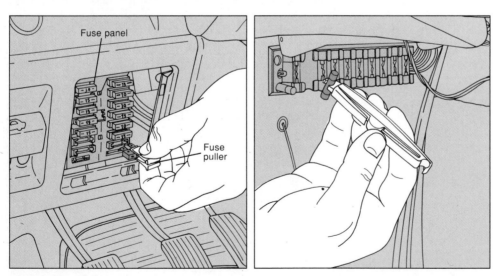

Fuse panel

Fuse puller

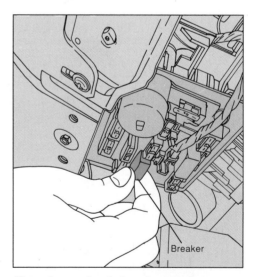

Breaker

Changing a fuse. The fuse panel cover or your owner's manual will indicate which circuits are protected by each fuse, and the amperage (rate of current flow) through those circuits. If your car has automotive-type fuses, which are flat, use the fuse puller provided in the fuse box or buy a plastic puller. Fit the puller over the base of the fuse, pull it out *(above, left)* and push a new fuse with the same amperage rating into the vacant slot. If the fuses are the glass-cartridge type, which are round with a metal cap at each end, remove them with a fuse puller especially designed for this type of fuse *(above, right);* do not use your hands, since glass fuses can break. Some circuits are protected by a fusible link—a short, thin length of wire soldered to the main wire. When it is blown, the insulation will blister or char. Consult a mechanic to determine the cause and replace the fusible link.

Changing a circuit breaker. When the cause of a tripped breaker has been corrected *(page 108),* or to test the circuit, pull out the old breaker with your fingers *(above)* and push an identical replacement into the slot. Some breakers are mounted with nuts to a panel under the hood of the car; remove the nuts with a small wrench.

REPLACING FLASHERS AND RELAYS

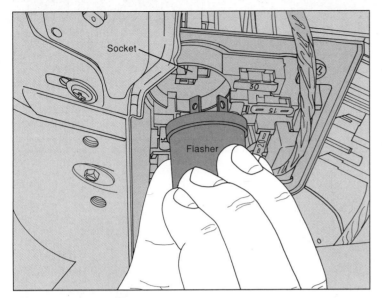

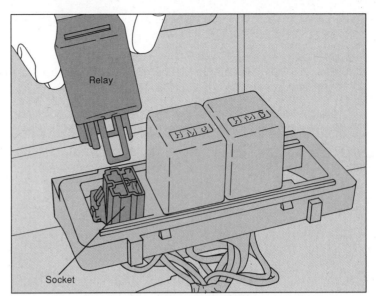

1 **Changing a flasher.** Look for the emergency and turn-signal flasher units in or around the fuse panel, under the dashboard, or around the fire wall of the engine compartment. Flashers are made of metal or plastic and are cylindrical in shape. Pull a defective flasher out of its socket by hand *(above)* and insert an identical replacement by lining up its prongs with the socket holes and pushing it firmly into place.

2 **Changing a relay switch.** This small plastic or metal box is wired into some high-amp circuits. It allows a high-current accessory (such as a horn or headlight) to be controlled by a lower-current circuit and switch. Look for a relay switch near the fuse box, under the dashboard, or along the fender panels or fire wall of the engine compartment. Turn the accessory on and off, and feel whether the relay clicks. If not, release the clip or unscrew the nuts holding the relay to the socket, and pull out the relay *(above)*. Disconnect the wire, if any, and plug in an identical replacement relay.

REPLACING SENDING UNITS

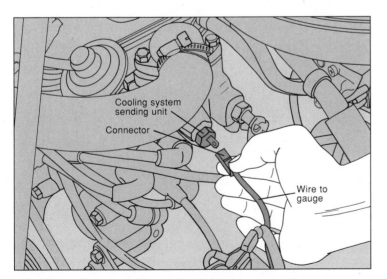

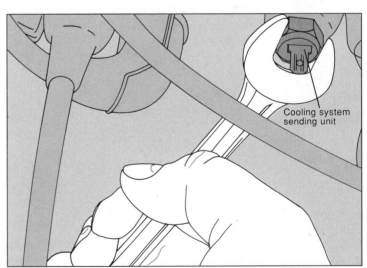

1 **Removing a sending unit wire.** Each warning light and gauge on the instrument panel is operated by a sending unit on the component it monitors (for example, the cooling system or the engine oil system). A sending unit is connected by wires to the gauge or light and is usually bolted to the engine block, below the spark plugs. In the cooling system, the sending unit acts as a switch; when triggered by high temperature, it lights the telltale bulb on the dash to indicate a hot engine. In the oil system, the sending unit senses low oil pressure and switches on the oil pressure light. To remove the wire leading from a sending unit to the dashboard, pull the wire connector from its terminal on the sending unit *(above)*.

2 **Replacing a sending unit.** Before removing the sending unit from a liquid system (such as coolant or oil) have a pan ready to catch any overflow. Or, in the case of the cooling system, drain coolant from the radiator first *(page 84)*. With an open-end wrench, unscrew the base of the sending unit from its mount *(above)*. If it is very tight, tap the end of the wrench with a hammer to jar the unit loose. Reverse the procedure to insert the new sending unit, top up the fluid and reconnect the sending unit to the gauge.

TRACING AN ELECTRICAL CIRCUIT

Reading a wiring diagram. A wiring diagram is a schematic drawing that uses symbols to show how the car's wires and electrical components are connected. A car's entire wiring circuitry diagram is very complex, but many manufacturers now publish manuals that isolate individual circuits into manageable groups. If you buy the service manual for your car, which contains the wiring diagrams, also obtain a wiring supplement if there is one.

The wiring diagram is a road map of the circuit, or loop, that electric current travels from the power source, through a series of switches, fuses and electrical devices back to the power source. By tracing a circuit from start to finish, you can test the components in sequence and thus pinpoint your problem quickly. The diagram below represents a

typical windshield washer pump circuit; the illustration on page 97 shows how the various components in this diagram actually appear in the car. Wires often disappear behind panels or into clusters of other wires, so recognizing the components and individual wire colors along a particular circuit is crucial. To discover how far along the circuit power can travel before it is stopped by a broken wire or faulty component, use an unpowered test light. Poke the sharp probe through the insulation into the wire; also touch it to exposed metal connecting terminals along the circuit. The following pages guide you through specific uses of the test light and wiring diagram at connectors, fuses, sockets and wires along a circuit. **Caution:** Never insert the probe in ignition system parts or wires when the ignition switch is on.

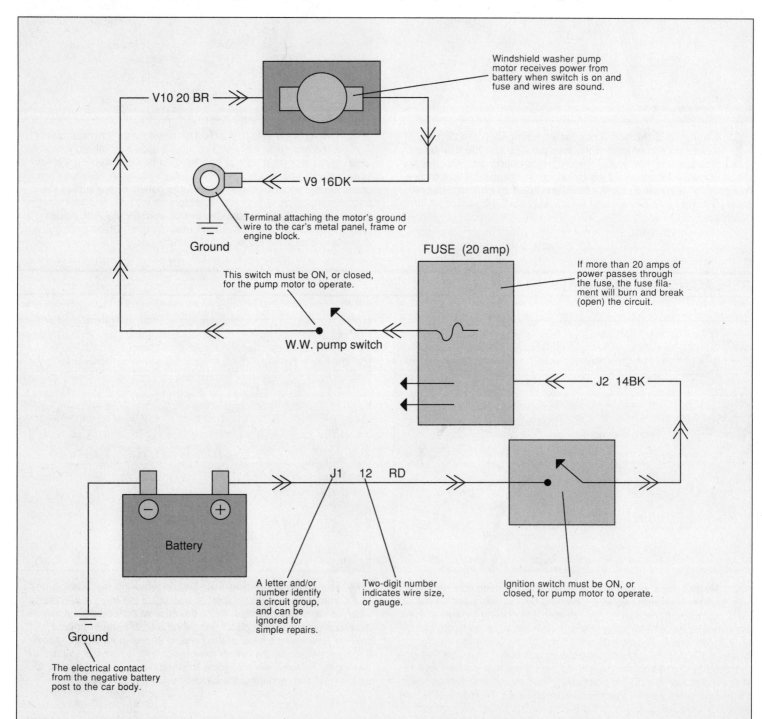

Windshield washer pump motor receives power from battery when switch is on and fuse and wires are sound.

V10 20 BR

V9 16DK

Terminal attaching the motor's ground wire to the car's metal panel, frame or engine block.

Ground

FUSE (20 amp)

If more than 20 amps of power passes through the fuse, the fuse filament will burn and break (open) the circuit.

This switch must be ON, or closed, for the pump motor to operate.

W.W. pump switch

J2 14BK

Battery

J1 12 RD

A letter and/or number identify a circuit group, and can be ignored for simple repairs.

Two-digit number indicates wire size, or gauge.

Ignition switch must be ON, or closed, for pump motor to operate.

Ground

The electrical contact from the negative battery post to the car body.

TESTING AND REPAIRING A CIRCUIT

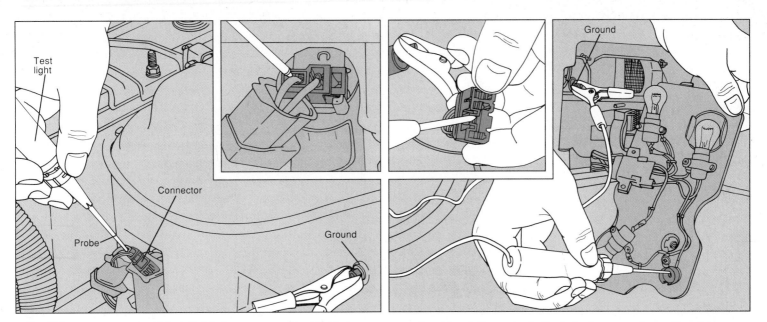

1 **Using an unpowered test light.** An unpowered test light shows where electricity is flowing by lighting up when its probe touches a "hot" part of a wiring circuit or accessory and its alligator clip is attached to a good ground—any unpainted metal bolt fixed to the car's metal panels, frame or engine. Refer to the pertinent wiring diagram in your service manual to determine which color wire is hot and which is ground. Or identify the ground wire by tracing it to the car body or engine. To test an accessory (the windshield washer pump motor in this example) turn on the ignition, then attach the alligator clip to a

ground and touch the probe to the hot wire connector on the motor *(above, left)*. To test a light, determine which contact in the socket is served by the hot wire and, with the test light clip grounded, touch that contact to determine whether power is reaching it *(above, right)*. If there is no power at an accessory, test the wiring by touching the connecting terminals located along the wiring, working your way back to the battery. If electricity is flowing, but the accessory does not work, test the ground side of its circuit *(next step)*.

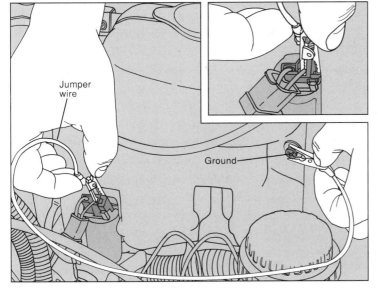

2 **Testing for a good ground.** Every electrical device requires a good ground connection to the car's metal panels, frame or engine. If electricity flows to an accessory that does not work, do not replace it until you test it with a substitute ground connection. To create the alternate ground, attach one alligator clip of a jumper wire to the grounded connecting terminal of the accessory *(inset)* and the other alligator clip to a nearby bolt or metal part of the car *(above)*. If the accessory now works, repair or replace the original ground wire *(page 110)*, or make a new ground for the circuit *(step 3)*; if the accessory still does not function, replace the accessory.

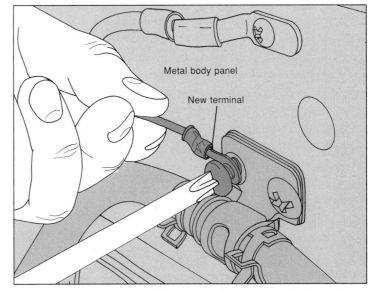

3 **Making a new ground.** If the ground wire connecting terminal on the car's metal panel, frame or engine is corroded, but the wire itself is good, cut the wire off its corroded terminal. Find and remove an uncorroded metal bolt or screw that is attached to the car's metallic body and which the wire can easily reach. Measure the circumference of this new fastener and buy an appropriate size round terminal. Attach the new terminal to the end of the wire *(page 111)*. If the wire is damaged or will not reach a new grounding fastener, splice a new length of wire of the same gauge *(page 111)* to a good section of the old, or replace the wire and its terminals entirely *(above)*.

TESTING AND REPAIRING A CIRCUIT (continued)

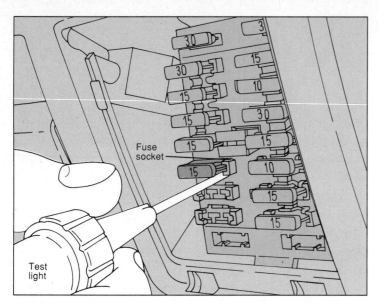

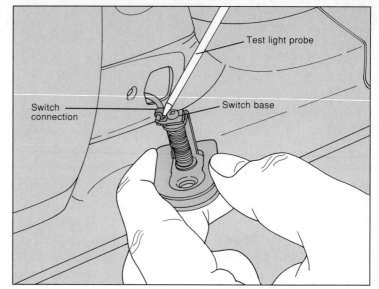

4 **Testing fuses.** If power is not reaching an electrical accessory, use the test light at the fuse box. Turn on the ignition and all switches on the circuit, and touch the grounded test light probe to the retaining clips at each side of that circuit's fuse or breaker *(above)*. If only one side lights the test light, the fuse or breaker is blown; insert a replacement *(page 106)*. If both sides light the test light but the accessory is not receiving power, the break is somewhere else in the circuit. Test the connectors on the wires leading to the accessory and test the wire at several points in between by pushing the probe through the insulation into the copper strands, until the break location is discovered. Repair the break with a splice *(page 111)*, or replace the entire section of wire where a break is not accessible *(below)*.

5 **Testing a switch for good contact.** To access the back of a switch for testing, pry or unscrew it from its panel. Then turn on the ignition switch and touch the probe of the grounded test light to the switch terminals. If the test light shines at one terminal but not at the other, the switch is faulty; replace it. A door jamb switch grounds the wire from the dome light circuit. Detach the switch by removing its retaining screw and pulling the switch out. Touch the probe of the grounded test light to the end of the switch where the wire is attached *(above)*, then to the base of the switch where it contacts the mounting screw. If the test light glows only on the first test, the switch is faulty; replace it. The dome light will glow when the test light does because the test light completes the ground circuit.

REPAIRING DAMAGED WIRING

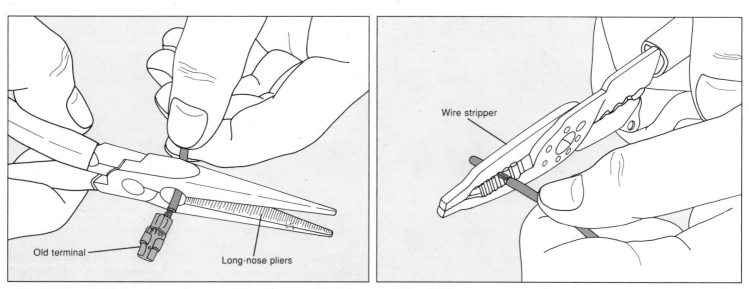

1 **Cutting and stripping a wire.** Check for brittle, frayed or exposed wiring along an affected circuit. Cut off damaged wire and corroded terminals with wire cutters or long-nose pliers *(above, left)*. Prepare the wire for a new terminal by peeling 1/4 inch of insulation from the end with a wire stripper *(above, right)*. Insert the wire into a matching slot, close the tool and twist it back and forth until the insulation is severed and can be pulled off the wire.

REPAIRING DAMAGED WIRING (continued)

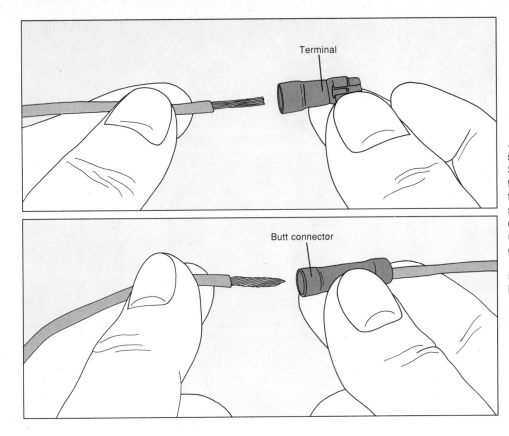

Terminal

Butt connector

2 **Attaching a terminal.** Terminals come in a variety of shapes and wire sizes, male and female connector styles, and with or without plastic sleeves. So-called "solderless" terminals and connectors are crimped to the wire *(step 3)*, although they can also be soldered *(step 4)* for added security. Soldered terminals should always be crimped first. Whatever type of terminal you use, place the stripped wire end into the back of the terminal up to the crimping tunnel *(left, top)*. To splice two wires together, strip 1/2 inch of insulation from each wire and place both into a butt connector from opposite ends *(left, bottom)*. Crimp the terminal or connector *(step 3)*.

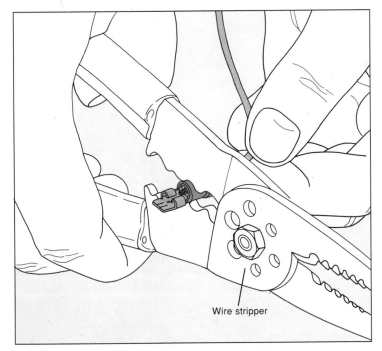

Wire stripper

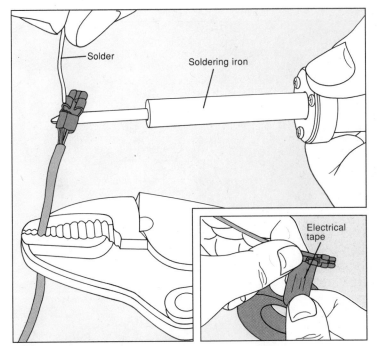

Solder

Soldering iron

Electrical tape

3 **Crimping a terminal.** Use the crimping jaws of a wire stripper to pinch the connector near the end of the wire *(above)*. Crimp again where the wire enters the connector. Give the wire a firm pull to test the crimp. If crimping fails to hold, cut off the sleeve of the terminal with a utility knife and solder the terminal as well.

4 **Soldering and taping a terminal.** Clamp the crimped terminal loosely with locking pliers *(above)*. Hold a hot soldering iron or gun against the back of the terminal and touch acid-core solder to the face of the terminal and the exposed wire. When the solder melts into the wire and over the terminal, remove the heat and allow the connection to cool. Wrap a generous amount of electrical tape over the wire to protect any exposed portion from the elements.

SERVICING THE ALTERNATOR DRIVE BELT

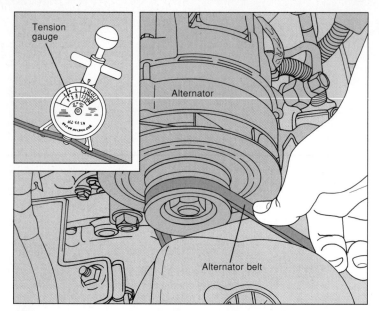

1 **Testing belt tension.** Check the condition of drive belts at least once a year. A quick check can be made by pressing down with your thumb midway along the belt's longest span *(above)*. The belt should have no more than 1/2 inch of play. Obtain a more accurate reading of the belt's tension with a tension gauge *(inset, and page 89)*. Follow steps 2 through 4 to tighten a loose belt. If the belt is cracked, brittle, soft or otherwise damaged, replace it.

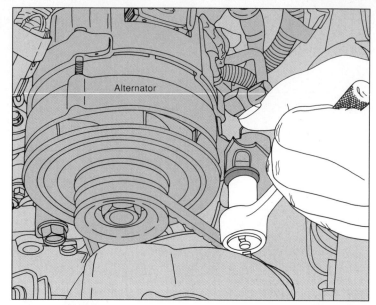

2 **Loosening the alternator adjustment bolt.** The alternator is mounted with two bolts—the adjustment bolt near the top, and the pivot bolt on its base. Loosen the nut on the adjustment bolt with a socket wrench *(above)*, pulling hard on the ratchet and giving it a bump with the heel of your other hand, if necessary. Try to push the alternator against the belt with your hand, as in step 4, or pry it with a tool handle. If the alternator moves and the belt tenses, tighten the adjustment bolt. If the alternator will not budge, try loosening the pivot bolt as well *(next step)*.

3 **Loosening the pivot bolt.** Grip the pivot bolt with a socket wrench and extension *(above)*. You may need to use a lot of force, or a sharp blow against the ratchet handle with the heel of your hand, to loosen it. Turn the pivot bolt only one-half turn, or until the alternator moves with hand pressure.

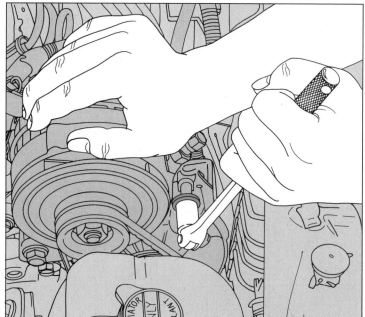

4 **Tightening the belt.** Press against the alternator with one hand until the belt is taut, then tighten the adjustment bolt slightly *(above)*. Repeat the thumb test *(step 1)*. If the belt is too loose, press the alternator harder; if too tight, apply less pressure before tightening the adjustment bolt. When the tension is correct *(step 1)*, tighten both the adjustment and pivot bolts securely.

GAPPING AND REPLACING SPARK PLUGS

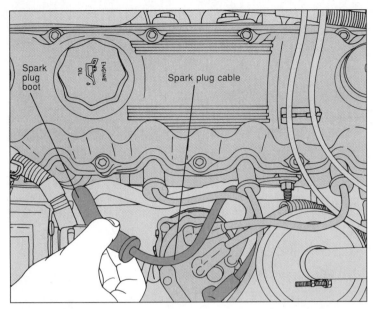

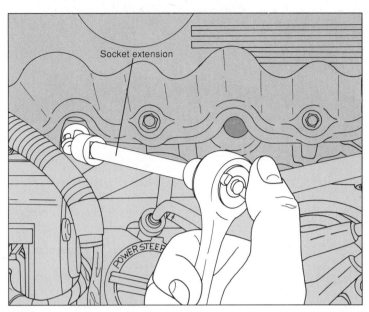

1 **Disconnecting a spark plug cable.** Made of nylon filament and filled with carbon, spark plug cables are fragile. Their performance deteriorates quickly if they are pulled or twisted, or become wet, dirty or oily. To remove a cable from the spark plug, grasp only the protective boot and twist it back and forth while pulling it off the plug *(above)*. On some cars, you must lift off the air cleaner *(page 75)* to gain access to the spark plugs.

2 **Extracting a spark plug.** Fit a spark plug socket (either 14mm or 18mm in size, depending on the specifications in your service manual) onto the spark plug, turning it until its rubber insert grips the plug firmly. Use a socket wrench, with extension and universal joint, if necessary, and strong hand pressure to loosen the plug *(above)*; twist out the loosened plug by hand.

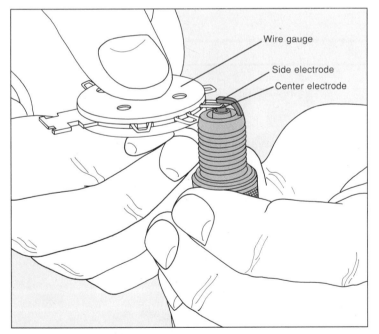

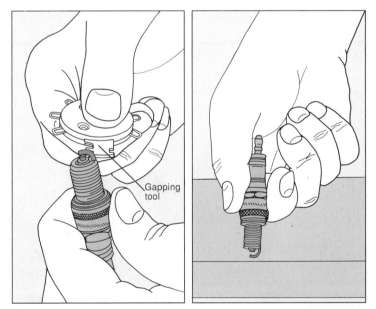

3 **Checking spark plug gap.** Apply parts-cleaning solvent to a used spark plug and rinse it clean; brush the electrode end with a wire brush. Determine the correct gap width for your car's plugs in your owner's manual. Use only a wire gauge to measure the gap between the electrodes *(above)*. The wire should touch both electrodes but pass between them smoothly; if it passes through without touching, the gap is too wide. Always check the gap on a new set of spark plugs before installing them.

4 **Adjusting the gap.** To widen the gap between the electrodes, use the gapping tool on the wire gauge. Widen the gap by gently bending the side electrode away from the center electrode *(above, left)*. Narrow the gap by holding the plug and pressing the top electrode gently against a hard surface *(above, right)*. Check the gap again with the wire gauge.

GAPPING AND REPLACING SPARK PLUGS (continued)

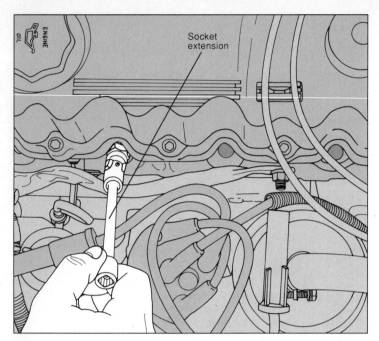

Socket extension

5 **Reinserting a spark plug.** Before fitting the plug back into the spark plug socket, smear the spark plug threads with anti-seize compound so they will not bind. Insert the plug into its hole and turn it clockwise by hand with the socket extension *(above)*. When the spark plug is fully seated, fit the socket wrench ratchet onto the extension and tighten the plug no more than one-quarter turn if it has a gasket. If the plug has no gasket, tighten it no more than 1/16 inch; overtightening will damage the plug hole threads.

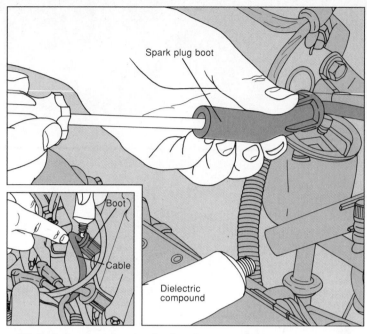

Spark plug boot

Boot

Cable

Dielectric compound

6 **Lubricating the spark plug boot.** To protect the plug from corrosion, apply a thin layer of dielectric compound to the inside of each spark plug boot, using a stick or screwdriver *(above)*. Push the boot firmly onto the plug until you can feel or hear it click over the tip of the plug. Spread a drop of silicone sealant where the cable and boot meet to block moisture and dirt *(inset)*. If the spark plug boot and cable are molded together, a sealant is not needed.

REPLACING SPARK PLUG CABLES

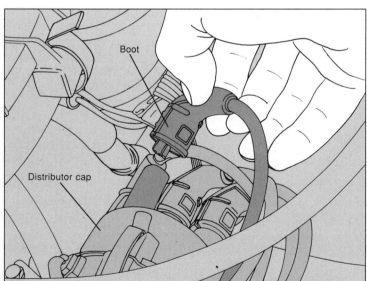

Boot

Distributor cap

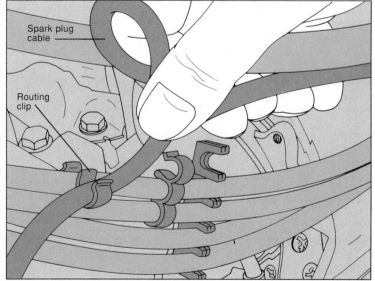

Spark plug cable

Routing clip

1 **Installing new spark plug cables.** A car has one cable for each spark plug, plus one cable that leads to the ignition coil. Inspect each cable from end to end. If any cable is damaged or corroded, replace all cables with a new set made for your car's make, model and year. Disconnect and replace one spark plug cable at a time. If the distributor has a protective cover, remove it to expose the cap. Release the first cable from the distributor by grasping its boot firmly, twisting it slightly and pulling it off *(above, left)*. Then unthread the cable from the routing clips *(above, right)*. Follow the cable to its spark plug and pull the boot off the plug. Select a new cable of equal length, and spread dielectric compound inside both boots. Attach the new cable by reversing the steps you followed to remove it, making sure the boots are secure and the cable is threaded through the routing clips. Replace each spark plug cable the same way, one at a time.

REPLACING SPARK PLUG CABLES (continued)

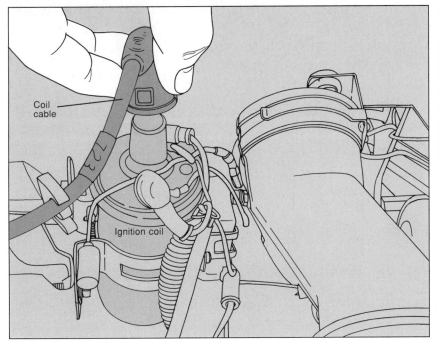

Coil
cable

Ignition coil

2 **Installing a new coil cable.** The center cable on the distributor runs to the ignition coil. As you did for the spark plug cables, disconnect its boot from the distributor and unthread the cable from the routing clips. Follow the cable to the ignition coil and disconnect its boot from the coil *(left)*. Spread dielectric compound inside the boots of the new coil cable. Install the new cable, reversing the steps you followed to remove it. Make sure the boots are secure and the cable is threaded through the routing clips.

REPLACING THE DISTRIBUTOR CAP AND ROTOR

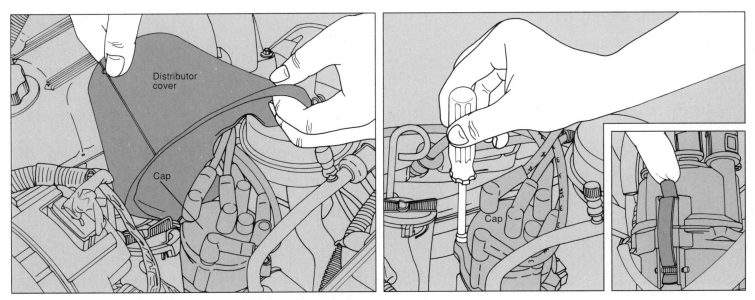

Distributor
cover

Cap

Cap

1 **Removing the distributor cap.** The distributor and rotor send high-voltage current to the spark plugs. Both should be checked periodically for wear or damage. Remove the rubber or plastic protective cover over the distributor cap with your fingers *(above, left)* or, if it has fasteners, use a screwdriver. Release the cap from the distributor, leaving the spark plug cables in place: Undo the retaining screws around the base of the distributor with a screwdriver or a nut driver *(above, right)*; the screws will remain in the cap. Or, if two spring clips hold the cap in place, push them outward to free the cap *(inset)*. Some distributor caps have spring-loaded fasteners; push them down and twist them with a screwdriver one-half turn in either direction to release the cap.

REPLACING THE DISTRIBUTOR CAP AND ROTOR (continued)

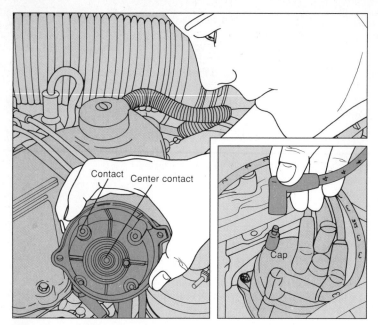

Contact Center contact

Cap

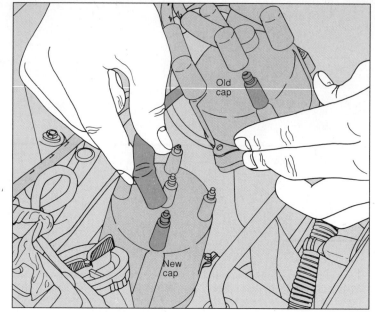

Old cap

New cap

2 **Inspecting and replacing the distributor cap.** Turn over the distributor cap and inspect it *(above)*. Check for signs of deterioration: burns or pits on the metal contacts, and carbon tracks (black lines burned by high-voltage sparks) on the cap. Next, twist the cable boots off their towers one at a time *(inset)* and look for carbon tracks and cracks or other damage to the cap. If the cap is in good condition, clean it inside and out with a dry rag. If the cap is faulty, replace both the cap and the rotor *(step 4)*. Place the new cap on its base, rotate it to fit into the alignment notch, and tighten the screws or snap on the spring clips.

3 **Transferring the cables to the new cap.** With the new cap installed, hold the old cap and cables beside it. Remove the boot of one cable at a time from the old cap and fit it snugly onto the corresponding tower on the new cap *(above)*.

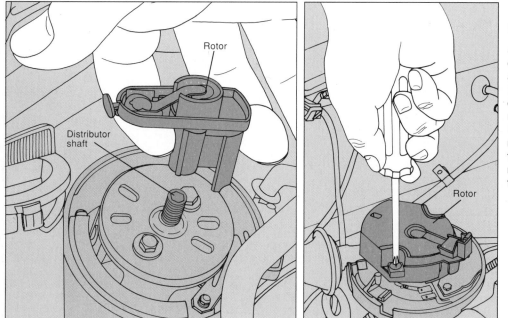

Rotor

Distributor shaft

Rotor

4 **Replacing the rotor.** The rotor receives high voltage from the coil at the center post of the distributor cap and distributes the power to the spark plug cables as it rotates. Grasp the rotor as shown and lift it straight off the distributor shaft *(far left)*. Inspect the rotor for pits, carbon tracks or other visible damage. If the rotor is faulty, replace both the rotor and the distributor cap. Place the new rotor on the distributor post, rotate it until they are aligned and gently slide the rotor down. Some rotors *(near left)* have retaining screws; remove the screws, position the new rotor and screw it in place.

COMPUTER DIAGNOSIS OF CAR PROBLEMS

Cars and computers. In the computer-equipped car, an electronic control module (ECM) controls certain functions in the fuel, ignition, emission, suspension, heating, cooling and brake systems, and supplies instrument panel information. In addition, the computer records malfunctions, storing this information as trouble code numbers that represent individual problems. (To interpret each code for your make and model of car, consult your service manual.) If the car has been overheating, for example, the computer will store in its memory the number corresponding to overheating, and inform you of the problem when you activate the diagnostic process. On some makes of car, the trouble codes appear on the instrument panel *(step 2)*. With others, you must use a special diagnostic scanner to access the trouble codes *(below)*. Professional mechanics use the scanner to obtain specific readings of a car's entire computer-controlled operation. For example, the scanner not only records that the car has been overheating, but will also note the temperature reading at which the thermostat switches on the cooling fan. Diagnostic scanners for use on most computerized American cars can be purchased at auto supply stores.

Using a diagnostic scanner. The scanner *(left)* is a hand-held instrument that looks much like a pocket calculator. It usually connects to the cigarette lighter for power and to a connector located under the dashboard *(step 1)* or under the hood—your service manual will indicate the exact location. When you buy a diagnostic scanner for your car, you will also receive the appropriate adapter to plug it into the car's computer, and generous instructions on its use and code information. On command, the scanner will enable you to test various switches and circuits, and to determine battery voltage, ignition timing, coolant temperature and engine speed.

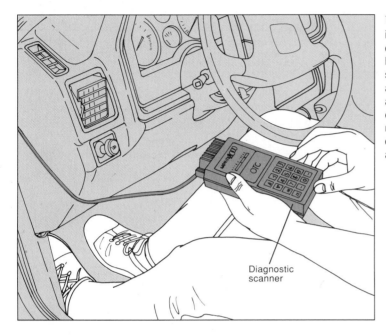

Diagnostic scanner

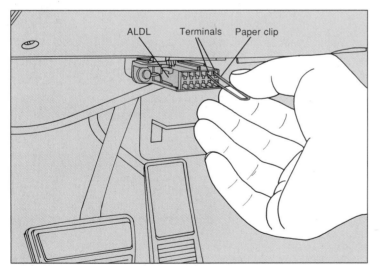

ALDL   Terminals   Paper clip

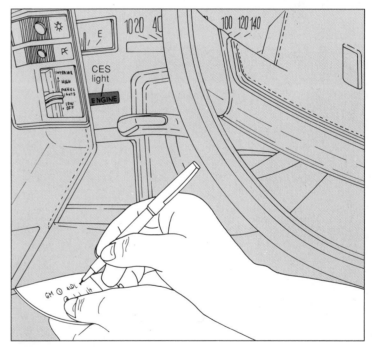

CES light

1 **Activating the diagnostic mode (GM cars).** General Motors cars that are computer-equipped have an assembly line diagnostic link (ALDL) under the dashboard. The ALDL has a connector with several terminals. To activate the diagnostic process on most GM cars, turn on the ignition switch but do not start the motor. Bend a paper clip into a U and use it to connect the two top right terminals, marked A and B *(above)*. The "check engine soon" (CES) light, or similar telltale light on the instrument panel, will flash on and off as long as the paper clip remains in place. On GM models with electronic climate control, the diagnostic process is activated by pressing the OFF and WARMER buttons together; the trouble code numbers are then digitally displayed on the fuel information panel.

2 **Reading the code.** The CES light will flash on and off quickly once and, after a short pause, flash on and off twice in quick succession. This is a Code 12 (or one-two), which indicates that the diagnostic mode has started and is ready to go. After a longer pause, Code 12 will flash two more times, with longer pauses after each flash. If the computer has stored a trouble code, that code number will appear next. For a Code 15, representing overheating on some GM models, the CES will flash once quickly and, after a short pause, five times in quick succession. The sequence will be repeated three times, with longer pauses after each sequence. Watch the light and write down each trouble code that appears *(above)*, then refer to your service manual or a professional mechanic. The sequence will end with a code 12. A continuous code 12 indicates that there are no malfunctions. If you disconnect the battery, however, all trouble code numbers stored in the computer's memory will be lost.

BODY AND INTERIOR

A car door that doesn't latch, or wipers that don't clean the windshield, can keep you off the road as surely as a dead engine. And from an economic point of view, the market value of a car in good running condition can drop to near zero if the body is rusted, or the interior leaks.

Even the car's paint is more than just cosmetic—it is the only barrier between the body's steel panels and invading rust. A simple preventive measure, regularly washing and waxing your car will keep rust at bay, maintaining the value and appearance of the car. As you wash, check for scratches and dings and touch them up *(page 131)* before they rust.

Each time you wash the car, clean the interior as well. Vacuum the carpet and cloth upholstery, and wipe all vinyl surfaces with a moist cloth. If an occupant of the car smokes, wash the inside surface of the windshield with a commercial glass cleaner at least once a week; smoke residue greatly reduces visibility. Car upholstery is chemically treated to repel spills and retard burning. Wipe spills immediately; if a stain does set, treat it as you would a stain on upholstered furniture.

The illustration below points out the often-neglected mechanical parts of the car body. Hinges and locks, window and mirror mechanisms, weather stripping and windshield washers should all be inspected and cleaned or lubricated periodically—the steps in this chapter show you how. If a part breaks or goes out of adjustment, find the symptom in the Troubleshooting Guide, which will direct you to the repair procedure. Most doors, hoods and trunk lids can be adjusted by loosening their hinge bolts. Some cars have welded or riveted door and trunk hinges, and some windows are riveted to their lift channels; these must be aligned professionally.

A water leak can greatly damage the car's interior. Most leaks are admitted by weather stripping that is dried out, torn or misaligned. Periodically inspect all the weather stripping, including that on the windows, hood and trunk lid. Replace a faulty strip with an exact match. Finding the source of a leak is a painstaking process. Use the garden-hose test on page 125 to locate the water's probable point of entry, and examine the weather stripping in that area.

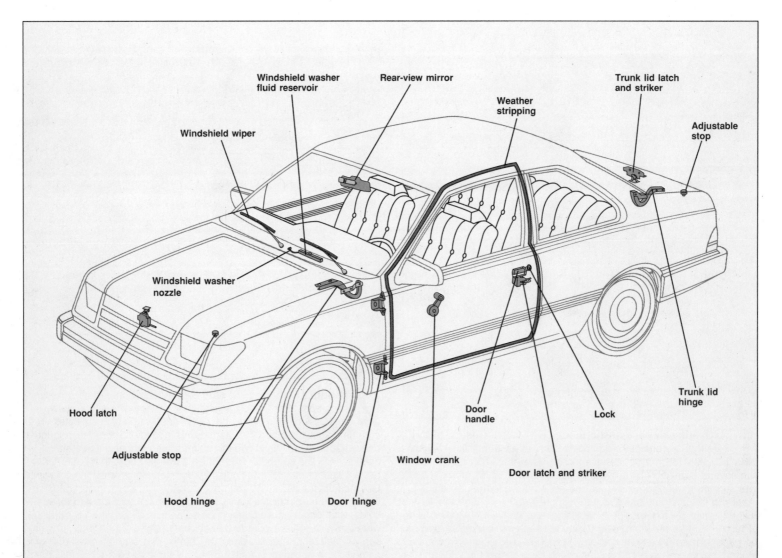

TROUBLESHOOTING GUIDE

SYMPTOM	POSSIBLE CAUSE	PROCEDURE
Interior door panel damaged		Remove and replace panel *(p. 120)* □○
Door sags	Hinge misaligned	Adjust hinge *(p. 123)* □○
Door hard to close; door rattles when closed	Latch mechanism or striker misaligned	Adjust latch or striker *(p. 123)* □○
	Hinge misaligned	Adjust hinge *(p. 123)* □○
Hood or trunk lid too high or too low	Hinge misaligned; adjustable stops misaligned	Adjust hinge *(p. 124)* □○; raise or lower stops *(p. 124)* □○
Hood or trunk lid hard to close or rattles when closed	Latch mechanism or striker misaligned	Adjust latch or striker *(p. 124)* □○
Hatchback lid doesn't stay up	Seal on damper cylinder leaks	Replace damper *(p. 125)* ◲○
Draft through closed window	Glass tilted too far backward or forward	Align window *(p. 121)* ◲◑
	Weather stripping loose or damaged	Inspect weather stripping; glue it, if loose, or replace it, if damaged *(p. 126)* □○
Window rattles	Weather stripping loose or damaged	Inspect weather stripping; glue it, if loose, or replace it, if damaged *(p. 126)* □○
	Glass stabilizers loose	Adjust stabilizers *(p. 121)* □○
Window difficult to move up or down	Window mechanism dirty or corroded	Remove door panel *(p. 120)* □○; lubricate mechanism *(p. 121)* □○
	Glass stabilizers too tight	Adjust stabilizers *(p. 121)* □○
Window doesn't open or close all the way	Glass tilted too far backward or forward	Align window *(p. 121)* ◲◑
Window won't go up or down at all	Window mechanism badly corroded or broken	Do not force jammed window; have window serviced professionally
Window broken		Remove and replace window *(p. 122)* ◲◑
Water leaks into car interior	Weather stripping damaged	Trace source of leak with a garden hose *(p. 125)* □○; replace damaged weather stripping *(p. 126)* □○
Lock jammed	Lock mechanism dirty or corroded	Lubricate lock *(p. 122)* □○; replace if necessary *(p. 122)* ◲◑
Windshield wiper streaks glass	Squeegees dirty or worn	Clean squeegees with mild detergent-and-water solution; if worn, replace squeegees or blade assembly *(p. 127)* □○
Windshield wiper chatters or cleans glass unevenly	Wiper arm bent	Straighten wiper arm *(p. 127)* □○; or have wiper replaced professionally
Windshield washer fluid doesn't reach glass, or hits glass in wrong place	Windshield washer fluid level low	Check fluid level; top up with commercial windshield washer fluid
	Nozzles blocked or out of position	Clear nozzles and re-aim nozzles if necessary *(p. 127)* □○
	Fluid reservoir tube disconnected, kinked or broken; filter inside fluid reservoir pick-up tube clogged	Straighten or replace tube; clean filter *(p. 127)* □○
Rear-view mirror loose		Tighten mirror-adjustment joint *(p. 128)* □○
Rear-view mirror missing		Install new mirror *(p. 128)* □○
Vinyl upholstery torn		Repair upholstery with commercial vinyl repair kit *(p. 129)* □○
Cigarette burn on carpet		Fill burned area with carpet fibers *(p. 130)* □○
Small scratch on body		Remove rust; apply primer and touch up paint *(p. 131)* ◲○
Rust spot on body		Remove rust; apply primer and touch up paint *(p. 131)* ◲○

DEGREE OF DIFFICULTY: □ **Easy** ◲ **Moderate** ■ **Complex**
ESTIMATED TIME: ○ **Less than 1 hour** ◑ **1 to 3 hours** ● **Over 3 hours** *(Does not include drying time)*

REMOVING AN INTERIOR DOOR PANEL

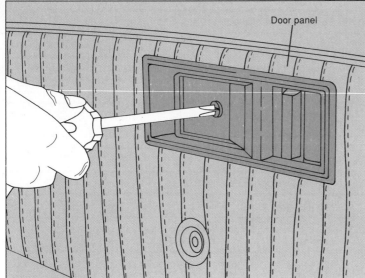

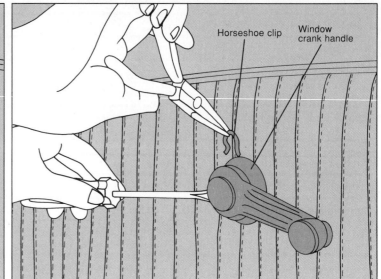

Door panel

Horseshoe clip   Window crank handle

1 **Removing door-panel screws.** Locate the screws securing the door panel to the door frame. Some of the screws may be hidden. Common locations are inside the door handle *(above, left)*, in the arm rest and at the corners of the door panel. Use a screwdriver to remove the screws, and a nut driver or wrench to remove bolts. Unscrew and remove any door-mounted radio speakers.

In most cars, the window crank handle is secured to the window mechanism by a horseshoe-shaped clip. Pry the handle away from the door slightly with a screwdriver, then use long-nose pliers to pull out the clip behind it *(above, right)*. A coat hanger wire bent into a hook can also be used to remove the horseshoe clip. Pull off the window-crank handle.

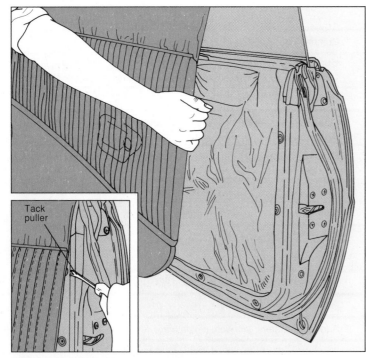

Tack puller

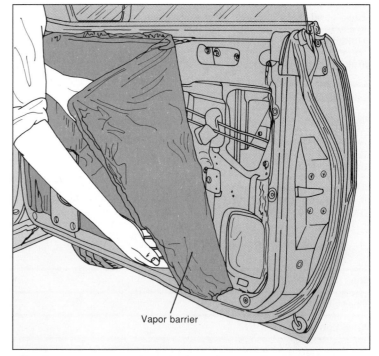

Vapor barrier

2 **Removing the door panel.** Most door panels are attached to the frame by metal or plastic clips that grip the edges of the panel and plug snugly into holes around the edge of the frame. With a tack puller or special door panel removal tool, gently pry the clips out of the holes *(inset)*. If any clips break, buy replacements at an auto parts store. With all the clips removed, grasp both sides of the door panel and lift it off the door frame *(above)*.

3 **Removing the vapor barrier.** A thin sheet of plastic, foam or treated paper is taped or glued to the door frame to protect the window mechanism from moisture. To access a window mechanism, gently peel off any tape and lift away the vapor barrier *(above)*. If the vapor barrier is glued, score its edge with a razor blade as you separate it from the frame. If the barrier tears, repair it with silver duct tape or replace it. Replace the old panel if damaged. To reinstall it, align the panel clips with the holes in the door. Press the panel into place and gently hammer its edges with a rubber mallet. Reinstall the parts that you removed in step 1.

ADJUSTING A WINDOW

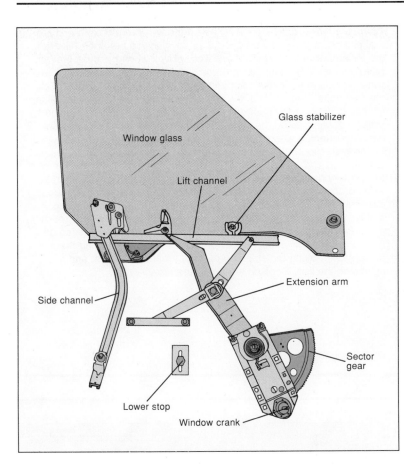

Window glass

Glass stabilizer

Lift channel

Side channel

Extension arm

Sector gear

Lower stop

Window crank

Troubleshooting window problems. There are two types of movable car windows. Framed windows are surrounded by a metal channel that guides the glass. Frameless windows are guided by a mechanism inside the door. Window-winding mechanisms vary, too, but most operate on the same basic principle; the example at left is typical. The window-crank handle (or electric motor, on power windows) is attached to a sector-gear and extension-arm assembly called the regulator, which is connected to the lift channel. The bottom of the glass is bolted or riveted to this channel, which can be cranked up or down. You can adjust a bolted window, but if the glass is riveted to the channel, have the window professionally realigned. On some models, a slotted tape or cable replaces the regulator. Both framed and frameless windows may have glass stabilizers that press gently against the inside of the window to hold it steady.

If the window glass is misaligned—tilted too far forward or backward, or positioned too tightly against an inner or outer edge of the channel—go to steps 1 and 2 below. If the window is difficult or impossible to move up and down and there is no obvious misalignment, lubricate the window mechanism. Remove the door panel *(page 120)* and spray penetrating oil on all accessible joints and gears. Then spray silicone lubricant on the same parts. Insert the spray can through access holes in the door frame to reach less accessible parts. Finish by applying water-resistant grease to the joints. Crank the window up and down. If the window moves smoothly without sticking, reinstall the door panel, and lubricate twice a year. If the window still moves with difficulty, the regulator may be damaged. Have it checked and, if necessary, replaced by a professional. Never force a stiff or jammed window—this can break the regulator.

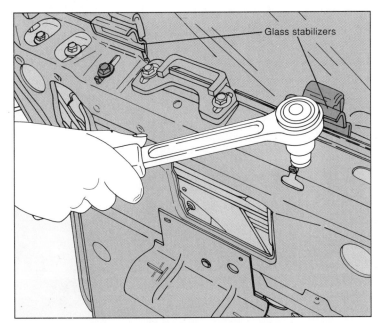

Glass stabilizers

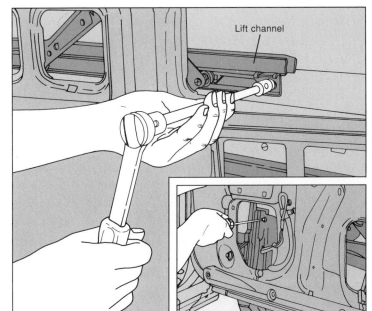

Lift channel

1 **Loosening the glass stabilizers.** Remove the door panel *(page 120)*. The door frames of some large cars have glass stabilizers that grip and center the glass as it moves up and down. If your car does not have glass stabilizers, go to step 2. Glass stabilizers can be loosened slightly if the window moves stiffly, or tightened if the window rattles. Locate the bolts or screws attaching the stabilizers to the door frame. Use a socket wrench *(above)* or screwdriver to loosen or tighten the stabilizers slightly, by moving the bolts in their slots. To adjust the window, loosen the stabilizers, then go to step 2.

2 **Loosening channel bolts.** The bolts are located on a central lift channel *(above)*, and possibly on one or two side channels *(inset)*. Have a helper hold the glass while you slightly loosen the channel bolts. Gently move the window to its proper position in the channel (check the angle on the opposite door's window for comparison). Push the glass out to the weather stripping. Set the glass stabilizers so they just touch the glass and tighten them. Tighten the channel bolts. If the glass has upper or lower stops, loosen the bolt in the stop, move the stop into position around the glass, and tighten the bolt.

REPLACING A WINDOW

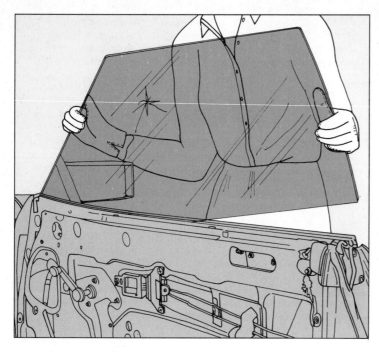

Lifting out the damaged window. If the window is broken into several pieces, or broken glass has fallen down inside the door, take the car for professional service. Wear work gloves when handling broken glass. Remove the door panel *(page 120)*. With a helper holding the window, loosen the glass stabilizers, if any, and locate and loosen all channel bolts *(page 121)*. If the window is frameless, have your helper lift it straight up out of the door *(left)*. If the window has a frame, there may be guide clips on the sides of the frame (the clips help to keep the glass running straight up the frame). Insert a flat-tipped screwdriver under each clip and pry it off the frame. Tilt the glass out of the frame and lift it up and out of the door. The replacement window must match the old window exactly; specify the make, model and year of your car when ordering. Have your helper insert the new window into the door channel and position it so that it just touches the weather stripping. Tighten the channel bolts. Set the glass stabilizers so they just touch the glass, then tighten the stabilizers. On a framed window, snap on the guide clips. Adjust any upper or lower stops by loosening the bolt in the stop, moving the stop into position around the glass, and then tightening the bolt. Replace the door panel *(page 120)*.

SERVICING A LOCK

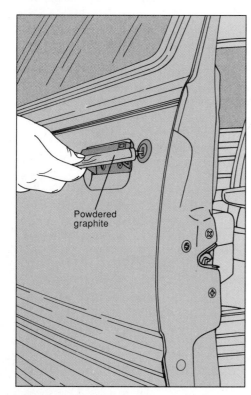

Powdered graphite

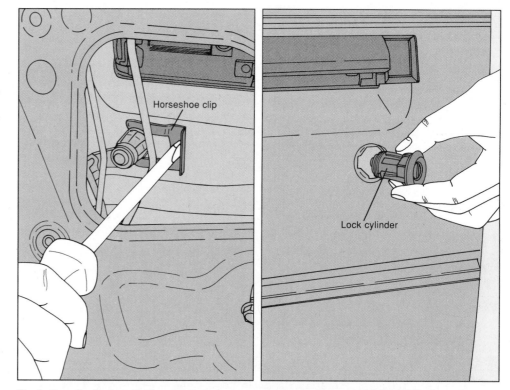

Horseshoe clip

Lock cylinder

Lubricating the lock from the outside. Insert a puff of powdered graphite or a few drops of silicone lubricant in the keyhole *(above)*. Move the key in and out a few times to spread the lubricant. In icy weather, squirt a few drops of lubricant or antifreeze into the lock every 2 to 3 weeks. In other seasons, lubricate the lock every few months.

Replacing the lock cylinder. Many locks are now key-coded, and a new key may be needed for a new lock cylinder. Ask the locksmith whether the new cylinder can be set to match the old key. Remove the door panel *(page 120)*. The lock cylinder is attached inside the door with a horseshoe clip. Pry off the clip with a screwdriver *(above, left)*, holding the clip to keep it from falling inside the door frame. Pull the lock cylinder out of the door from the outside *(above, right)*. Insert the replacement lock cylinder through the lock opening and snap the horseshoe clip back in place. Lubricate the lock, inside and out, with powdered graphite or silicone lubricant *(left)*. Replace the door panel *(page 120)*.

ADJUSTING A DOOR HINGE

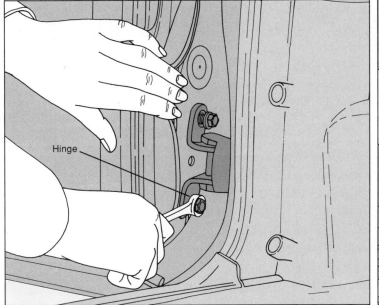

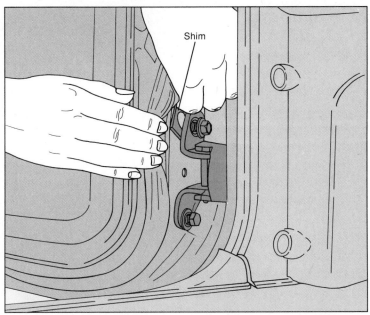

Loosening the hinge bolts. The door hinges on many GM cars, Chrysler K cars and some Fords are welded or riveted to the door and body. Have this type of hinge professionally adjusted. A door that doesn't close properly needs its position adjusted within the frame. Determine the direction in which the door needs to be adjusted: up or down, backward or forward, in or out. A door that sags should be moved up; a door that hits the car body along the top should be moved down. A door that doesn't latch properly may need to be adjusted forward or backward. A door that is loose and rattles when closed needs to be moved in or out of the frame. A door that rattles may also have worn hinge bushings; check them and have them replaced, if necessary. If a misaligned door has worn the hinge, have the hinge replaced.

To adjust the door either up and down or forward and backward, slightly loosen the hinge-to-body bolts. To move the door in and slightly loosen the hinge-to-door bolts *(above, left)*. Open the door and have a helper hold it steady. Depending on the type of hinge bolt, use a screwdriver, open-end wrench or hex wrench to loosen it. To correct minor misalignment, insert a U-shaped shim (available at auto parts stores) behind the hinge, around the shank of the bolt *(above, right)*. Tighten the bolt and gently shut the door to check the fit. Add more shims as needed. When the fit is correct, tighten the bolt snugly.

To correct more serious misalignment, loosen the bolts just enough so that your helper can move the door in the necessary direction and hold it there, then slightly tighten the hinge bolts. Gently shut the door and check its fit. If the door is not aligned properly, adjust it again. When the fit is correct, open the door, have your helper hold it and tighten the bolts snugly. If the door does not latch properly, adjust the striker *(below)*.

ADJUSTING A DOOR-LATCH STRIKER

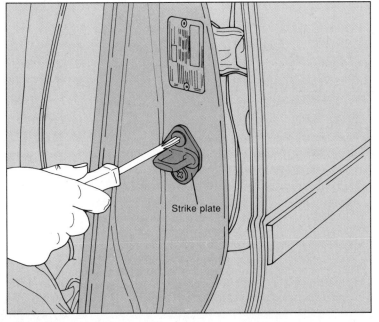

Adjusting the strike plate. If the door doesn't latch securely after the hinges have been adjusted *(above)*, adjust the striker. Door strikers are made in several styles, but all are adjusted by moving the strike plate—the rigid part of the latch mechanism attached to the door post. Slightly loosen the screws or bolts that attach the plate to the door post; depending on the striker, use a screwdriver *(left)*, hex wrench, or a socket wrench fitted with a Torx bit. Move the plate to the correct position. If the plate is difficult to move by hand, tap it lightly with a rubber mallet. Gently shut the door to check the adjustment. Make further adjustments as necessary. When the fit is correct, tighten the strike plate bolts or screws.

ALIGNING THE HOOD OR TRUNK LID

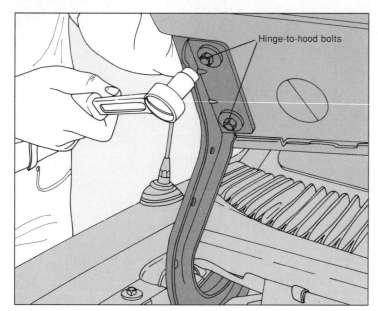

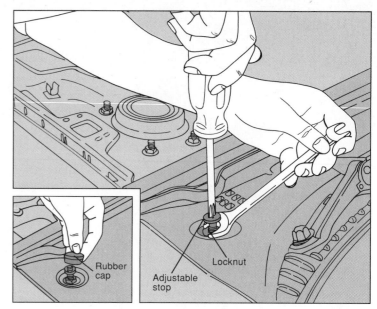

1 **Adjusting trunk lid and hood hinges.** To raise or lower the hood, slightly loosen the hinge-to-body bolts; to move the hood forward or backward, loosen the hinge-to-hood bolts *(above)*. With a helper holding up the hood, use a socket wrench to loosen the bolts just enough to shift the hood into position. When the fit is correct, tighten the bolts snugly. Move the trunk lid forward or backward as for a hood. To raise or lower a trunk lid have a helper hold it up, and slightly loosen the hinge-to-trunk-lid bolts. To lower the lid, remove the U-shaped shims from under the hinge; insert extra shims (available at auto parts stores) to raise the lid. Tighten the bolts snugly.

2 **Unscrewing the adjustable stops.** Many cars have adjustable stops at each corner of the hood and trunk lid to help them sit flush with the body of the car. If the stop is covered by a rubber cap, pull off the cap *(inset)*. If there is a locknut under the stop, loosen it with a wrench; if there is a clip, use a screwdriver to pry it off. Depending on your car, use either a screwdriver or your hand to move the stop up or down as needed *(above)*. Gently shut the hood or trunk lid to check the fit. Make further adjustments to the stop as necessary. Tighten the locknut or replace the clip, and snap on the rubber cap. Adjust other stops if necessary.

ADJUSTING A HOOD OR TRUNK-LID LATCH AND STRIKER

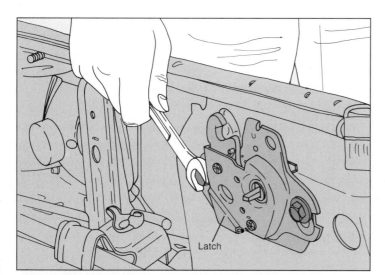

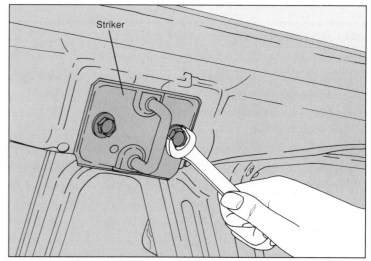

1 **Adjusting the hood or trunk lid latch.** If adjusting the hood or trunk lid hinges or stops does not improve the fit, adjust the latch assembly. Open the hood or trunk lid; with a screwdriver or wrench, slightly loosen the bolts or screws that secure the latch *(above)*, then move the latch assembly up or down as needed. Close the hood or trunk lid and check the fit. Make further adjustments as necessary. When the fit is correct, open the hood or trunk lid and tighten the screws or bolts snugly. If the hood or trunk lid doesn't close without slamming, or is still loose when closed, go to step 2.

2 **Adjusting the hood or trunk lid striker.** Place a lump of clay or modeling putty on the latch. Gently lower the striker onto the clay. If the mark left in the clay is not centered on the latch, adjust the striker. Loosen its screws or bolts *(above)* and shift it into the correct position. If the striker is hard to move by hand, lightly tap it with a rubber mallet. Shut the hood or trunk lid to check the adjustment. When the striker is centered, tighten the screws or bolts snugly and shut the hood or trunk lid. If it still does not latch properly, the assembly may have to be replaced.

REPLACING A HATCHBACK DAMPER

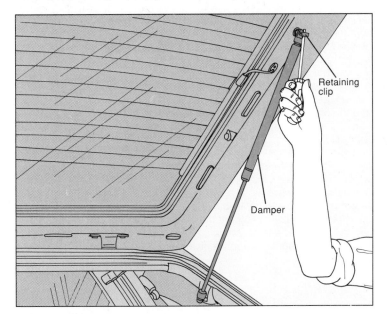

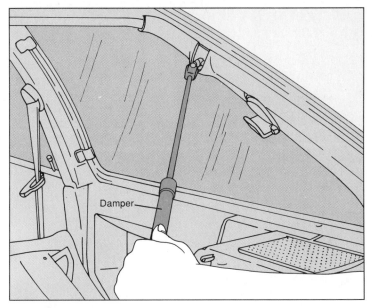

1 **Snapping off the damper clip.** Hatchback rear lids, as well as some trunk lids, have a damper, a gas-filled cylinder with a piston rod that moves up and down. The damper works as a shock absorber when the lid is closed, and as a lift when the lid is opened. If gas escapes as a result of a blown seal or a puncture, an open lid will fall shut. Dampers may be attached to the car in a number of ways. Have a helper hold the lid open while you remove the top retaining clip or bolt *(above)*, then remove any bolts attaching the damper to the body of the car.

2 **Removing and replacing the damper.** With your helper still holding the lid open, pull out the damaged damper. Install the retaining clip or bolt from the top of the old damper onto the new one. Position a clip-on damper against the lid and hit it sharply with an open palm to snap it into place, or use a wrench to screw the bolt in place. Reinstall and tighten any bottom bolts. Lubricate the cylinder and pivot points with white grease. Take the old damper to a service station for proper disposal.

DIAGNOSING WATER LEAKS

Locating a leak with a garden hose.
Water or air can seep into the car through misaligned doors and windows, cracked or worn weather stripping or places where rust has eaten through the metal.

A leak does not always originate at the point where the water enters the car; therefore, finding the source of a leak can take time. A simple test with a garden hose can help identify the original source of a leak. Have a helper sit inside the car and tightly close all the windows and doors. With a garden hose, run a gentle stream of water over the window gaskets, around the doors, along the roof seams, around the trunk and along the body where the trim is screwed onto the panels. Concentrate the water on each spot for several seconds. Have your helper mark the spots where the hose is pointing when water enters the car. Check the entire car.

Check the condition of the weather stripping at the points marked. Torn or loose weather stripping can be fixed with silicone sealant *(page 126)*. More seriously damaged weather stripping will have to be replaced *(page 126)*. If the problem is a misaligned window, go to page 121; to adjust a misaligned door, see page 123.

REPAIRING DAMAGED WEATHER STRIPPING

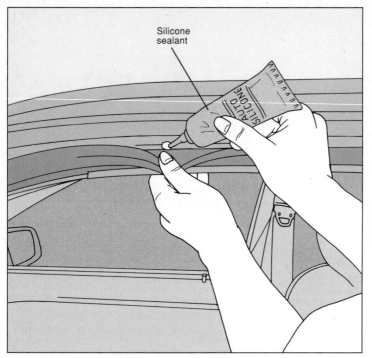

Silicone
sealant

Reattaching loose weather stripping. Resecure loose weather stripping with silicone sealant. The sealant is available at auto parts stores in clear or black, to match the color of the weather stripping. Lift the edge of the loose weather stripping. Scrape off any old adhesive with a stiff bristle brush and wipe the area clean with a damp rag. Let dry. Grasp the edge of the weather stripping and apply a thin bead of silicone sealant to both the car body and the weather stripping *(left)*. If one length of weather stripping has several leaking spots, apply a thin, even bead of sealant all around the car body and the entire length of the weather stripping. Carefully press the weather stripping back into place. Let the sealant dry for 15 minutes. If the weather stripping is cut or torn, fill the area with silicone paste (available at auto parts stores) and reattach it as above. Repeat the garden hose test *(page 125)* and, if the leaks remain, check and seal the weather stripping again, or replace it *(below)*.

REPLACING WEATHER STRIPPING

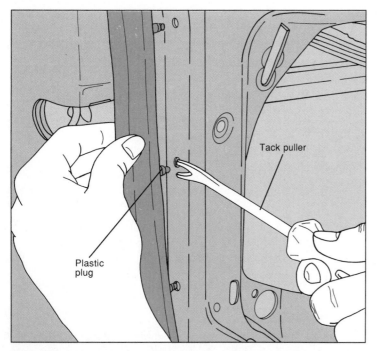

Tack puller

Plastic
plug

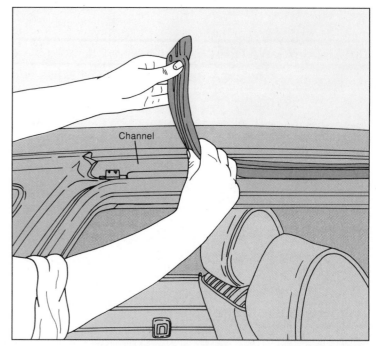

Channel

Removing damaged weather stripping (snap-in type). Hard rubberlike weather stripping has small plastic plugs along its length. The plugs snap into holes in the body of the car. To remove the weather stripping, pull up one edge by hand; place a tack puller or upholstery fork around the plastic plug *(above)* and pull the plug out of the hole. Continue along the length of damaged weather stripping. Line up the plastic plugs on the replacement weather stripping with the body holes, and press the plugs into the holes. Spray new weather stripping with silicone lubricant to weatherproof and preserve the rubber.

Removing damaged weather stripping (pull-out type). A common type of firm weather stripping fits into a channel along the door frame, without any plastic plugs or adhesive. Grasp the end of the damaged section of weather stripping by hand, and lift and pull it out of the channel *(above)*. Slide the replacement piece into the channel from one end. Spray the new weather stripping with silicone lubricant to weatherproof and preserve the rubber.

SERVICING A WINDSHIELD WIPER

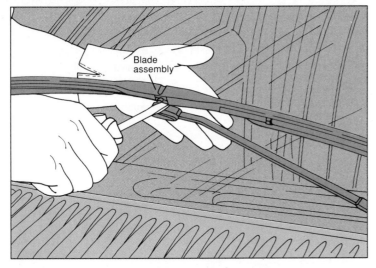

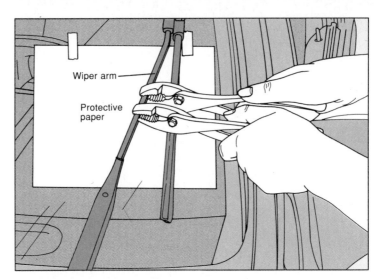

Removing the blade assembly. If they are available, purchase new squeegees to fit your car's blades; however, on newer cars the entire blade assembly may have to be replaced. Lift the wiper arm away from the windshield. Depending on your car's model, remove the blade assembly from the wiper arm by either pushing a button on the blade assembly or using a screwdriver to depress a small lever or clip on the blade *(above)*. Take care not to bend or break the clip. Pull the blade assembly out of the arm and snap in the new assembly.

Straightening the wiper arm. If the wiper arm is not parallel to the windshield, the squeegee cannot clean the windshield effectively. Chattering sounds may be a symptom. Place a towel or piece of paper across the windshield to protect the glass; lift the wiper off the windshield and, with two pairs of pliers, gently bend the wiper arm *(above)*. If the arm is bent because of rust, have it replaced professionally.

SERVICING THE WINDSHIELD WASHER

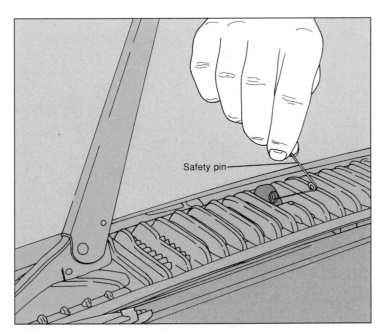

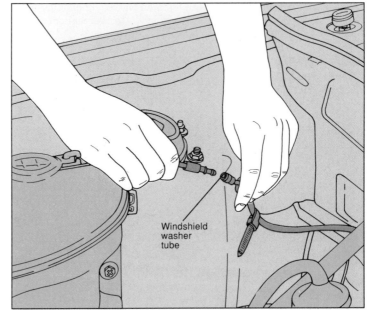

1 **Aiming the washer nozzles.** The washer nozzles may be directly in front of the windshield, as shown above, or on the wiper arm itself. To unplug a nozzle, insert a clean pin into the nozzle hole *(above)*, being careful not to widen the opening. Compressed air (available in cans) can also be used to clear a blocked nozzle. If the nozzle is not aimed correctly, use a screwdriver to loosen the nozzle clamp, if there is one, and then gently bend the nozzle back into position by hand or with a pair of pliers. If windshield washer fluid still does not coat the windshield properly, go to step 2.

2 **Unblocking the washer tube.** Open the hood and check the plastic tube that carries the windshield washer fluid from the fluid reservoir to the nozzles. If the tube is loose, push it back on the nozzle connection *(above)*. Straighten out any kinks in the tube. If kinks don't come out or the tubing is damaged, pull the tube off its connections and replace it. Remove the fluid reservoir cap and check the filter screen inside the pick-up tube in the cap. If the filter is clogged, flush it with water and reinstall it.

REPLACING THE REAR-VIEW MIRROR

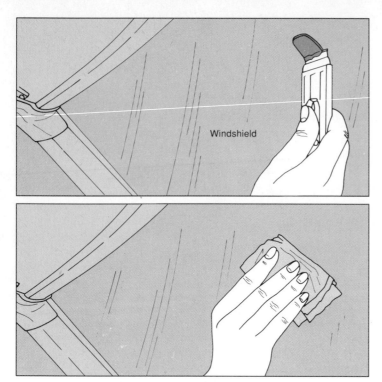

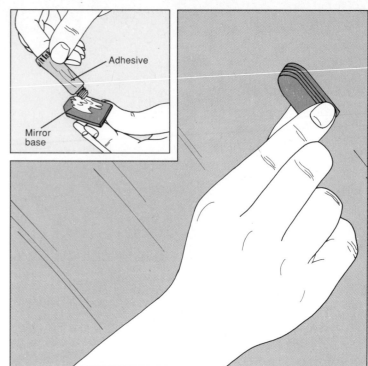

1 Preparing the surface. Most rear-view mirrors are glued to the windshield. Buy a rear-view mirror installation kit at an auto parts store. Before removing the old mirror, measure its exact position on the windshield so you can replace it accurately. Apply the cleaning solvent from the kit to loosen the base of the old mirror and soften the old glue. Use a razor blade to scrape off all gummy residue *(top)*. With a rag lightly dipped in solvent, clean the area carefully *(bottom)*. Wipe the glass completely clean and dry—any moisture, old glue or grease from your fingers will prevent the adhesive from bonding.

2 Installing the new mirror base. The rear-view mirror kit contains a small perforated mirror base and a tube of glue. Spread the glue evenly over the mirror base *(inset)* and firmly press the base of the mirror onto the proper spot on the windshield *(above)*. Let the glue dry for the time indicated by the kit instructions (between 6 and 24 hours).

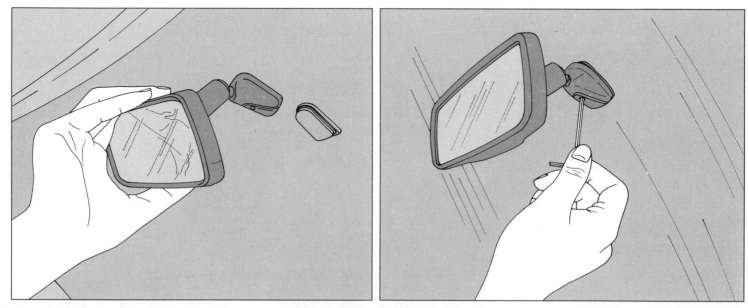

3 Inserting the new mirror. Check that the mirror base is secure—gently try to move the base with your fingers. If the base moves, let the glue continue to dry. When the base is firmly glued, mount the neck of the mirror on it *(above, left)*. Tighten the mirror with the appropriate size hex wrench *(above, right)*, and adjust it to the angle needed for driving. Lubricate the mirror joint once a year with a spray lubricant to prevent stiffness and rust. Tighten the joint when the mirror gets loose.

REPAIRING TORN VINYL UPHOLSTERY

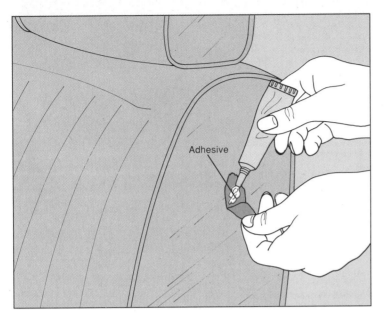

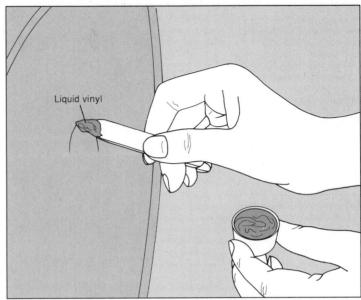

1 **Applying the adhesive.** If the damage to vinyl upholstery is extensive, see a professional. To repair small scratches and tears, buy a vinyl repair kit at an auto parts store. If the scratch is narrow and the upholstery has not lifted, go to step 2. If pieces of upholstery have lifted, trim the ragged edges of the torn vinyl with a small pair of scissors. Apply the adhesive to the underside of the edges *(above)*. Lightly press down the torn vinyl until the adhesive sets (approximately two minutes). Let the adhesive dry for about 10 minutes; check the kit for specific instructions.

2 **Covering the damage with liquid vinyl.** To make a good color match, it may be necessary to blend several shades of the liquid vinyl. Follow the color guide in the kit for mixing instructions. Apply a smooth, even layer of liquid vinyl over the entire damaged area *(above)*. Do not apply too thick a coat—the repaired area should blend invisibly into the surrounding surface. If you are using the heat transfer tool in the kit, go to step 4. If using a hair dryer to heat the liquid vinyl, go to step 3, then step 4.

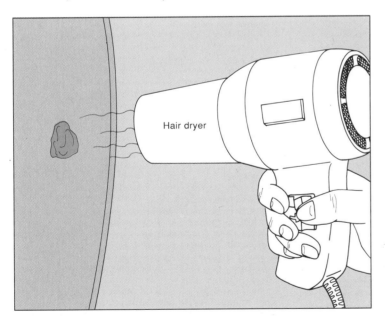

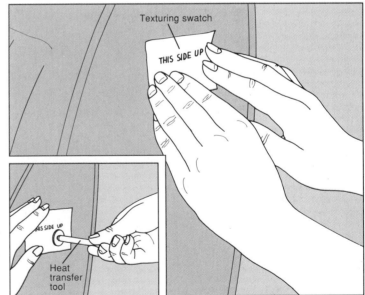

3 **Heating the repair with a hair dryer.** Aim a hair dryer about 6 inches from the vinyl patch; set the hair dryer on a low setting and heat the patch *(above)*. Do not put the hair dryer on a high setting or hold it too close to the vinyl—the patch can melt. When the vinyl patch has a shiny, smooth consistency, turn off the hair dryer. Do not dry out the patch, and do not use a heat gun—it can burn the vinyl.

4 **Texturing the repaired area.** If you used a hair dryer (step 3), select the swatch from the kit that matches the original texture of the vinyl. Firmly press the swatch onto the softened vinyl *(above)*. When the swatch is cool, lift it off. If the tear or crack is still noticeable, repeat steps 2 through 4 until it disappears.

If you are using the heat transfer tool, heat the tool with the car cigarette lighter. Select the swatch from the kit that matches the original texture of the vinyl. Place the swatch on the vinyl, and press the heated transfer tool against it for one minute *(inset)*. Heat all parts of the damaged area. When the swatch is cool, lift it off. If the tear or crack is still noticeable, repeat steps 2 and 4 until damage disappears.

REPAIRING BURNED CARPET

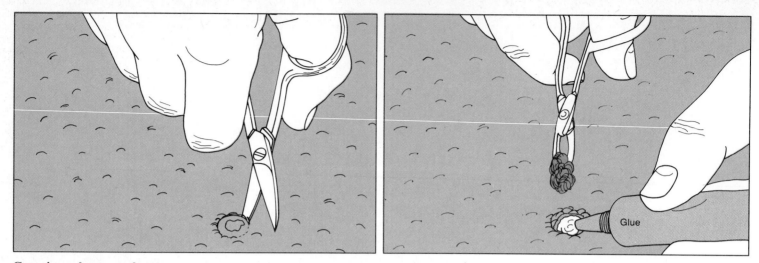

Covering a burn mark. With a small pair of scissors, snip away the charred and discolored carpet tufts around the burn *(above, left)*. From a less visible portion of the carpet, such as under the seat, cut enough loops of undamaged carpet to fill in the burn hole. Apply clear-drying waterproof glue to the hole. With a pair of tweezers, delicately add the cut carpet strands to the glued area *(above, right)*. Hold the strands in place until the glue sets (about two to three minutes).

WARDING OFF CORROSION

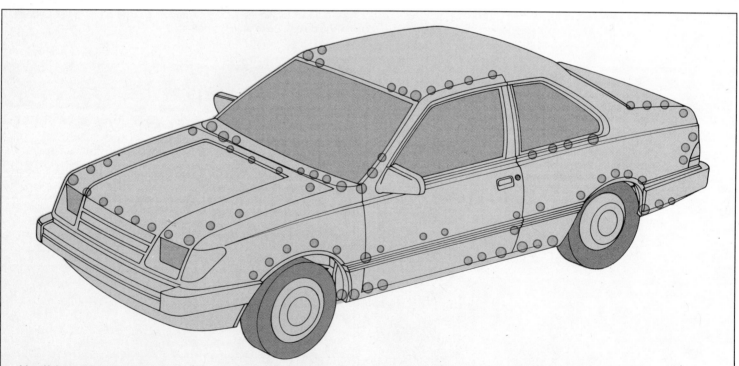

Identifying rust-prone areas. Rust most often forms around fenders, behind bumpers and around wheel wells, where road salt, mud and water accelerate corrosion. Other common locations are along trim and molding, around lights, side-view mirrors and the aerial, and in the underbody. Although some rust is inevitable, there is much that a vigilant car owner can do to minimize and prevent rust formation.

Rustproofing is applied by many service stations. Choose one with an excellent reputation; a shoddy rustproofing job can encourage more rust than it prevents. Rustproofing techniques vary, but essentially it is a process that coats the car to prevent contact with moisture. Some rustproofing is a chemical treatment; other types are oil-based, creating a protective shell that can crack and break off when it becomes brittle with age. The surest way to protect your car from rust is through regular maintenance. Hand wash the car regularly, and dry it quickly and thoroughly. (In winter, have it washed every three weeks if you live in an area where salt is spread on the roads.) Remove all traces of mud and asphalt. Repair small dents and dings *(page 131)* before they become pockets in which rust can form. Clear all drain holes and ventilation holes in the trunk and along the bottom of the doors. Thoroughly hose off the underbody of the car every six months. To make the surface of your car water-repellent, and add rust protection that can last for months, wax cars with acrylic finishes using a high-quality polymer-based wax; on other finishes, use a carnauba wax.

REPAIRING A SCRATCH

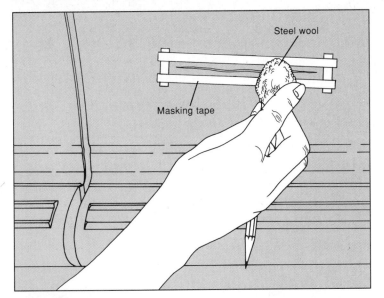

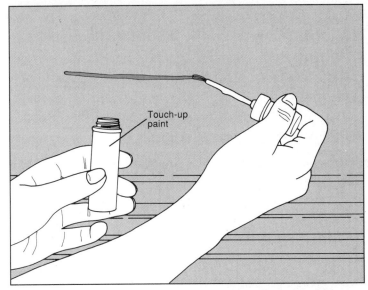

1 **Removing rust with steel wool.** Touching up small scratches in the paint prevents rust from forming on the bare metal. If the spot is not yet rusty, clean it with enamel thinner and let dry, then go to step 2. If the scratch has rusted, protect the area around it with masking tape. Wrap a bit of 3/0 steel wool around the eraser end of a pencil and rub the scratch lightly until all rust is gone *(above)*. Rub down to the bare metal. Brush away dust, then clean with enamel thinner and let dry. Peel off the masking tape.

2 **Applying primer and touch-up paint.** Use a rust-inhibiting, lacquer-based primer. Apply a thin coat of primer to the bare metal, being careful not to get it on the surrounding paint. Let the primer dry. Small bottles of touch-up paint that match your car's original finish are available from the dealer or at an auto parts store. Touch-up jobs are rarely a perfect match because car paint fades over time. Brush a thin coat over the dried primer *(above)*. Let the paint dry completely, then buff with polishing compound.

REPAIRING A PATCH OF RUST

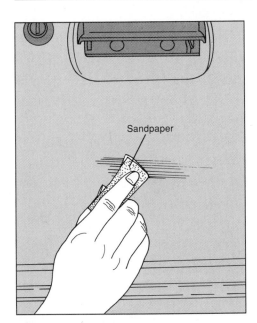

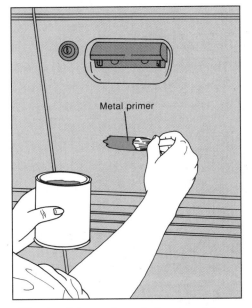

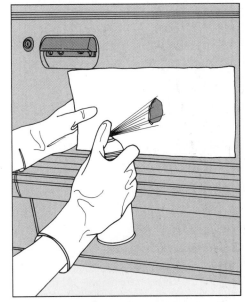

1 **Sanding off the rust.** With coarse (80 grit) sandpaper, remove the rust. Then sand with medium-grit (180-220 grit) sandpaper; finish with fine (400 grit) sandpaper. Feather the edges of the patch, lightly etching the paint so that the new paint will blend well with the old. Brush away dust.

2 **Applying primer to bare metal.** With a small paintbrush, apply a thin, light layer of rust-inhibiting, lacquer-based primer to the bare metal *(above)*. Let the primer dry, then sand it lightly with fine sandpaper. Apply two more coats, sanding after each coat dries.

3 **Feathering paint through a cardboard mask.** Cut an irregularly shaped hole, slightly smaller than the sanded area, in a piece of cardboard. Hold the mask 6 to 8 inches from the car and move it in a circular motion while you spray paint through the hole *(above)*. Apply several light coats of paint—a thick coat will drip and run. Let each coat dry.

TOOLS & TECHNIQUES

This section introduces basic tools and procedures for do-it-yourself car care, from setting up a safe home garage to removing stubborn fasteners. A maintenance schedule on page 135 provides a calendar of routine checks and services; telltale leaks and squeaks are diagnosed on pages 140-141. And, if all else fails, learn how to talk to a mechanic—or complain effectively—on page 136.

You can handle most of the repairs covered in this book with the basic tools shown below. Although some, particularly the wrenches and screwdrivers, may resemble items found in an all-purpose tool kit, these tools are designed for automotive use. Specialized tools, such as a hydraulic jack or vacuum gauge, can often be rented from the same auto supply dealer where you buy replacement parts.

Clean metal tools with a rag moistened with a few drops of kerosene or light oil (but don't oil the handles). To remove rust, rub with fine steel wool or emery cloth. Protect tools in a sturdy plastic or metal toolbox, with a secure lock if stored around children. Tools are usually cheaper purchased in sets than bought individually, especially wrenches. Buy filters, belts and engine oil at sale prices and store them in the garage until needed.

Almost every new car built in North America, and all foreign cars, are made to metric standards. Although many metric nuts and bolts seem to be the same size as those measured in inches, they are not interchangeable. Do not try to loosen a stubborn metric nut with a standard wrench; you will likely round off the corners of the nut and make it even more diffi-

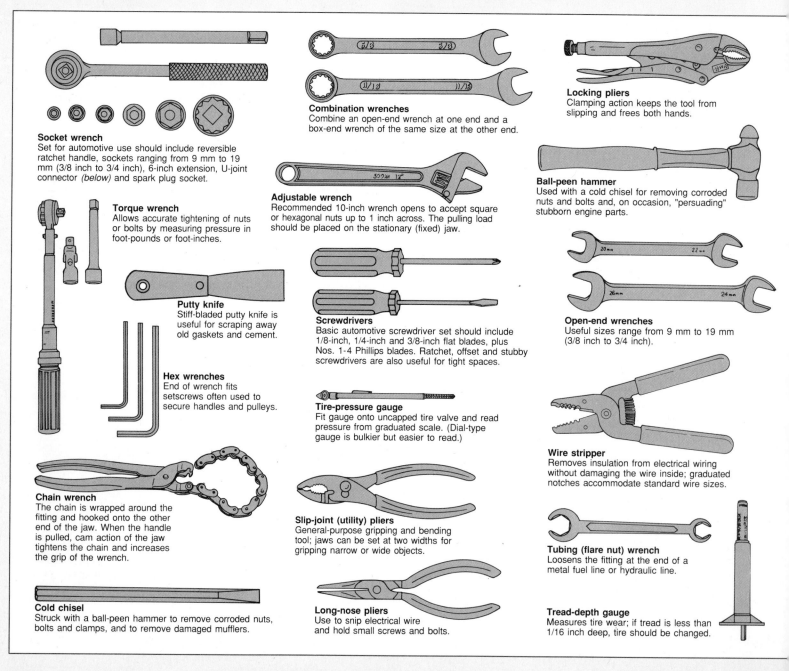

Socket wrench
Set for automotive use should include reversible ratchet handle, sockets ranging from 9 mm to 19 mm (3/8 inch to 3/4 inch), 6-inch extension, U-joint connector *(below)* and spark plug socket.

Torque wrench
Allows accurate tightening of nuts or bolts by measuring pressure in foot-pounds or foot-inches.

Putty knife
Stiff-bladed putty knife is useful for scraping away old gaskets and cement.

Hex wrenches
End of wrench fits setscrews often used to secure handles and pulleys.

Chain wrench
The chain is wrapped around the fitting and hooked onto the other end of the jaw. When the handle is pulled, cam action of the jaw tightens the chain and increases the grip of the wrench.

Cold chisel
Struck with a ball-peen hammer to remove corroded nuts, bolts and clamps, and to remove damaged mufflers.

Combination wrenches
Combine an open-end wrench at one end and a box-end wrench of the same size at the other end.

Adjustable wrench
Recommended 10-inch wrench opens to accept square or hexagonal nuts up to 1 inch across. The pulling load should be placed on the stationary (fixed) jaw.

Screwdrivers
Basic automotive screwdriver set should include 1/8-inch, 1/4-inch and 3/8-inch flat blades, plus Nos. 1-4 Phillips blades. Ratchet, offset and stubby screwdrivers are also useful for tight spaces.

Tire-pressure gauge
Fit gauge onto uncapped tire valve and read pressure from graduated scale. (Dial-type gauge is bulkier but easier to read.)

Slip-joint (utility) pliers
General-purpose gripping and bending tool; jaws can be set at two widths for gripping narrow or wide objects.

Long-nose pliers
Use to snip electrical wire and hold small screws and bolts.

Locking pliers
Clamping action keeps the tool from slipping and frees both hands.

Ball-peen hammer
Used with a cold chisel for removing corroded nuts and bolts and, on occasion, "persuading" stubborn engine parts.

Open-end wrenches
Useful sizes range from 9 mm to 19 mm (3/8 inch to 3/4 inch).

Wire stripper
Removes insulation from electrical wiring without damaging the wire inside; graduated notches accommodate standard wire sizes.

Tubing (flare nut) wrench
Loosens the fitting at the end of a metal fuel line or hydraulic line.

Tread-depth gauge
Measures tire wear; if tread is less than 1/16 inch deep, tire should be changed.

cult to remove. To free a rusted fastener, first try tightening it before loosening it, or apply penetrating oil.

The owner's manual provided with every new car is must reading for the do-it-yourselfer. It provides a maintenance schedule for your car, and locates filters, belts, hoses, fuses, fluid reservoirs and other components. If you are a serious weekend mechanic, consider buying a service manual (also known as a shop manual) for your make and model. These manuals range in price from $25 to $45 and are available from car dealers, auto-parts suppliers and bookstores.

Car care can be dangerous unless you observe basic safety precautions. Many engine parts become red-hot in normal use; others have sharp edges or spin at tremendous speeds. Most of the fluids you will be working with are poisonous, corrosive,

flammable or explosive. To reduce the risk of injury, work slowly and deliberately, and follow all **Caution** warnings throughout this book.

To prevent accidents, keep your work area well-lit, clean and free of clutter. Don't smoke or cause a spark, particularly around gasoline or solvents, and keep a class ABC fire extinguisher in the garage. Skinned knuckles and minor cuts are a part of car repair; have a first-aid kit close at hand. When a job requires working under the car, always use sturdy drive-on ramps or jack stands, and chock the wheels that are on the ground *(page 136)*. Never crawl under a car that is supported only by a jack. If you must run the engine during a repair, open the garage door or attach one end of a flexible exhaust hose to the tail pipe and feed the other end outside.

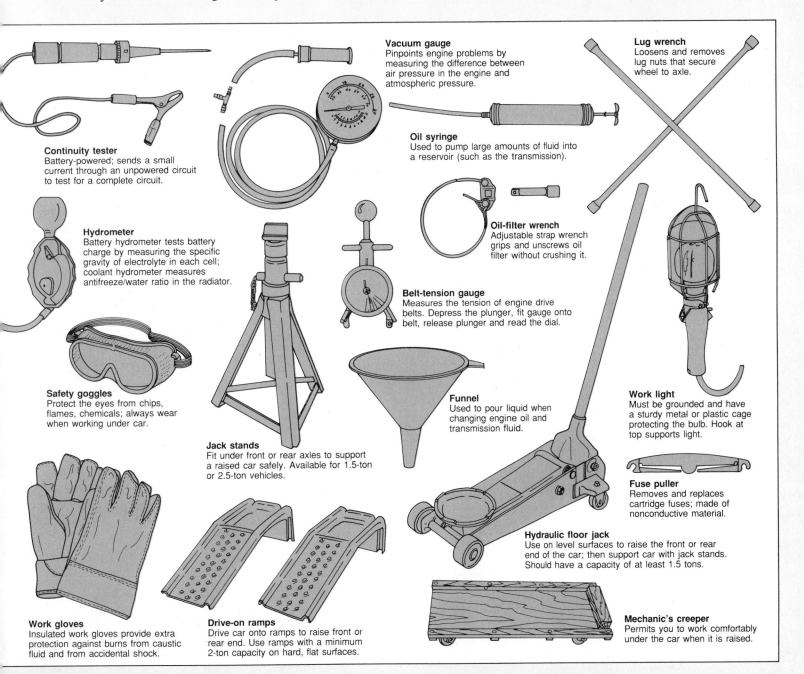

Continuity tester
Battery-powered; sends a small current through an unpowered circuit to test for a complete circuit.

Hydrometer
Battery hydrometer tests battery charge by measuring the specific gravity of electrolyte in each cell; coolant hydrometer measures antifreeze/water ratio in the radiator.

Safety goggles
Protect the eyes from chips, flames, chemicals; always wear when working under car.

Work gloves
Insulated work gloves provide extra protection against burns from caustic fluid and from accidental shock.

Vacuum gauge
Pinpoints engine problems by measuring the difference between air pressure in the engine and atmospheric pressure.

Oil syringe
Used to pump large amounts of fluid into a reservoir (such as the transmission).

Oil-filter wrench
Adjustable strap wrench grips and unscrews oil filter without crushing it.

Belt-tension gauge
Measures the tension of engine drive belts. Depress the plunger, fit gauge onto belt, release plunger and read the dial.

Jack stands
Fit under front or rear axles to support a raised car safely. Available for 1.5-ton or 2.5-ton vehicles.

Funnel
Used to pour liquid when changing engine oil and transmission fluid.

Drive-on ramps
Drive car onto ramps to raise front or rear end. Use ramps with a minimum 2-ton capacity on hard, flat surfaces.

Hydraulic floor jack
Use on level surfaces to raise the front or rear end of the car; then support car with jack stands. Should have a capacity of at least 1.5 tons.

Lug wrench
Loosens and removes lug nuts that secure wheel to axle.

Work light
Must be grounded and have a sturdy metal or plastic cage protecting the bulb. Hook at top supports light.

Fuse puller
Removes and replaces cartridge fuses; made of nonconductive material.

Mechanic's creeper
Permits you to work comfortably under the car when it is raised.

SETTING UP A SAFE SHOP

A well-organized home garage *(below)* is the safest and most convenient place for do-it-yourself maintenance chores and most of the repairs illustrated in this book. The first step is to clear away the bicycles, lawn mowers and garden tools that clutter most garages. Fit a workbench along one wall and install a pegboard above it to hang frequently used tools within easy reach—and out of the reach of children. Narrow shelves or second-hand kitchen cabinets provide additional storage space.

Paint the walls and ceiling white or another light color with semi-gloss latex or alkyd paint to reflect as much light as possible. Scrub slippery oil and grease spots off the concrete floor with trisodium phosphate (TSP), patch all cracks, then seal the floor with two coats of light-colored epoxy resin paint. Install a large fluorescent light

fixture in the center of the garage and a smaller one over the workbench. A work light with a long extension cord will provide additional light for working under the hood or chassis. If the garage's wiring is not sufficient to handle the extra load generated by power tools, install outlets with GFCI (ground-fault circuit interrupter) protection to prevent accidental shock.

Make sure the garage is adequately ventilated. Open the door when running the engine or working with toxic chemicals. Keep a large box fan handy to help expel fumes. Wear an approved respirator when using paints or solvents. Keep a class ABC fire extinguisher and a first-aid kit close by and install a smoke detector. Dispose of oily rags and other flammable materials promptly, storing them temporarily in a metal can with a tight-fitting lid.

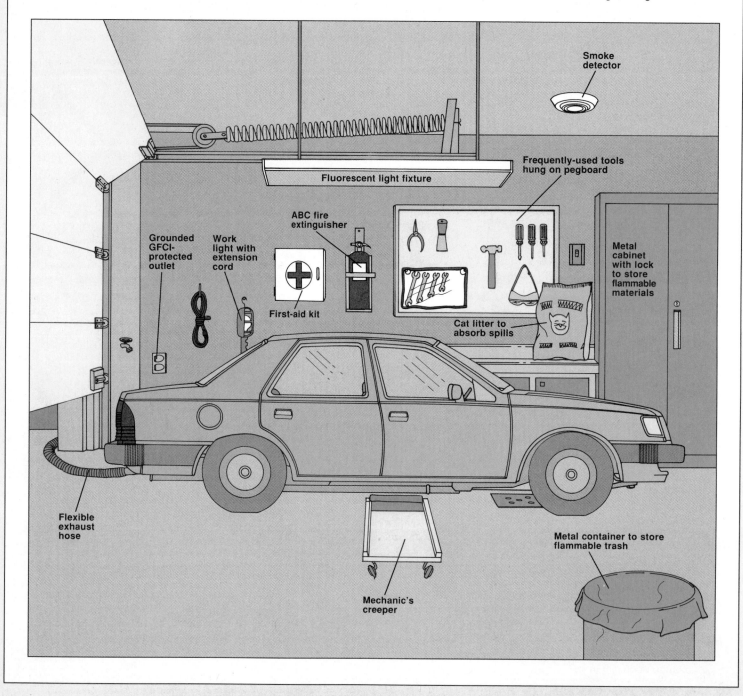

Smoke detector

Fluorescent light fixture

Frequently-used tools hung on pegboard

ABC fire extinguisher

Grounded GFCI-protected outlet

Work light with extension cord

First-aid kit

Metal cabinet with lock to store flammable materials

Cat litter to absorb spills

Flexible exhaust hose

Mechanic's creeper

Metal container to store flammable trash

MAINTENANCE CHART

INTERVAL (time or mileage)	MAINTENANCE CHECK OR SERVICE
Every week or 250 miles	With engine off: Check oil (p. 58) and windshield washer fluid levels
	Clean lights and windows; check tire pressure (and spare) with gauge (p. 26)
	With engine on: Check fuel gauge, warning lights and instrument panel lights
	Test windshield wipers and washer; sound horn; check headlights and signal lights
	Check for fluid leaks under the car (p. 140)
	With car stopped: Check brake pedal and steering wheel for excessive play
	On the road: Be alert to brake, steering and transmission performance, and unusual noises and smells (p. 141)
Every month or 1,000 miles	Top up windshield washer fluid
	Check brake fluid level (p. 29), brake pedal action and parking brake (p. 33)
	Check coolant level (p. 83), cooling system hoses and connections (p. 86)
	Check electrolyte level in battery and look for corrosion on terminals (p. 100)
	Check power steering belt (p. 38), fan belt (p. 89) and air conditioning belt (p. 94)
	Check tires for wear and damage (p. 26)
	Touch up minor paint chips or rust spots (p. 131)
Every 3 months or 3,000 miles	Change engine oil and filter (p. 59)
	Check automatic transmission fluid (p. 50), power steering fluid (p. 38) and differential fluid (p. 52)
	Inspect vacuum hoses (p. 49); check exhaust system for leaks (p. 79)
Every 6 months or 6,000 miles	Inspect fuel filter (p. 65) and air filter (p. 74)
	Clean and regap spark plugs or change if using leaded gasoline (p. 113); check carburetor (p. 54) and distributor (p. 115)
	Lubricate door locks (p. 122) and hinges (p. 123)
	Check windshield wiper blades (p. 127); adjust headlight aim (p. 103)
	Rotate tires and have wheel alignment checked (p. 27)
Every 12 months or 12,000 miles	Tune engine and replace spark plugs
	Inspect brake linings and shoes (p. 31) and adjust parking brake (p. 33)
	Flush radiator and replace coolant (p. 84)
	Have wheel bearings repacked and chassis points lubricated at a service station
	Check PCV (p. 77) and EGR (p. 78) systems
	Have air conditioning system recharged with refrigerant
	Each spring, thoroughly wash road salt from underbody
	Repair major rust spots
Every 24 months or 24,000 miles	Replace coolant hoses (p. 86), PCV valve (p. 77), automatic transmission fluid (p. 50), manual transmission oil (p. 48), brake fluid (p. 29) and differential fluid (p. 52)
Every 36 months or 36,000 miles	Refer to owner's manual for any long-term maintenance checks or services

HOW TO TALK TO YOUR MECHANIC

Americans spend some $65 billion each year on automobile maintenance and repair. Unfortunately, a large part of this fortune is spent on unneccesary parts and labor because, far too often, motorists are victims of dishonesty or incompetence. Surveys indicate that you have less than a 50-50 chance of getting fair, competent service on your first try.

You can improve your odds significantly with a working knowledge of your car. Read the owner's manual—and this book— to learn the names and locations of the various systems and the basic geography of the engine compartment. Even if you don't plan to do your own repair work, follow a regular maintenance plan to prevent minor problems from becoming expensive emergencies. According to the U.S. Department of Transportation, the three leading causes of breakdowns are flat tires, running out of gas and cooling-system problems. All three could be avoided by the kind of routine checks outlined on page 135.

If you cannot repair a problem yourself, find an honest, competent garage and patronize it regularly. (If the car is under warranty, return it to the dealer for repair.) Ask for recommendations from friends or neighbors—especially those who keep their cars in good shape. Contact your local Better Business Bureau, auto club or consumer protection group, who keep lists of reputable (and disreputable) garages.

Call the garage to make an appointment. Keep all written records of previous work in the glove compartment so that the mechanic will have a precise case history of your car. A good mechanic, in turn, will solicit information about you and your car.

Be precise in describing your car's symptoms. Is there a specific sound, smell or action associated with the problem? Does the problem occur as soon as you turn on the engine or must you travel some distance before it begins? Is it constant or intermittent? Is the problem triggered by weather conditions such as excessive heat or cold? Give the person you're dealing with a written copy of the symptoms. Unless you are knowledgeable, refrain from telling the mechanic what you think is the exact cause; you may find yourself paying for an unnecessary repair. Like-wise, do not hover over the mechanic while he works. You are taking up his time, and his time is your money.

Before you sign a service order, ask for a written estimate and an assurance that no extra work will be done without your permission. Don't be intimidated by a shop that refuses to give an estimate; take your business elsewhere. The garage should also give you a written guarantee before you authorize the work. (The guarantee is valid only if written.) Save both the bill and guarantee in case the repairs are faulty.

When the job is completed, road-test the car. If the problem persists or you are not reasonably satisfied with the repair, return it to the garage right away. Should the problem recur after a few days, call the garage and explain, politely but firmly, what has happened. If the garage refuses to take the car back, or tries to charge you again for the same problem, don't be intimidated. Your recourse is to complain *effectively*. Inform the shop that you will contact the Better Business Bureau, auto club or other authority.

RAISING A CAR WITH DRIVE-ON RAMPS

Placing the ramps. If the wheels need not hang free, you can raise one end of a car simply by driving it up onto ramps. These must be at least 12 inches wide to accommodate most tires, and 18 inches high to allow room to work. Park on level ground and place the ramps close to the wheels *(above)*, making sure the ramps are perfectly in line with the tires. With someone guiding you, slowly drive up the ramps until the tires dip into the wells at the top. Set the parking brake and shift an automatic transmission into park or a manual transmission into reverse. For added safety, place wooden chocks (mitered at a 45-degree angle) snugly behind the tires on the ground.

RAISING A CAR WITH JACK STANDS

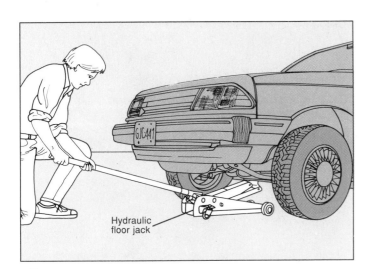

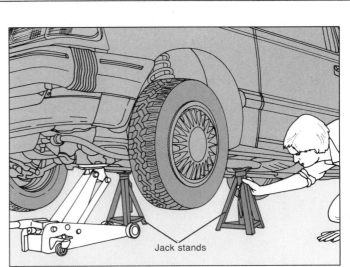

Hydraulic floor jack

Jack stands

1 **Raising the car.** Park the car on level ground, set the parking brake and place the transmission in gear. A scissors jack or hydraulic jack *(above)* is safer and easier to use than the bumper jacks that come with most cars. Center the jack under a solid support point, such as the differential or the lower suspension arms. Turn the jack handle clockwise to lock its hydraulic action and pump it up and down to raise the saddle up to the supporting point. Continue to pump until the tires are about 8 inches off the ground.

2 **Adding jack stands.** Slide two jack stands under the raised axle as close to the wheels as possible. You can also place stands on opposite sides of the frame *(above)*. With both stands in place, lower the hydraulic jack by slowly screwing the handle counterclockwise until you see the raised end of the car descending. With the car's weight on the jack stands, rock it gently to assure yourself that the setup is secure. Remove the jack and chock the wheels on the ground.

REMOVING STUBBORN FASTENERS

File

Damaged nut

Hanger

Mini-hacksaw

Nut splitter

Using a file, hacksaw or nut splitter. To get better purchase on a nut or bolt that has been rounded off, file two opposite sides flat with a rough metal file *(above, left)*. Test the fit with the next smaller size open-end wrench until the wrench fits snugly (or use an adjustable wrench). Use a mini-hacksaw with a carbon steel blade to cut through rusted clamps, such as the hanger that connects the muffler to the exhaust pipe *(above, center)*. A nut splitter, tightened onto a frozen nut with a wrench *(above, right)*, cuts through the nut without damaging the bolt.

REPLACING A DRIVE BELT

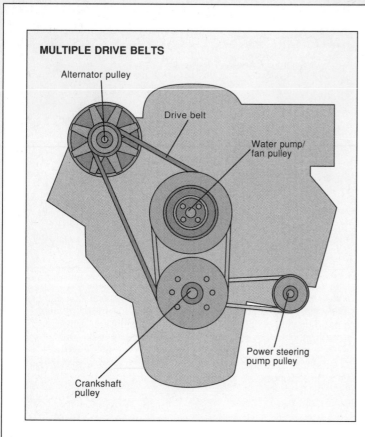

MULTIPLE DRIVE BELTS

Alternator pulley

Drive belt

Water pump/
fan pulley

Power steering
pump pulley

Crankshaft
pulley

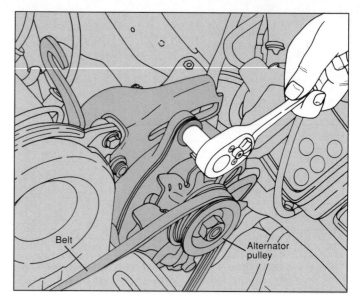

Belt

Alternator
pulley

1 **Loosening the mounting bolts.** Powered by the crankshaft, drive belts operate various engine components such
as the fan, water pump and alternator. To replace a loose
or broken belt, first loosen the mounting bolts on all accessories
driven by the belt (the alternator, in this example). If the belt to be
removed is behind other pulleys and belts, you must remove these
belts first. Use your hand or a pry bar to push the alternator
toward the engine block to slacken the belt.

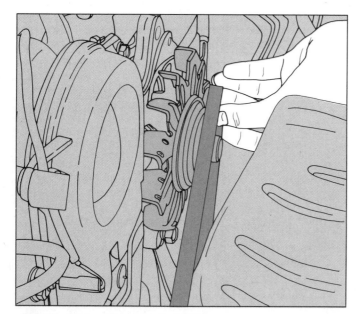

2 **Removing the damaged belt.** When it has enough slack,
pull the old belt off the alternator pulley. If this is difficult,
and the alternator is pushed toward the engine block as far
as it will go, simply cut the belt with a utility knife.

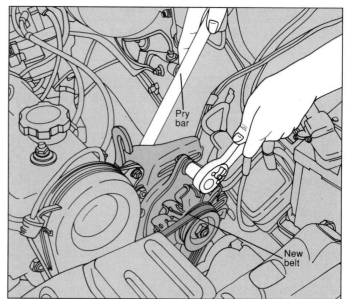

Pry
bar

New
belt

3 **Installing the new belt.** Buy the correct replacement belt
for your make and model. Fit the new belt in the grooves of
the stationary pulleys first, then finish by rolling the belt over
the accessory's pulley. Pry the accessory away from the engine
block and attach a tension gauge *(page 94)* to the center of the
belt. With one hand, apply enough pressure to stretch the belt to
its proper tension; with the other hand, tighten the mounting bolts.
Run the engine, then recheck the belt tension.

REPLACING A SERPENTINE DRIVE BELT

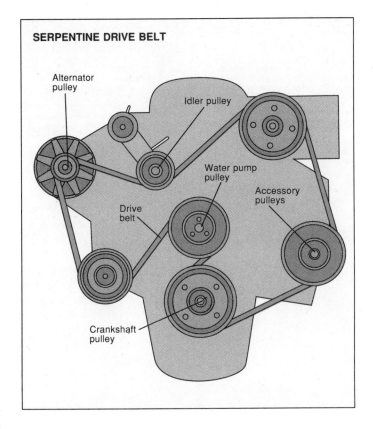

SERPENTINE DRIVE BELT

Alternator pulley

Idler pulley

Water pump pulley

Accessory pulleys

Drive belt

Crankshaft pulley

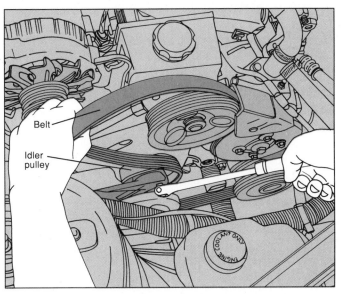

Belt

Idler pulley

1 **Freeing the old belt.** In some car engines a single long, serpentine belt drives all the accessories. A spring-loaded idler pulley maintains constant tension on the belt. Before you remove a serpentine belt, first draw a sketch of its position around the various pulleys. Some idler pulleys have mounting bolts and a slot for a pry bar; others are loosened with a ratchet handle *(above)*. Push the loosened pulley toward the engine block; when there is enough slack, slip off the belt.

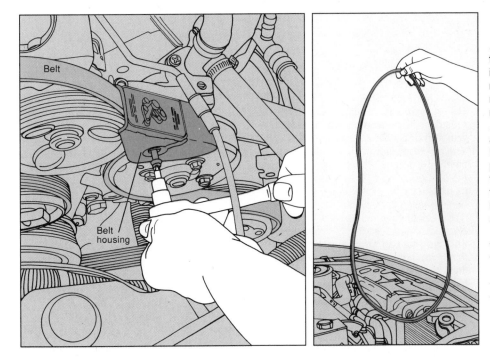

Belt

Belt housing

2 **Installing the new belt.** A metal or plastic housing may cover part of the belt. Fit a screwdriver bit onto the ratchet handle and remove the housing *(far left)*, then pull the belt from the remaining pulleys. Buy the correct replacement belt for your make and model, and remove any kinks before installation *(near left)*. Thread the new belt on the engine according to your diagram, starting at the lowest pulley and working up to the idler pulley. If the belt is grooved, make sure it fits snugly into the pulley tracks. Reattach the housing. Using the ratchet handle or pry bar, tighten the idler pulley against the belt and check the belt for proper tension *(page 94)*. With one hand, apply enough pressure to stretch the belt to its proper tension; with the other hand, tighten the mounting bolts. Run the engine for three to five minutes, then wait 30 minutes before rechecking the belt tension.

IDENTIFYING LEAKS

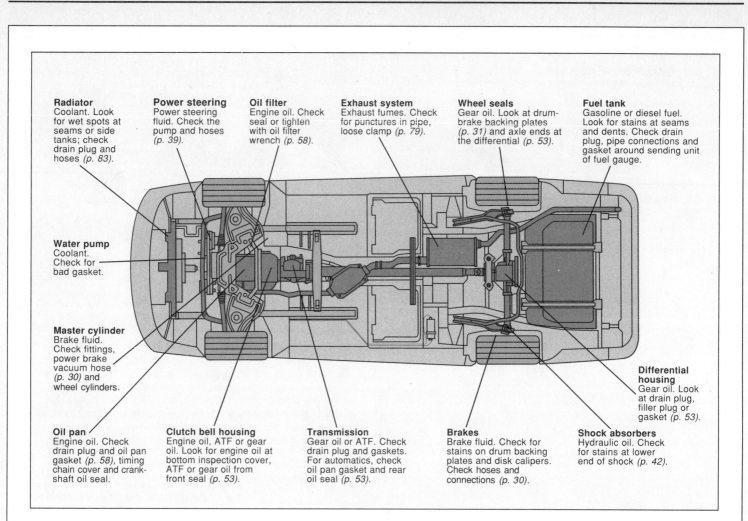

Radiator
Coolant. Look for wet spots at seams or side tanks; check drain plug and hoses (p. 83).

Power steering
Power steering fluid. Check the pump and hoses (p. 39).

Oil filter
Engine oil. Check seal or tighten with oil filter wrench (p. 58).

Exhaust system
Exhaust fumes. Check for punctures in pipe, loose clamp (p. 79).

Wheel seals
Gear oil. Look at drum-brake backing plates (p. 31) and axle ends at the differential (p. 53).

Fuel tank
Gasoline or diesel fuel. Look for stains at seams and dents. Check drain plug, pipe connections and gasket around sending unit of fuel gauge.

Water pump
Coolant. Check for bad gasket.

Master cylinder
Brake fluid. Check fittings, power brake vacuum hose (p. 30) and wheel cylinders.

Differential housing
Gear oil. Look at drain plug, filler plug or gasket (p. 53).

Oil pan
Engine oil. Check drain plug and oil pan gasket (p. 58), timing chain cover and crankshaft oil seal.

Clutch bell housing
Engine oil, ATF or gear oil. Look for engine oil at bottom inspection cover, ATF or gear oil from front seal (p. 53).

Transmission
Gear oil or ATF. Check drain plug and gaskets. For automatics, check oil pan gasket and rear oil seal (p. 53).

Brakes
Brake fluid. Check for stains on drum backing plates and disk calipers. Check hoses and connections (p. 30).

Shock absorbers
Hydraulic oil. Check for stains at lower end of shock (p. 42).

Overlooking a leak can be hazardous to your car's health. Leaks in the cooling system can cause the engine to overheat, shortening its life. An engine oil leak, if left unchecked, will increase friction between moving metal engine parts to the point where the parts fuse from the high heat. The only normal "leak" is water from the air conditioner on a hot summer day.

Fluid leaks are noticed as puddles or stains on a garage floor or a frequently used parking space. Identify the fluid by placing a small container or a sheet of white paper under the car where the leak occurs. Remember, however, that a fluid may run along pipes or flanges before appearing elsewhere in the car. Other leaks are even harder to detect. For instance, a fluid leak can enter the vacuum power booster and get burned in the engine. The fluid level will drop, but there will be no visible leaks. To spot this type of leak, check inside the power booster vacuum hose for dampness.

Antifreeze/coolant can be clear or tinted yellow or green. It is thicker than water and has a slightly sweet smell.

Automatic transmission fluid (ATF) is red and has an oily feel and distinctive odor. Check the transmission dipstick to confirm. *Battery acid* is clear with a pungent, sulfurous odor. If the acid comes in contact with skin or clothing, flush with water. *Brake fluid* is clear, thinner than oil and smells like alcohol. Identify by checking the master cylinder. *Diesel fuel* is a light oil that has a distinctive smell similar to home heating oil. Sniff the filler cap on a diesel car to confirm. *Gasoline* is a thin, clear liquid with a strong, aromatic smell. Sniff the filler cap to confirm. Gasoline fumes are highly flammable. *Gear oil* is thick and clear, light brown when new, black when used. It is found in axles, manual transmissions, steering gearboxes and differentials. *Grease* has a black color caused by dirt or additives. It is found in axle boots and rear wheel seals. *Power steering fluid* is a light oil with a distinctive odor. Automatic transmission fluid, which is often colored red, is sometimes used as power steering fluid. Check the power steering pump reservoir to confirm. *Shock absorber fluid* is a light oil that leaves a

dark stain on tubular shocks. *Windshield washer fluid* is a detergent-and-water solution with alcohol added to prevent freezing. Clear or sometimes tinted blue or green, it has a slippery feel.

Not all leaks from a car are fluid leaks. Gases can escape from certain parts of a car and be potentially harmful. *Air* can leak slowly from tires, causing a soft hissing sound. A daily visual check of tires and a weekly check with a tire pressure gauge *(page 26)* will catch the problem. *Exhaust fumes* contain deadly carbon monoxide. If you notice an exhaust smell inside the passenger compartment, check the exhaust pipe for blockages or punctures *(page 79)* and repair any damage immediately. *Refrigerant* turns into a colorless, odorless gas when it leaks from the seal in the air conditioning compressor or the air conditioning lines. Check the pressure in the system with a pressure gauge *(page 95)*. *Vacuum* leaks make a hissing noise when air is sucked into hoses that operate the emission control system, power brake boosters and heater system valves. Check these hoses with a vacuum gauge *(page 57)*.

DIAGNOSING SOUNDS AND SMELLS

SOUND	POSSIBLE CAUSE
Bang: loud explosion	Spark plugs misfiring (p. 113); incorrect fuel mixture not burning properly (p. 62); broken distributor cap (p. 115); broken valve or valve spring (p. 60)
Buzz: high-pitched vibration	Leak in exhaust pipe (p. 79); exhaust pipe contacting engine or chassis; loose dashboard or heating system component (p. 90); loose accessory bracket
Chatter: rapid clicking	Limited-slip differential filled with wrong lubricant (p. 52); wear in valve train (p. 60)
Chirp: rhythmic, shrill whistle	Loose drive belt on power-steering pump (p. 38)
Click: rhythmic, high-pitched metallic tapping	Loose hubcap; defective wheel bearing (p. 28); bent or loose fan blade (p. 90); low oil level in engine (p. 58); loose manifold heat-control valve (p. 75)
Clunk: dull thump	Defective universal joint on rear differential (p. 53)
Grind: grating crunch	Defective clutch (p. 47); worn brake pads or linings (p. 31); worn bearing in alternator (p. 112) or air conditioning compressor
Growl: low, muffled sound	Worn front wheel bearings (p. 27); worn rear differential (p. 53); worn axle shaft bearings (p. 53); defective speedometer cable or gears
Hiss: sharp, high-pitched release of air	Leak in pressurized component such as radiator (p. 83), tire (p. 26) or vacuum line (p. 51)
Howl: low- or high-pitched moan	Snow tires on bare road surface
Knock: heavy pounding	When engine is in gear or under load: worn crankshaft main bearing; when engine is not in gear: bad connecting rod or loose bolts in torque converter; also: fuel octane rating too low; bent push rod on fuel pump (p. 67); incorrect ignition timing (p. 117); defective spark plug (p. 113); failure of electronic knock-control (p. 117); carbon buildup on pistons, rings and valves
Moan: steady, low-pitched hum	Low power steering fluid level (p. 38)
Rap: rhythmic, metallic tapping	Worn piston connecting rod
Slap: sharp, rhythmic smacking	Piston moving against cylinder: when engine is cold, normal; when engine is hot, worn cylinder
Squeak: high-pitched rubbing	Defective drum-brake linings; chassis needs lubrication (p. 40); worn suspension bushings (p. 41)
Squeal: high-pitched whine	Underinflated tires (p. 26); misaligned wheels; loose or worn power steering belt (p. 38); worn fan belt (p. 89) or air conditioning compressor belt (p. 94)
Thud: low, metallic thump	Loose pulley; worn crankshaft bearing; loose exhaust pipe (p. 79)
Whine: continuous, high-pitched hiss	Defective overhead camshaft belt

SMELL	POSSIBLE CAUSE
Burning insulation (plastic)	Short circuit in electrical system (p. 108)
Burning oil	Low engine-oil level (p. 58); transmission overheating due to low transmission fluid level (p. 50); oil leaking on hot engine part
Burning rubber	Rubber hose contacting hot engine (p. 86); hot tire due to locked brake shoe
Exhaust odor in passenger compartment	Puncture in exhaust pipe under passenger compartment (p. 79)
Gasoline odor in passenger compartment	Evaporation-control canister worn or defective; plugged air filter in carburetor system (p. 74)
Rotten eggs (hydrogen sulfide gas)	In new car, over-rich fuel mixture breaking down active ingredient in catalytic converter; in older car, catalytic converter needs replacing
Slightly sweet odor (ethylene glycol)	Leak in cooling system (p. 83)

INDEX

Page references in *italics* indicate an illustration of the subject mentioned. Page references in **bold** indicate a Troubleshooting Guide for the subject mentioned.

ACKNOWLEDGMENTS

The editors wish to thank the following:
.Canadian Automobile Association, Toronto, Ontario; Glenn Carpenter, Dero Shell, Dorval, Quebec; John E. Graham, Montreal, Quebec; Honda Canada Inc., Scarborough, Ontario; Hyundai Auto Canada Inc., Toronto, Ontario and Boucherville, Quebec; Claude Lachapelle, Brossard Toyota Inc., Brossard, Quebec; Wilfrid Massie, Service Department, Park Avenue Chevrolet Oldsmobile Cadillac, St. Leonard, Quebec; James Mullett, Western Radiator Reg., Montreal, Quebec; Nelson Garage Inc., Montreal, Quebec; Paul Preuss, Product and Technology Department, North American Public Affairs, Ford Motor Company, Dearborn, Michigan; Gilles Proulx, Montreal, Quebec; James R. Rogers, Graphic Arts and Administrative Services Department, Ford Motor Company, Dearborn, Michigan; Toyota Canada Inc., Scarborough, Ontario; Robert E. Waite, Jr., Ford of Canada Ltd., Oakville, Ontario; Ken Waldchen, Graphic Arts and Administrative Services Department, Ford Motor Company, Dearborn, Michigan; Stuart Woodman, Chubb Fire Security, Toronto, Ontario.

The following persons also assisted in the preparation of this book: Claude Bordeleau, Fiona Gilsenan, Julie Leger, Solange Pelland, Natalie Watanabe and Billy Wisse.

Typeset on Texet Live Image Publishing System.